The Void Between Breathing in and Breathing Out

KaDawna Gasson

I am dedicating this book to the nurses and doctors that spent tireless hours holding onto the thread of life that snapped. The ones who watched over me day and night. The ones that prayed for me and my baby. Thank you to the NICU nurses who helped my baby survive and thrive. Thank you to my mother and grandmother who also never gave up hope and fought for me every step of the way. Even when that next step was in total darkness. Thank you to Jewell who advocated for Meadow and I the best she could. Who held and cared for the other pieces of my heart and kept them warm in the darkest of winters. Thank you, Rayne and Louts, for finding the strength inside yourselves and with each other. Thank you for the circumstances that showed me the other side, and my true strength. Thank you The One for holding onto me and throwing me back. Thank you for giving me more time with the ones I love.

$\mathcal{C}$ontents

The Void Between Breathing in and Breathing Out

Betrayals

I woke up screaming. I sat bolt upright hands to throat. Through the piercing blackness just my oxygen cord hisses at me. I catch my breath. Was I breathing, or just scared that I had stopped breathing again? Would I ever let go of this fear of drowning in my own body?

I take a moment to reorient myself. It is so dark that dawn must be scratching at the windows. I sit cross legged on my uncomfortable bed that sags in the middle, with its bright orange thin fitted sheet. My comforter has found refuge at the end of my bed. The other sheet that I usually sleep with is nowhere to be found. The baby has scrunched up against me, now taking over half my pillow.

This is all okay. You see I woke up. I was using my lungs. I was breathing. I am still here to terrify my girls if they could hear me. I strain in the dark listening for any noise from the other two. Nothing moves. Even the moon seems stuck in a limbo right now.

I gently move the baby over to the other pillow. Then I lay back down, after unlooping the oxygen cord from around my neck. I synch it up under my chin. That way it won't fall off. I now lay on my back, pull the blankets back up, and fold my arms over my chest. A new way that I have been trained to sleep. Sleeping on my stomach puts weight on my ribcage making it more difficult to breathe.

Isn't breathing funny? How many times did you breathe reading that last paragraph? Now that you are aware of breathing can you feel your chest expand? Can you hear the rush of air as you breathe in and out? Then there is that little tiny pause. The void as I like to call it. A void between breathing in and breathing out.

When we are scared, happy, or sad what happens to our breathing.

Do we breathe in slow shallow breaths as we creep around in the dark? When we are crying, don't we try to smoother our strange breathing pattern, if we don't want others to know? How about all the different meanings of sighing. All the different meaning behind screams. What about the breath we use for laughing, and talking, and smelling?

Some believe that we do not enter our body until our first breath. When one dies the first thing we look for is the rise and fall of a chest. We lean against it hopes of hearing the exchange of air. Sometimes we even try to breathe for those that aren't doing it themselves.

We can live weeks without food, days without water, but just minutes without breathing. Without oxygen to feed our cells; without the blood exchange of eliminating waste, and replenishing everything, our brain and other vital organs die. It is so important to our bodies, yet we have some control over it.

How many times as kids have you tried to be the one to hold your breath the longest? In yoga classes they try to bring your awareness to it, and train you to stretch in rhythm. Think of all the ways you use your lungs.

I breathe deep and slow before I chance something outside my comfort zone. It seems to bring me back to my center. The deep air rushing through my nose and down. The pressure as my chest expands, and the oxygen rush, all seem to ready me for what's ahead.

I breathed in the first time. I don't remember how it came about. I celebrate it every year. The day after my mother's birthday. I hear the story. I have seen scar like a smile resting on the top on her hip bone. I get scoffed playfully for being logged up in her ribs and refusing the dissent downward. I had yet to learn how important it was to a mother to hear her children breathing in the night or to squint in the darkness for a rise and fall of blankets.

My lungs have been something I have never thought much of in my childhood. In fourth grade we got worksheets showing the body, and a few strange demonstrations that explained how it all worked. I breathed into a meat paper bag; I thought. One way or another it went into my blood stream. They are delicate and wrapped in my ivory cage.

I was never supposed to smoke and all though school we were shown pictures of black lungs, and the horrible effects of what would happen. People with tubes in their throats, with cancer, that spoke like robots. That didn't affect me. I didn't want to smoke, because my parents did it. It was appalling. I stunk. Everything I had stunk. Our house stunk. Past the normal middle school trials, I never smoked.

I also never paid much care to my lungs except to breathe deep for the doctors. I had a bout of asthma that I vaguely remember when I lived in a hot dry desert when I was young. I remember how they hurt around every Halloween growing up. Sometimes I wanted to pass out. The cold dry air was like a knife lodged in the ivory cage that was supposed to protect them.

As reckless as I got as soon as I paid my dues to Mom and graduated, I am glad I had the ivory cage wrapped around them. I was promised magic once I turned this corner. Instead, I began to hit one dead end after another.

This was a small town that was impossible to find work in. I dressed up and applied everywhere. I didn't think I could manage college with my grades, and my lack of money. I had nothing. I drank, and wandered the streets bouncing from friend to friend.

It seemed to be that everyone turned that magic corner. They were starting college, married, had a job, or at least a dream. In the morning I heard the bus carry away a whole new group of promise. I was creeping around my house knowing fair well how unwelcome I was here. I hid in books and fake promises.

I tried to get out and meet people. I was going to gay prides with friends. One invited me to a LGBT meeting held on the university campus. I wasn't a student. He said it didn't matter he wanted me to come along. I sighed annoyed and agreed.

I held my breath when I met her. She came into the meeting last and very late. Hidden under sunburned skin in the body of a man. There was something deep. Strange flukes in our day had brought us together. Eye to eye we couldn't separate as the souls reconnected. I felt as though we had lived lifetimes stitched together. I tried to push her away, but it was there. Proof that love did exist.

We shared a love of the earth, and God. We kissed on cold starry nights. I loved to feel her breathing on me, as we snuggled together. We played and eventually married in a quietly moving creek. We slept with the earth even as it grew cold. We got to know animals of all kinds. We felt as one in play and passion. It was no surprise when someone wanted to join in the love.

I fell pregnant three months later. Rayne was born first. To an immature 19-year-old in 2004. One hot day in August as I swayed and rocked. I took a hot shower letting the water relax my muscles. I wanted to take a bath and relax in the water before heading to the birthing center. I thought I would have hours of pain before giving birth. Jewell sensed the changes in me and hurried me out the door.

I came in dilated to 8cm. No time for backing out. No time for medicating. After three hours of labor and fifteen minutes of pushing I was born again. She kicked inside me as they cleaned her nose and mouth before pulling her the rest of the way out. Her eyes caught mine. They put her on my tummy while they toweled her off and she rooted for her first sips of milk.

I held her in awe. I counted fingers and toes. I carried her for 42 weeks. She was a roly-poly perfect 7lb baby. I tried to feed her sloppily. Eventually she drifted off to sleep. I placed her in my lap, as she slept. I didn't dare pick her back up until Mom had arrived.

I was too shy in from of Jewell, or her mother, to admit I knew nothing about babies. I had read tons of books, but the real thing. My brand-new daughter. That was too intimidating.

I asked Mom, who thankfully came in alone, how I do I pick up a newborn. I blushed, but Mom seen no shame. She cupped her hand around Rayne's head, and hoisted her up gently. Then she put her back down, and I practiced. Next was the bath and the diaper. Poor Rayne was my experiment. She flowed with me, dealt with me, as I changed and grew.

I wanted to make a great life for her. I started college. I never thought I could, especially with her growing inside me. Jewell signed me up for classes. She paid tuition and bought everything I needed. I put my all into stitching together a comfortable life. It was no longer me. I now had a family.

Juggling school and a baby, I took on a job. I climbed to the top rung in a matter of months. I was doing it. With hardly any time for sleep, I pushed on.

I worked too hard. I pushed too far, and I gained a cough. I was taking five college classes. I was working as hard as I could for money, so that I could stitch together my tiny time of a holiday season.

I was coughing while getting ready for work. I just couldn't pull my pants on without getting too dizzy. I gave up. I crawled into bed and found my cellphone. I called in. Me. I never called in before.

I lay here for two or three days. I hardly get up. I spit phlegm. I am burning up. I try to clean house at least, but quickly give up. I don't even cook. Jewell brings me food.

She tells me to go into town for help. I stumble dizzily to the car. The ride is blur. The window is so cold. I lean my heavy head against it. I an attempt to try to cool my body.

The Urgent Care Center is tiny and cramped. No windows. Certainly, its crawling with germs. There is a line of people that I join as we wait. I lean against the wall and wait. The line is long. People are coughing. I try to cough inside my shirt. We are all so crammed in here. I want to sit. I want to sleep. I sidestep closer and closer. I feel like my skin is on fire.

I think an hour has passed on my feet. I am forced into another smaller room. A nurse checks me over and asks me lots of questions. She scratches away at her clipboard then leaves.

The doctor comes in after another grueling long wait. I want to sleep so badly. There is nothing comfortable. Where I am sitting; if I doze, I will fall off onto the germy hard concert floor. I am glad to finally see her.

The doctor on the other hand is almost spitting venom, and anger from the moment she walks in. It doesn't even cross my mind until I realize she hasn't said a word to me directly. She listens to my lungs and looks in my throat. She reads the chart, and then begins to write on a small pad speaking more out loud then directly to me. She tells me that she is giving me an antibiotic, and codeine cough syrup.

"Codeine cough syrup?" I ask surprised. I had never heard of it.

"Are you sick are not!" She yells across the room.

She is frozen glaring up at me. So much hatred, and anger are burning my already on fire body. I feel like I will be ashes.

I snap my mouth shut and look stupidly at the tiles on the floor. I shiver at how many germs may be there. I hear the rip of her prescription pad. She pulls her seat back with a horrible scrapping sound, and she roughly hands me the prescriptions. I dare not make eye contact. She leaves in huff with a door slam. I spent three hours here for that. I climb in the truck and collapse in the seat. I barely manage the seatbelt.

Jewell brought me my favorite coffee. I throw the scripts angrily on the dashboard. I lay against the cool truck window and begin to gulp the mix of espresso and chocolate ice-cream. Anything to cool my body. I am half tempted to throw the prescriptions out the window.

"Don't you want those filled?" She says staring at them curiously.

"No. I guess I'm not that bad." I choke back tears.

She looks at me concerned for a long while then speaks.

"Okay? Look I got you a humidifier. I heard they help people who have asthma, and this is a dry climate." She ends on a high note in hopes this box contains the answers to my problems.

I smile at her though my tired red eyes. As soon as we get home, I shower in the hottest water possible. I breathe in the steam, trying desperately get a good deep breath of air. Dizzy and tired I pass out next to my new humidifier.

I get up early in the morning. I force myself to dress. Then I drag myself coughing and spiting to work. They are threatening me. I cannot lose my job. I know I am contagious, so I try to stay back and away from food. I wash dishes, scrub floors, and full force use my manager powers tell people what to do. I drag myself home. The days are blurring together.

Jewell has snuck back into town and filled my scripts. They are there next to my humidifier when I get home. Pills that are huge. I choke one down, but only because she was kind enough to trek 30 minutes back into town for me. I open the cough syrup and guess-timate a tablespoon. I take the horse pills to work.

My friend takes a look at the antibiotic that I bring in. He tells me I have either walking pneumonia or bronchitis. With my cough he was guessing bronchitis.

"The way the doctor acted with me I thought I was just wasting her time. I didn't think I was actually sick." I moan into a sink of hot dishes, as my boss eyeballs me from the cash register.

He shakes his head and tells me I shouldn't be anywhere near here.

"Then who will run the place." I say with a heavy sigh as dry my hands off while glaring back at my boss.

I heave myself on two egg crates stacked together. My body language tells him I am on the verge of walking out and crying. I work all the time for him keeping this hell hole together.

I'm in a sick drugged stupor. This is the first time my lungs had betrayed me this badly. It takes me weeks to recover.

The next year I end up in the E.R. I think it was an asthma attack. A migraine from the stress and wait causes me to throw up.

They thought I was crazy, and they gave me a number for a psychologist. No help. Just this number. I throw it away as I leave.

The curtains of the world were forced open, as Rayne clamped onto my skirt. We boarded a train. Trains have always been my favorite mode of transportation. They are sleepy and bumpy. They are slow. They leave you the freedom to walk around, mingle with others, and bring what you want to eat on board. They are tucked away from the fancy world that loves airplanes.

Now, no longer did the world happily end in town where we got groceries. It went on for hours and kept going even as the sun had long gave us its last rays. She looked at me worried, but I knew it was all long overdue. I now owned 20 acres in Colorado at 8,200 feet.

Rayne, now four, stares out the window as the lights of a city blur past. She takes mostly after my other half. A dirty blonde with a strong philosophical side. She is great with tools and has even helped turn a car into a solar powered one. She has one blue eye and one green eye. Short tempered, quick witted, and likes to eat her veggies. I am always so blessed to have this little wild spirit stop all activity just for a hug or a quick snuggle.

We were a family of three. I didn't think it could get any better. I was wrong. In 2009, my heart expanded even further. I realized I was expecting again. Now I was sure my family was complete. Two kids were everyone's norm. Even as this little being turned out to be another girl. I named her after my wife, just switching her middle and first name.

Lotus Jewell turned out to be very impatient. She came into the world a week early. The day before Thanksgiving of 2009. After just one hour of labor, I delivered her myself in the cab of the truck that we took our first date on.

When my water finally broke, I felt the ring of fire, and barely had time to catch her. I placed her on my bare chest under my shirt. Everyone touched the top of her head as a welcome to Earth. The town was almost empty. For a moment we were the only ones who knew she was here.

My mom was waiting at the hospital. She opened the door expecting an angry pregnant woman. Instead she got a new angry mother worried about a wet baby in the cold. She ran into the E.R. and got a couple of nurses and a bed. They helped me out of the truck. I left the cord attached and had not yet delivered the placenta. They immediately covered me with lots of blankets. Then they ran me into the E.R. before moving me to the maternity ward.

All the nurses that took care of me in that hospital knew me as the one that didn't make it. They thought I was in shock because I was so calm. I knew it could happen with my first birth being so fast. Women all over the world from the beginning of time gave birth unassisted. I was ready for minor emergencies like a cord wrap.

They didn't want to release me right away. I spent Thanksgiving eating their version of turkey, mashed potatoes, and gravy. I enjoyed the quiet three days we spent together with no one, but the nurses.

This little person holds my strong tomboy nature. She is short fused, and obstinate. Favorite hobbies include bending the rules and finding my candy stash. We both favor potatoes and pasta. We love to write, and draw, and create. She seems to be an amazing blend of the two of us that in turn makes her totally unique.

I was comfortable, and confident in my role now as a mother. Birth, or a lack of one is so important to a woman's identity. I was a mother who had two fast rather uneventful births. My babies were full term. A term I wouldn't use until my third birth. That one I was not present for. That birth still haunts me. I didn't know it then. That was a good thing. I was convinced I was done forever with babies.

Instead we focused our energy on building a house together. Bit by bit it would come together. Both of us laying foundation, gathering help and materials. We put together walls, floors, and a strong sturdy roof. Finally, it felt like we had a mini empire hidden away in the trees.

We were homesteading. We loved nature. For us living with the earth was essential in our sense of spiritual wellbeing, our family dynamic, and even as catapult to encouraging others in our community to be more self-reliant. Hard as it was, it gave us a true sense of purpose. Rain or snow there were hungry animals to tend too. We built loving bonds as the fuzzy, feathery creatures all became family.

Money suddenly became harder and harder to get. People were selling animals at the livestock auction left and right. Hay was sitting in fields left to rot. Jobs were again impossible. Even now with my college degree.

The house building was stalling. We had places that still were leaking air, and uninsulated. Our car was even giving up on us. At our tenth year together, things became more and more frayed.

January 2013, we are cleaning up a hay field. Hay for work was a deal we couldn't pass up. I couldn't lift a bale of hay. I was lethargic again. This time Jewell was pointing the finger at me. I was being lazy. She turned her nose up at me after my unhelpful fiasco in the fields. I was still homeschooling, cooking, and cleaning. Though I lay on the couch most of the day. I feel guilty. I am also worried.

I arrange for my friend to come and take me into town. My best friend that we met when we first arrived here, He had eventually become my lover, as I dared venture into an open relationship, for the last two years. Older than me, but very much male, and very much from a more traditional family. He took me into the Convenient Care Center here in Colorado.

My wait was surprisingly only 30 min, and I was able to rest in a chair. The waiting rooms were open wide, with windows and plenty of places to sit. Not many people were waiting. There was a TV quietly playing the Denver news.

When I was ushered in, the rooms were large and clean feeling at least. The nurse showed me this time that my lung was partially collapsed. She pointed to the monitor sighting an 88-92% oxygen rate.

She left, and soon came back with a machine I had never seen before. A nebulizer. I breathed in deep the steamy medicated smoke. It was a miracle. I was coming out of my brain fog. I could breathe again!

The doctor was quick to see me. He was kind. He walked me through the inhaler he was going to give me. He told me why I was getting the medications.

Walking Pneumonia. He even gave me his business card if I got sick again. He told me if it got any worse to go straight to the E.R. I left feeling good.

"Well, are you sick?" My friend snapped at me coldly.

I snarled at him, and then grumbled I had a script to fill at the store. I hid it all away until everyone had gone to bed. I pulled out the inhaler and cleaned the long chamber it attached to. I used it twice. Then I took one of my pills and crawled into bed. It took me longer to fight it this time.

It wasn't because it wasn't working. It was because I didn't care. Jewell was cold to me now. My other partner had also turned away. Things were crumbling out from under my feet. No one cared. It was as if they were watching with excitement to see me fall.

I couldn't give in. I crawled my own way slowly out of the ditch and struggled on. I had built my own little empire. I wasn't going to let it just evaporate. I was lost, but I still put one foot in front of the other. I knew if I just kept going, I would see light eventually. Right?

One by one the dominoes seemed to fall around me. I broke up with my lover. I was determined to find a way to take the kids and leave Jewell. I would get pregnant again. My dad would die. 2013 was year of hell. A year that could have finished me completely. I just keep pushing and shoving myself forward.

I was grabbing pieces. I was desperately trying to knit what I could back together for just a little while longer. I called a truce with Jewell. Our issues were going to wait. We would turn a blind eye, and instead focus on the holiday season that was fast approaching. It seemed to pull us back together for a common cause again.

I counted the days tell Christmas 2013. It was going to be wonderful and the last one with our family of four. I was big and warm. Every day I felt the new baby kick stronger and stronger. Now the other two could feel their new brother/sister. They took delight in talking to, and occasionally poking at this curious stranger.

I had a vague list of names for a boy or girl, but nothing else at the time. I would buy all the stuff I needed for the new baby in January.

Then I would set it up as nesting took full effect. I would be ready for her/him in March. I was fully focused on soaking up every last moment with Rayne and Lotus.

The girls and I were going to make sugar cookies, and big soft ginger cookies. I would give them each a Christmas Eve bags with a new washed pair of pajamas, snacks, one toy, and some new crayons and a coloring book. I couldn't wait.

I imagined the kids pouncing on me in the morning. I would wiggle out of bed. The best someone as pregnant as I could. After a quick bathroom trip, I would waddle to the tree. The kids would tear open my gifts disguised as Santa's. I would fantasize over the new being, and silently count roughly how many months the baby would be next year.

I imagined a ham slow cooking in the oven. I would peel potatoes as Jewell cleaned up wrapping paper. The kids would bounce off me to help with this piece, and that. I would dodge their remote-controlled trucks. They would sugar out. Then we watch our yearly traditional movie together. Finally, with new stuffties clutched to their chests they would sadly say goodbye to Christmas and drift off to sleep.

I had it all planned and neatly organized. How everything was going to go. I had my home school calendar all set up for the year: books to buy, field trips, breaks, and goals. Everything color coordinated. I had a good idea of when I would go into labor.

Everything was organized, scheduled, and bendable. Now it was only two weeks until Christmas. Little did I know that with a shift of breeze all my thoughts, fantasies, and carefully constructed plans, would simply turn into dandelion wishes delicately dancing away in the wind.

The Burden You Carry

The burden you carry is your cage.
Truths unraveled is night's fate.
Watch the colors fade.

The creature creeps snarling rage.
Smoldering smiles hide the hate.
The burden you carry is your cage.

Switch the candy with the mace.
Losing is simply fate.
Watch the colors fade.

The rush desired is just a haze.
Death is creeping half past late.
The burden you carry is your cage.

Ripples turn to waves of rage.
Tearing down the ragged gate.
Watch the colors fade.

Night envelopes you in a haze.
Stars hang on strings of fate.
The burden you carry is your cage.
Watch the colors fade.

Christmas and Death

Little did I know that I was counting down the days until I died. While kids were jumping on their parents and running for the tree as the groggy eyed moms, dads, guardians, and grandparents, followed behind. Doctors and nurses who had forfeited their holiday fought to save my life. Nobody in their wildest of imaginations would have imagined this.

Around 7:15am the NICU was paged stat to my bedside. After a brief 29 weeks they pulled my baby out in seconds. I won't know anything for another two weeks. My mom would follow this new being, and not know for hours whether or not she would have to plan one funeral or three.

Death wears so many hats. We only want to see one. The one where we grow old and death is our mercenary. I had seen it in many forms. In the last four years I had lost numerous people. I had seen inside the casket of my great grandmother. I watched my grandmother cry as she sat there at the funeral. I hoped that one day my legacy's white haired would be crying over me. I think deep down it is the card we hope we draw.

The market is abuzz with things that add years to your life. Things that are supposed to increase our chances of pulling the death card late in the game. Pills and herbal tinctures. Exercise programs. Having a pet. Relaxing music even.

I didn't smoke, and I hardly drank. I for one loved juicing carrots, making salads, and smoothies. I cooked from scratch and didn't use any dairy that wasn't the best quality. We drank raw goat milk from our goats only, and ate our own eggs brought in by Lotus daily. I used to run. Even pregnant I still lifted 60lbs with ease. Before this even happened, I was sharing ripe pomegranates with my girls. I arrogantly thought I could escape death for many years.

My first death experiences on the human scale came at 17. In the spring I got to see a cadaver dissection. Our Junior Biology class was invited up to a medical school. I remembered them showing us his brain with the eyes still intact. Deep blue eyes attached to a gray brain floating around in a large jar. The lungs were unimaginably big. Surprisingly through it all only one girl in our class fainted. It wasn't me. I was too grossed out and simultaneously fascinated.

My best friend's dad had killed himself in a motel just a month after that. I stood in awe as my best friend's mother drunker than usual was fumbling over paperwork. Cigarette dangling shakily out of her mouth. My buddy, Kate, was in shock. She was 12. It happened in May which was when the schools closed for the summer, and the forest closed due to drought.

I stayed with her all summer long. Her mother called it a job and paid me even though I balked heavily at the thought. I used the money to buy us candy, and music. Kate didn't care she was just happy to have me with her.

His ashes appeared on the kitchen table one day. I shuddered thinking about the brain and eyeballs. It was in a tight locked clear jar, so you could see all the gray power. I shook him around and thankfully there was only gray powder, and small fragments of bone.

He sat like a vase would on the table all summer. We said hi to him as we microwaved some freeze-dried soups her mother left us. We sat at the table and chatted with him as the soups cooled, so we wouldn't burn ourselves.

When we watched movies, she would put him in his favorite chair. We got bold and would take him outside for walks, or to watch as I pushed her on their rusty green swing set. Eventually, we would put him in a backpack, for fear of adult eyes, and carry him to his favorite field. The grass was deep and the woods around us stretched on forever. We would place him in the grass next to us.

Then we would feast on the sugar filled snacks and soda I bought. As the breeze of the June air rustled our unkempt hair the day would slip away. I kept a close eye on the time, so he could be back on the table before her mom came home. I didn't want the fuss her mom might make.

All summer he was a part of our daily rituals. Kate's needs were my top priory. I began to come over to cook her dinner or clean her room. We would sometimes walk around outside in our pjs at 1am. No one seemed to care about us. My senior year came in August, and the forests eventually opened. I still came to care for her when she needed it. Now, he was gone. Thrown in the wind.

My best friend is now motherless. She wouldn't stop drinking and smoking. I remember the last time I saw her. She was in the last stages of cancer. Mouth cancer, I think, maybe throat. So weak that she could barely walk. and yet she made it to the kitchen to get a beer. It wasn't really drinking she said to me, as she struggled to keep her legs in some kind of order.

I wished I could break the beer bottle over her head. How many times had my buddy and me drug your drunk dumb ass to bed, I thought, as I watched her chug it down while smoking cigarettes. I sighed. What was done was done.

It wasn't long after that I heard she died. It was a month before her fiftieth birthday. It was in the first year I was mother of two. I imaged my friend going into her room and finding her asleep. I wished that was the truth. Oh, how I wished it was the truth. Her death was a lot more dramatic, and now Kate has to carry those scars with her forever.

I really try to shelter my kids. No horror movies, or bloody video games. I try to make death holistic, and without the fear that mainstream tagged to it. But we live on a farm. A goat farm. It's there. Sex, birth, and death is an honest part of their existence. One you cannot escape. Most of our plants are born in the spring and lay dead after the first hard frost.

Rayne had bounded outside one bright spring day to play with her favorite little goat. The mother had rejected it. She was five at the time. They were in an unconditional love loop. Rayne fed, and cared for her. The goat loved her and was always there in return.

Instead of giggles I heard a scream. I ran outside. My heart was too scared to follow. I saw the hooves dangling and turned 360 back for the house. Jewell was there. They were trying to hold her weight up. I grabbed the first sharp thing I could find. I wrenched open a kitchen drawer and pulled out a knife.

It was too late as she was cut free. In a freak accident she had hung herself by frolicking in the back of the truck. One weird way or another, she jumped out with a rope around her neck. There were just a few unforgiving inches, and a nasty knot to seal her fate. Rayne's face usually covered in dirt now was cried clean. I knew years later it still affected her.

Maternal death and the loss of a baby is something we experience on the farm. Brutally cold winters at our altitude had caused some pregnant goats to catch pneumonia and die. One or two had bloated. A kid born before we found out in a cold storm, easily meant death. Even if we warmed them and made sure their bellies were full. They would often still slip through our fingers.

No one wants to lose a child. Baby goats, and even a lost baby chick, upset us horribly. Such deaths I blocked in the human world. I would curiously peek at it hearing a story. Twirl it around in my mind, then let it go. Preemie babies were only for an unlucky handful. No way could it happen to me.

I had that all figured out too. I envisioned myself crying over my mom who would pass away at a very old age. I never thought my mother would be contemplating if I would live through another night at 28 years old. That she was bracing to help my wife raise her three grandchildren. If and only if the youngest made it, and Lotus who was also walking a tightrope on needing hospitalizing too.

I met death again as I heard it crackle in the voice of my dad, as I wished him what I knew was going to be his last Father's Day. He had been diagnosed with cancer of some kind last year. He was vague, and he made me promise I wouldn't say anything to anyone. It was his story to tell not mine. An easy promise.

I thought he would have a good fight. He would out smart it like he did everything else. I could see him at least 75 laughing at the doctors. Like his triple bypass. He would laugh as he would choke on his cigarette. Then hastily put it out. His usual habit. Full of stubborn pride.

This is where my paddle up shit creek comes in. It's June 30th, 2013. My period is now three days late. I decide that it is officially time for me to panic. I run to get a dollar store test. It's obvious as soon as my pee is sucked up the stick. I am staring now at two pink lines.

The nauseating days. The night sweats. It all makes sense now. It's more than summer. It's more than stress. I cannot believe such luck. I have two kids. My youngest is finally out of diapers. I didn't think this was going to happen again. I didn't want it to happen again.

Money was so tight. I was skipping meals to see the kids never had to go without. I didn't even want to be here. Be with her. Another mouth? Could I snuggle all three kids at the same time? Could I see that they all got a great education? What about hand holding while crossing the street? Would I have to go to a minivan now? Things come in packs of fours, not fives.

What about the joy of holding a newborn? The new baby smell. The sweet "I love you". The innocence. The everlasting bond that siblings can have. The chance it might be a boy. The simple idea of a new energy, and personality adding to our family.

I quietly make the kids lunch as I mull over it in my mind. I can make a grilled cheese like nobody's business. Perfectly brown and full of gooey cheese. I can easily add another, child that is. I let go and find joy. I can be excited for the first time this year. I smile and hug them. I give lots of hugs, so they don't think this is a special moment for me. I am just giving thanks that they are all with me.

I keep it from the kids for now. I have had a miscarriage before. I wanted to hold out until I reached the 12 week hurtle. They would all find out in due time. I keep it quiet. I know I won't meet with much support from my community. Jewell is thrilled. It is our little secret.

At ten weeks pregnant, in unmercifully hot August, I boarded a train. I try not to throw up with the mix and mash of smells. The rocking. I sleep and giggle at a couple of new mothers as they tried unsuccessfully to make their littles behave. I catch one mom glaring at me in a way that said I didn't have any reason for my smirk. I feel like flashing her my old stretch marks and burgeoning belly.

I decide to pass her by and go for a quick cup of soup. It is hot in my hands. I hope for no sudden stops, as I slither through the passenger car quiet as a mouse. Some people are sleeping or attempting too. The soup seems to take forever to cool. It's salty. Probably not the best for the baby. It helps my ever-queasy stomach. I am sure this is a sign it is going to be a boy. I have never had morning sickness. I slurp it down as I squint out at the dark trying to piece together Flagstaff, the town I was raised in.

Not much more than two hours later I was greeted by my mom. It was a long 20-hour train ride to dry scorching Bull Head. It's now roughly 2am. She brought burritos for me to eat. I was now too nervous to eat. I kept the bag of goodies close knowing it wouldn't be long before hunger would strike again.

I listened intently on the updates, as we rumbled and bounced through the sleeping town in her tiny Jeep. I was still fighting to keep my soup down. She told me how she had lost her job and had to move out of her place. She barely got all of her stuff at her mom's (Grandma) before coming out here to join in this mess.

We pulled up into the driveway. The air still hot, despite the blackness that rushed in to fill the void that her headlights turning off caused. A second later the porch light flicked on. I drew my breath as I wiggled out of the Jeep. There stood the big looming little brother that I hadn't seen in years. He hugged me. Then turned to Mom to complain about Dad.

From the sounds of it Dad had taken over his amount of medication. Death was waiting patiently for him. There was nothing left except skin pulled over bones. Leukemia and COPD did an amazing job taking a strong, slightly overweight attitude, down to the humble helpless mess before me. I bent over and gave him a kiss on the forehead like I always have.

He asked three times if I had made the trip out. Three times he smiled at me like he hadn't seen me in years. Three times I kissed him on the forehead and let him know I was there.

No mistake about it. The gruff cowboy was still there. I still snuggled up next to him and showed him pictures of the farm. I asked him his expertise on whether my "Gouck" was a duck or a goose. He, impatient as usual, told me to look at the bill. It was obviously a duck.

He loved kids and animals. He enjoyed being a grandpa. He hadn't seen Rayne since I was pregnant with Lotus. I showed him pictures of Lotus. The wild free running clone of me. Sadly, he would never meet her, or the new one.

On Monday it was his last birthday. He had made it 69 years. He wanted his birthday present. What he thought was a pill to end his suffering that night. We were almost all kicked out of the room when the hospice nurse only came up with morphine. That was cleared by the doctor. Mom and I took turns giving him a strong dose every two hours.

On Tuesday he was bright and happy. He wanted to go dancing. Mom and I looked at each other worried he would try to get up again and fall like he usually did. He must have learned his lesson from the last time. We all continued to spend as much time as possible with him.

He was on his way down in a blink of an eye. By Wednesday night we both went in his room to find him too asleep to rouse. I swabbed his lips and gums with a special hydrating gel.

In the morning Mom cleaned him one last time. I held his hand and stood beside him. Rubbing the backside of his hand gently I told him quietly how much we all loved him and how much it was going to be okay.

His heart stopped. My world stopped spinning for a moment. I folded both hands across his chest. Then blurry eyed I ran to find Kyron and Mom. It was finally over.

The hospice nurse came over quick. She was light and bright in attitude, as usual, wearing pink floral scrubs. She worked in a field that even doctors have trouble with. She was a secret that no one wants to hear. The couple of times that I saw her she was happy and got a good giggle out of Mom and I. Once she had come to trust me of course. She was as content as a Labor and Delivery nurse. Respectful, and light in such dark times of people's lives. Or, was it dark times? Maybe she knew a secret we didn't.

She fascinated me. I sat on the bed and watched her work. She chatted with me. About what I cannot tell you. It went in one ear and out the other.

Instead of handing mom's new life and watching pink happy babies; she was leaning over dad checking for a heartbeat. Instead of swaddling babies; she was dressing him for leaving the trailer he called home for the last seven years. She gave us all hugs and smiles before she left.

Two funeral home workers showed up next to remove him. They were snappily dressed in all black. They handed us their card. They told us to go into the living room and try not to look as they removed him from the trailer. I thought it was odd, but I didn't want anything else haunting me.

We worked all day, for 5 weeks, to clean out his house. 20 or more years of clutter. There were more remotes and lighters than I had ever encountered. Broken glasses that were saved to be fixed at a later time that never came. Old, cracked, and dusty pictures of old times with people I would never meet.

There was a hole in his closet floor covered up with carpet that could have thrown me into the E.R. had I fallen in it. I found dust bunnies that have lived for so long they must have names. Dinosaur sized cockroaches skittered across the roof at night, casting terrifying shadows. It wasn't scary enough for me to leave my spoton top of air conditioning vent. Unless the damn thing tried to fly. Then it was squealing and scrambling.

As we worked, I lived on store bought pizza and whipped cream. I loved cooking and proudly took over for Mom but kept setting off the fire alarms. It kept us on our toes. Mom kept a broom handy to knock out the angry siren.

We also had toys that my younger brother clung to even in his twenties. He was a big guy looming over us at six foot, and three hundred some pounds. There was nothing little about my little brother anymore. A big snuggly comfort. Now he needed to spread his wings and fly. This nest needed emptying completely.

When we needed a break, we would walk three blocks down to the river. I would put on a pair of brown boy swim trunks, and my favorite sports bra. With lots of water to drink and a towel we would make our way down to the shore. The dividing line between Nevada and Arizona. Thankfully, I hardly ever sun burn.

The water cooled my hot skin. I was a never-ending ball of heat. The water would take the weight off my bones and ease my back. It was such a relief from the hard work. I would sometimes grab the snorkel and mask and look under the water. There were cinder blocks, and algae. This is the Nevada river. I bet there are dead bodies. I would pop up slowly. Matted hair and my mask and snorkel always caused my mom to go into a hard rib hurting laugh.

We finished putting Dads funeral together. I know he really didn't want one. Tough luck for him. We needed it. I am surprised that there is quite a bit of people. In his favorite little chapel, we sit. All three of us crammed into a little pew. We were elbow to rib with no room to do much more than breathe. We listened to the amazing preacher talk. I never met one as on his toes, honest, and kind as he. Well I don't think I have met very many to begin with.

It was an unspoken fact that I held most of dad's spirit. I got up and stood leaning on the pew. It was hard. I felt tears and choked as everyone stared. Kyron came and stood next to me. I buried myself in his big warmness for a minute to catch myself.

When I was ready, I turned back to the crowd. I told of how we met when I was four. He was my cowboy daddy. He took me under his wing and spread his love of the wild, of nature, and earth with me. We would scout and hike the woods. He taught me the songs of different birds. He taught me how to track. He showed me different plants. He taught me how to drink from ponds, and streams.

It didn't matter that I was a girl, and not his blood. I was his hunting buddy. I was great at finding rabbits he shot and helped him clean them. I was his fishing buddy. We would fill the freezer every year with our catch. He would brush my hair and walk me to the bus. That was our truce.

What I didn't say is what everyone knew. He could be cruel. He was very hard on me. He left bruises, mainly not on my skin, but on my spirit. There were many years where I hated him. He toughened me up. Painful as it was; I am grateful for the strength and gifts he has given me.

Finally, everything was done. I was exhausted. It wasn't until the beginning of October that I arrived back at home. Instead of the train back Mom and Dad agreed I could keep his little car. I used it as a trade for something more kid and farm practical. That took a little time to work out.

I have rough roads in and out. I needed a four-wheel drive. No one would plow my roads. I had a baby coming. I needed to get in and out in the middle of the looming winter ahead. March could be one of the wettest, and the worst for getting bogged down in soupy icy mud.

Finally, I made the trade. I got an emerald green '94 Jeep Grand Cherokee. I was in heaven. The AC worked. Leather seats with minimal damage. The mileage was high, and it clunked when it turned. I was in heaven. I could see fitting all three in the back seat. I imagined where I would put my new car seat.

I named her Alice. I tried at first to name her Forest. That turned into a fifteen-minute fiasco of trying to turn off the car alarm. That name was a no go. Alice on the other hand fit. I was considering moving. I wanted something tough enough to take me down the rabbit hole.

After a nonstop 18-hour trip with just a sandwich, and some fried back barring's I finally made it home. I was tired and sore. I collapsed into bed after a quick shower. I didn't get more than two hours of sleep. The kids were excited to see me, and what I had stuffed in the new car.

I brought back the hot wheel cars I played with as a child. I brought Halloween costumes, and bags of new clothes. I brought most of Dads camping stuff. His favorite knife was now nestled in my purse as my token. His ashes were in a white cardboard box, and in a necklace around my neck.

I also brought with me a bigger stomach. There was no hiding my pregnancy now that I was a big 18 weeks. Everyone eventually found out. Even who my best friend at the time. I tried to keep it from him, but there was no way my 5'3 frame was going to hide that much baby and water.

After a cold and awkward visit at his place Jewell warmed the van and we left. I hardly even looked back. As we crawled out of his place in the dark, we kept a careful eye out for his dog who was pure white. She liked to chase cars. Our minds on Pinot, and a good chat between us, for once, we almost didn't see it.

When we did, I screamed out, and prepared for it to come through the window. One hand on my face palm out, and the other on my stomach. Jewel hit the brakes. A lone wild horse black as this moonless night seemed to appear out of nowhere. His flank must have touched our bumper. He flicked his tail against the front of the van as he spooked on across the road.

We waited tell our hearts had stopped beating so hard. First, we looked on both sides of the road waiting for more horses. Oddly, there was none. We crawled on slowly still watching out. I had memorized the two main packs of horses that run around these parts. I never remember seeing a pure black horse like that. I shuddered deep and fiddled with the heater.

It was bitter cold as Halloween came around. We didn't make near as far as other years before. We were chilled even through winter coats. We could take no more, so we headed back to our warm wood stove. I picked out candy I wanted to keep sighting the fact that the baby needed to be apart too.

The next day as I washed the dishes, with a chocolate bar shoved in my cheek, a butterfly big and white came thumping on the window I daydream out of when my hands are full of soapy dishes. I was intrigued. To see a butterfly here was rare, and in this cold seemed impossible. I dried off my hands and swallowed my treat down. I went outside. It was easy to catch, and I brought it inside.

The girls loved to look at it and were careful not to touch. Finally, after a day it was still very much alive in my living room. So, I let it loose back outside. I watched as it fluttered off. Something fluttered in me. More than the baby stirring. A strange sadness I couldn't place perched inside me.

The beginning of November. I went in for my ultrasound at twenty-one weeks. I decided against finding out the sex. This was going to be my last baby, and I wanted a surprise. Not long after I dreamt, like I had done with all my babies at this point in my pregnancy, what it was and what it would look like.

I told Jewell one morning that it was a girl, and she looked just like me. I also told her that I felt this was going to be a C-section. The baby was not in my hips right. I felt like the hands and feet were not in the right places. At the edge of my consciousness something didn't feel right. I couldn't pull it in or push it out.

She on the other hand countered my thoughts. She was convinced it had to be a boy this time. She swore that she seen dangly bits in the ultrasound. She also reassured me that the baby had plenty of time left to move into the right spot, and not to worry about delivery. I had done great so far. She reassured me that everything was going to be fine.

My problems were minimal. My winter coat was getting hard to zip. A faded green canvas coat for the male frame and no giving way. I didn't know what I would do in January. By then it would be too small for me. Also, putting on winter boots seemed to be a prenatal yoga exercise in itself.

My hips loosened so intensely I was a newborn calf on ice. I slid around in the snow almost helpless. I made an igloo with Rayne. After an hour of scooping and putting snow in a big pile; she hollowed it out. It was perfect. Except for one spot. I leaned over to pack the snow down. Then I lost my balance and crashed into it. Thankfully, she wasn't inside. To make matters worse Rayne was laughing so hard, she could hardly rescue the stuck turtle.

I was happy. The holiday season with the kids always made me excited. Last year, Jewell took the girls to see his aging parents. So, I didn't have Christmas with them that year. Someone had to tend to the farm. I bought two big soft teddy bears, that I cuddled, while they were gone. This year I was so blessed to have them. I really wanted to show them that.

At night, I was intensely dreaming of Dad. I was sure it was the grieving processes. One morning he sat there on the edge of my bed as I was half awake trying to tell me something. He seemed so sad. My stomach tightened.

That same day Lotus found the talking fish that was his. I had it hidden. She played with it and wouldn't let me take it. I desperately wanted to throw it against the wall. The following night Dad was there again. He came as a black bear. I was catching and releasing rainbow trout. I woke with an immense sadness. A strange feeling that I just couldn't place or shake.

I called Mom and told her that he was haunting me.

"It's not Halloween anymore." I told her.

She laughed at me. Then she went on to tell me she thought it was twins. She kept telling me that the girl would reveal herself in December. I told her firmly I wasn't going to get anymore ultrasounds so there would be no "revealing" in December. I would change the subject then to a list of names I was pondering. I really liked Meadow, Brook, or Zeppelin. I had no boy names, but I would come up with one just in case.

For now, it was The Baby, or Cricket. My little bug. That was that. I was shifting my focus on the next holiday: Thanksgiving. It brought snow, and more bitter cold. Snow that wanted to stick around. Wind that could cut through anything we had. I stepped out for wood in my dad's coveralls and a shirt. I found it so funny that I couldn't zip it up with my belly that I had Jewell take a picture. I didn't know it would be one of only three pregnancy pictures.

As soon as December rolled around, I put up my poor ratty used to death plastic tree. It could last one more year. I had no choice in the matter. I wrapped some presents. I didn't tag them as I knew whose was whose just by the paper I used. I hid them in the attic. It nowhere entered my mind to think that someone else might have to deal with what I left behind. Even though I wasn't feeling up to par.

My asthma seemed to keep flaring up. I was using the inhaler more than ever. I just passed it off to cold dry air as usual. My doctor canceled an appointment I was going to talk more about it. As time wore on, I became more and more concerned. It seemed like all pregnancy related stuff, with a slight cold coming on.

Was it asthma I was fighting again? Was I overly tired from my final trimester? Was I just over doing it?

I knew I was simply tired to the bone that cold December morning of the 16th. Wrapping the rest of the presents could wait. I hid them all over the attic and laid down. Jewell made dinner, and I just snuggled with who ever came to lay with me.

The 17th wasn't much better. I felt something coming on even stronger. I used my inhaler twice and thought about using it a third time. Something was wrong. I was sick. I was still convinced it was a cold compounded on overdoing it in my oncoming last trimester. I was badly in need of naps. Even sweeping the floor was a chore that left me with no energy.

The 18th I developed a cough that hurt way deep down. I had never felt something so painful. I had suffered bronchitis and walking pneumonia in the past. This was new. This I was starting to take notice. The inhaler wasn't working anymore.

Earlier that month I had a Rayne and me day. We had lunch together. She happily showed off her budding pre-teen state by eating everything placed in front of her. We laughed, and she helped me along as I ran my errands.

Now, despite the tiredness, I wanted to have a Lotus and me day. We went into town. A long hour in and one hour back. I did laundry with her help. I bought a 50lb. bag of dog food and easily loaded it in the back of my Jeep. I got our propane tanks filled and easily loaded them in as well. I took the soon to be dethroned baby for a quick treat of hot French fries, and a frozen coffee.

I bought more fruit and vitamin C. I took two prenatal vitamins and thought that anything could be knocked out with the right herbs. It may be true, but it was too little too late for me. The cough was there, and it was dizzyingly painful. I had to stop everything to cough. I would cough deep into my coat, and quickly hand sanitize.

There was a baby in a cart I had not seen. As I coughed, I looked up to see the tiny thing looking at me. What if I passed it on? To this little creature without much immunity. It sent shivers down my spine. I needed to leave. I thought about stopping for a nebulizer treatment, but I was so tired that I told myself I would head straight for the doctor's office as soon as she was open at 9am tomorrow.

I was too tired to unload the food, and instead I showered and laid down. Rayne and Lotus came in wanting to snuggle and probably poke at the baby. I sent them out. Rayne was hurt that I didn't let her hug me.

Nothing was working. I was spiraling downhill at an incredibly fast rate. I was burning up, shivering, and the cough hurt beyond words. As I tried to get comfortable, to my horror, I coughed right in Jewell's face.

I couldn't lay down by the middle of the night. I got up and tried to sit on the internet and pass time. By the early morning hours, I was doing everything in my power to keep breathing sitting up in a chair. All my focus was on getting that next breath. Jewell got up. She sat next to me quietly for a moment. She breaks the silence asking me if she should call 911.

I was shocked. Could I be that sick? No, it was 4:30am I could wait 5 hours for 9am. Maybe I would go in at 8:30am, and bang on the door. I just need a nebulizer. 4:45am I am breathing in tiny puffs. It's getting harder and harder to complete each breath. I realize I am going to die, and worse kill the baby if I don't do something.

I called with Jewell beside me. I had never seen her this worried. I have to call three or four times as the phone disconnects numerous times. I pass the phone to her, and they manage to get a rough sketch of where we live. They keep me on the phone while the ambulance searches me out. They finally say the ambulance is as close as they are going to get. Now it's up to us to find it. They don't want to get stuck.

In my pjs, winter boots, and my winter coat I grab my purse. I take a long moment to look back at my living room. The kids are quietly sleeping. I resist the urge to walk back upstairs to hug them or watch them sleep.

I stop for a second, as I fight with my coat. I savor the last moments in my living room. The ratty Christmas tree, wood stove, and little hot wheel cars sprinkled around. I shiver. Not from cold. Terror has passed and has broken me open. It is no longer hidden deep inside me. Right at the surface I feel it. I know I may very well not come back. A strange feeling bubbles to the surface, more like a quiet song that I know I heard long before my first breath.

Watch the Weather Change

I feel it in my bones.
It is creeping up around me,
like vines,
it is cutting through my skin.
It is the winters breath,
cold and ghostly.
It burns inside me,
crackling, popping.
It flares.
Unexpected.
Everything is still.
No birds sing.
The deer lie down.
The storm foreseen.
Its powers hidden
whispers in the wind.

$\mathcal{P}$urging and $\mathcal{L}$etting $\mathcal{G}$o

I almost cannot stand the unbearable cold air. It is dark and slick outside. I shiver as I creep out the door toward the dark shape that resembles my car. Halfway there the headlights flick on, and Jewell starts it.

I feel a cold nose against my hand. My dog, Spot, as usual, wants to make sure I am okay. My response is almost automated. I touch his head and his ears. I run my finger over his head starting between his eyes where his white patch is. His fur is thick. His nose is cold and wet. He walks with me the rest of the way. It is hard to see the black lab without the spot of white on his head. Hence his name. I didn't name him. I wish I did. He is my guardian here on the farm. He must be five years old now. I touch him one last time as I reach my destination. A quick thank you.

I open the car door, and wiggle in the seat. Everything is ice cold to the touch. The car smells like older vehicles stink as they struggle to warm. As soon as the door is shut Jewell bolts out of the driveway. It whines and complains and bumps hard against the ground.

I stare longingly at the house we built. Spot runs to his favorite hillside area to watch us leave. Our farm is quiet. It looks desolate. Not even the goats stir from their warm barn. The chickens are still roosting. My nine-year-old daughter, and her four-year-old sister sleep soundly in their beds. We turn now hastily to the left, and the house is gone from sight.

I shiver and pull the ugly green coat as far over my belly as I can. I strain in the dark a few seconds more at the vague outline. Finally, I turn around, and I resituate in my seat pulling the belt over me laboriously clicking it into place. I begin to look out for the lost ambulance.

We slip, and bump, and turn, once more. Onto another dirt road. This one is older and more used. Jewell takes advantage of this slightly safer road and speeds up even faster. I glance at her and see fear. She is usually not so quiet. I don't know when I have ever seen her look this scared.

Two miles away Jewell and I spot the bright lights. They are waiting at the house we told them wasn't the right one. They must feel safer waiting there. As we speed down the road, they realize it is us who has called. They speed toward us.

As the sun creeps silently over the mountain to announce the new day we meet up. Jewell parks and gets out to help me. I kiss her quickly on the cheek. The back door of the ambulance is open, and a lady waits for me. I waddle toward the awaiting open door, and I heave myself up inside with her gloved helping hand.

I lean over the gurney and cough that painful cough. Up comes a gray boogie. Maybe, it was just stuck in my throat, and now I will be fine. I place it in a tissue and shove it in my pocket. I get up on the gurney. The door shuts before I can look out one last time. She begins to work on me.

The EMT who is not driving is an older woman with a white shirt, and black pants. She looks like someone should at noon. Fully awake, and ready to tackle the day. I wonder how much coffee it takes for such an effect at such an early hour.

My coat is stripped off me and placed on my feet with my purse. She begins to place super sticky patches on me to measure my heart rate and oxygen levels. Then I'm covered with blankets. On the bumpy road she manages to get an IV in effortlessly. I'm impressed. She runs her stethoscope down my back, stopping in certain areas, and going back over certain areas again.

I still feel silly, and I will be mortified if nothing is wrong with me. I am pregnant, so I can always use that as an excuse. I would rather be safe than sorry. As soon as my monitor is up it is obvious that I really am struggling to breathe. My oxygen stats are ranging in the 80's. The lower 80's.

They give me a nebulizer. It does not work. Another gray boogie painfully comes up. I can feel the change in road. We are on the highway now. I can't see much in the dusty small back windows. The EMT gives me a list of questions. I bring my focus back to her. She scratches my answers to them on her clipboard. I nod, or quickly answer through breathing with the nebulizer.

The scenery is blurred as we drive on. I cannot tell where we are at, or how fast we are going. I look around with great interest at this tiny ambulance encased in metal. I wonder how many people have died in here. I wonder if they really don't have regular bandages.

She listens again to my lungs. I can see she is worried as she looks at my stats marking away on her clipboard. She gives me one more nebulizer treatment to no avail. She worriedly tells me that the bottom lobes of my lungs are collapsed. She calls in to get a clearance for another nebulizer. They give an okay over the crackly receiver. She gives me my third one. No changes.

Now we are at the hospital. Tiny Alamosa. I am guessing 6am. No one but us is out in the cold. I am scared that the gurney is going to bump hard on the ground. They laugh playfully with me. They slide me down with effortlessness. I joke that they haven't done this much have they.

I am wheeled to a bed in the E.R. Before I know it someone else is listening to my lungs. My stats are still not looking promising. Maybe another nebulizer treatment will finally do the trick. They decide I will need monitoring and want to keep me overnight. I cringe at the thought of being here. I know I will not sleep.

From a crack in the curtain I see a nurse on the phone. They are debating where to put me. I am pregnant. They think I belong in the maternity ward. I am sick, and I don't want them to put me there with the new babies. I make it perfectly clear that if they try it, I will tear out my IV and leave. I pick a little at the tape. I wait and wait.

They finally agree that the maternity ward is not a good idea. They debate back and forth where I should end up. They think it is pneumonia but are not sure. I wait for answers. I wait for a bed away from the other germs and sick people.

They bring a nice OB nurse down to monitor my baby. I am only 28 weeks. The baby seems be moving around just fine. I can see the heart beating, as the machine spits out paper that looks like an earthquake monitor. The baby swims and kicks. So unaware and peaceful.

Next to me, behind the terrible brown, curtain, is an older man. He must have the same thing I do. He is coughing, and using tissues, and a spit bucket like me. But every time I cough the baby bounces into my ribs.

I spend five hours on the tiny cot. They give me two more nebulizers. It's not working. My back is killing me. My ribs are bruised. I hate having to use the bathrooms here.

Finally, they give me a gown. Green and stamped with SLV (San

Luis Valley). I keep my undies, and long johns on. I pile on blankets as I cannot keep warm enough.

They wheel me down to the x-ray room. It's cold. I hurt. I am dizzy and so tired, that my mind is swimming. They give me forms that say small radiation this and that. I sign. They have me breathe as deep as I can while I have my hands up on a pole. Turn this way. Now that. We're done. I am cold.

They put me in a normal room. Their small-town version of an ICU. Two beds, two white boards, two TVs, one bathroom. Thankfully, there is no one else in the room with me. I take over the bed closest to the window. I stamp the other bed as mine too with my bag of clothes.

I curl up in bed. A nurse with mask and gloves writes the date across the top. Then he writes the name of my main nurse, my certified nursing assistant, and my doctor. He shows me the call button.

He gives me an awesome SLV plastic cup with a straw. I had one from delivering Lotus here. Once I was done breastfeeding it seemed to fade away. That alone made it worth spending the night here. I ask him to fill it up for me. I am insatiably thirsty.

First, he puts a pulse oximeter on my finger, and plugs it into a machine. There are more nurses here now. One jabs a giant q-tip up my nose to swab for the flu. They take blood. They fill up numerous tiny vials. I am theirs now. Their pregnant guinea pig. It's okay for now. I still have six days before Christmas.

After all the drama has subsided; the nurse brings me ice. I fill my cup up. I situate the best I can. The bedside table I pack with a box of tissues.

I pull my phone out of my purse. If I don't tell Mom Jewell will. I don't want her getting upset, that I tried to hide it. Jewell will tell because I do, sometimes, try to hide things. I tend to recluse when I need to reach out the most.

I realize my battery is on half. The last thing on my mind was a phone charger. This battery will be dead by the end of the day. Mom is in Arizona, so the local phone is out of the question. I never took to electronics very quickly. Texting is still a laborious brand-new venture for me.

"In hospital. I think I have pneumonia. Bottom lobes of lungs collapsed. Doing okay. No worries." I text.

I try to sleep in this strange new world. I am badly exhausted, but I cannot unwind. Lack of sleep is finally catching up to me. Yet, I am too anxious to sleep.

I turn on the TV and get lost in an infomercial. I am surprised they can go an hour talking about some fancy toothbrush and vogue case. I see now why I do not have a TV. There is not much else to do. I look at the clock. I am now hanging in between breakfast and lunch. Why did they not think to feed the pregnant lady?

I hear a bleep. I pick my phone up and read the text from Mom.

"With a friend. Did they figure out if it's pneumonia? Will call in a bit. Make sure to eat well."

I am shaking now from the lack of sleep. I roll over and close my eyes. I am desperate for sleep. I doze off. I slip slowly into a deeper sleep. Then I am jerked dizzily out of it.

Every two hours a respiratory nurse comes in to give me a nebulizer. Then he checks my lungs. Every two hours, it's the same story. My heart rate is high. My oxygen is low. My blood pressure is fluctuating. The bottom lobes of my lungs are collapsed.

The phone rings. Its Mom. I can tell just by the ring tone. I know I have to be quick. The phone is dying.

"Hey, any news? How's the baby?" She says.

"Baby's fine. Their giving me steroids to open my lungs up. I heard with preemie moms that they help the unborn baby develop their lungs too." I say stifling a yawn.

"I had a dream last night about you. You died, and they brought you back with shock paddles." She pauses. "How true is this?"

"Very not true." I snap back angrily with the fear she just injected in my veins like ice water.

"You are eating right? You have to eat for that baby."

"I know Mom." There is a sarcastic tone, with an edge of anger in me now.

"Blow back up lungs. Is it pneumonia? How long are they going to keep you in there? Do you need me?"

"I don't know. My battery is dying out. I gotta go. I love you."

"Love you too. Call if you need me. I don't mind coming to be by your side. Just let me know, okay?"

"Okay. Will do. Love you too. Bye."

Truth was not so much the battery, but me not knowing the answer to anything. What is it I'm fighting? Why am I not getting any better? Do I need Mom?

Jewell and the girls come to see me on Friday the 20th. It's an hour from my house to here. Plus, the ice, and the holiday traffic danger. I told Jewell to wait. I was hoping when she did come, it would be to get me out of here. It sadly was just a visit.

I make everyone including me wear a mask. The girls hold their mask to their face as it's too big for them. I really want to kiss and hug them. I don't want them to get this. Whatever it is. I know I must seem cold to them, as I stand back. My arms folded across my chest instead of welcoming and touching.

I am worried about them. Lotus has a runny nose, and puffy red eyes. Jewell seems to be fighting it too. Rayne seems resistant, but I don't want to chance that.

Jewell brings me fresh fruit, juice, and my phone charger. She debates on whether she should go back out and get me some carrot juice. I tell her not to worry. I have plenty of goodies.

Jewell hugs me hard. I will not let her kiss me. I bury my face in her, and inhale that lovely farm wood smoke smell. I want to break down and cry. I want her to hold me forever. She is scared too. I see it in her eyes. I bite my lip, as tears swell up. She sees them. I blink them back with a few deep breaths. I smile. Jewell squeezes my hand.

I don't want the kids to know how freaked out I am. After a while they are wearing thin, and tired. We say our goodbyes without kisses. I do touch each one of their heads gently running my fingers through their hair.

Rayne reaches out and touches me. In her eyes I see a deep fear. I swallow hard and smile brightly for her. I know I am lying. I know she's not buying it.

Lotus hugs me tightly. Her skin is on fire. I know she misses me. She doesn't understand why I'm here. I for once am lost for words.

"I'll be home soon. I promise." I tell her also giving one of my fake smiles.

I grab my purse. I fish my debit card, and money out of my wallet. Jewell doesn't want to take it, but I don't want to worry over it. I don't need it now.

Jewell ushers them out of the room. The farm smell fades. I stare at the door replaying them leaving. I want them back. I feel guilty, like I was too cold. I cry. I have this strange feeling that I may not see them again.

I am crying more from anger. I cannot control this free fall. I don't know how to put into words what I feel creeping closer. I pull the blankets up as I shiver. I doze off for a few fleeting moments.

When I wake on my table now is the oranges Jewell left. I peel them, as I surf the web with my phone. I update my social media site with something half serious about my situation, yet lighted up with my sarcastic nature. I make note that the baby is fine. Only last month did

I tell everyone outside my main circle that I was even expecting another baby.

I chug my new bottle of lemonade. I cannot get enough water. I drink it with vitamin C packets and add lots of ice. Eating for me begins to fall away. I usually become an incessant eater this far in my pregnancy. The three meals they bring me in Styrofoam containers with plastic forks, would have not been enough.

In the maternity ward after I had Lotus all my meals were on real plates with metal forks. I realize this difference quickly. I know it's because I am contagious. What's scarier than that; I know I am not eating enough. Nothing looks good. I try to force the foods down me for the baby's sake. It gets harder and harder to do.

I cough so hard I cause my nose to bleed. I cough so hard I puke, and unknowing to me I aspirate it onto my right lung. I cough so hard that peeing the bed is becoming the normal. Those gray boogies are haunting me. I now know they are in my lungs.

The respiratory nurse comes in every two hours to give me my nebulizer. Then they run their cold stethoscope down my back. The same thing day and night. I don't get any better. They take turns announcing to me that I have pneumonia, or bronchitis.

Good I think to myself. Then give me antibodies and let me go home. They have switched so many times; I give up.

They even give me a load of questions that lead to Hantavirus. For a moment I panic knowing I have cats. Two of them: Flower, and Darkness. You could hardly tell them apart except for size. One was a year younger.

I have cats that care about my pregnancy. They want to see I am getting my protein. So, they have brought me numerous half dead mice in my bed; while I was sleeping. Not a fun thing to wake up to in the middle of the night. Especially, when you can't just bounce out of bed.

I ache for home. I want the smell of wood smoke, cold air, and warm farm animals. Not this overly sterile boxy room that reeks of chemicals. I want my bed. I want my pillow. Not these deflated scratchy ones that do not belong to anyone. I want unbroken promises that I'm all right. I want unsick kids. I want my perfect holiday season. I want a dark night with no nurse coming in every four hours.

I am tired, sore, and frustrated. In my anger I have hit the respiratory nurse. I have yelled at and fought just about everyone. I even thought about tearing out my IV and leaving. I picked at the tape, so temped. If I wasn't pregnant; I may have done just that.

The baby is like a small bolder slamming into my ribs. They are bruised from all the coughing. A nurse tells me to put a pillow on my stomach and hug it as I cough.

"Think happy thoughts." She says as she looks at my heart monitor concerned.

She changes my sheets for the second time, while I wait, in the chair. I have run out of long johns and underwear. She puts a mattress pad under me and gives me a pack to use as I need. The nurses have also gotten tired of me unplugging my pulse oximeter at will to go pee, so they give me a bedside commode.

At dinner, I roll some kind of chicken and noodles around my Styrofoam container with my plastic fork. The thought of me even putting it in my mouth makes me want to puke. I close the lid. I unplug my pulse oximeter and grab my IV pole. I take it over to the trash and throw it out. Then I get more water.

The nurse comes in grumpy that I have unplugged myself again. I ask for ice. She glares at me. Then she goes to get my ice. When she comes in again, I am back in bed all plugged in. I am dumping another vitamin C packet in my water.

She wants to look and see how much I ate. I shrug and vaguely tell her I ate enough. She replies with the stink eye again. I pretend not to notice. I turn on my TV. She takes it as a cue to leave.

Jewell talks to me on Saturday morning. The phone ringing startles me out of a rare deep sleep. Groggy, I reach over and pick it up. Her picture flashed across the screen. I poke the little green button.

"Hello." I say.

"Hey, babe how are you doing?" Jewell answers.

"I don't know." I choke back tears.

In the background I can hear Rayne grumbling that the eggs are burnt.

Jewell sighs and turns to Rayne.

"Pick the brown off." She gripes. "Be quiet! I am talking to your mom. I will give you the phone in a minute."

"Hey, I was doing some research." Jewell says, shifting focus back to me. "I read that it may be H1N1. The good thing is that if you have fought it this long; you will probably make it. It should let up soon."

My heart leaps with that little flicker of faith. Its only four days before Christmas. I tell her how to prepare the ham. I tell her where the presents are roughly located. She says we can wait until I get home. We exchange "I love you's." I talk to Rayne. She sounds small and meek on the phone. Then I am handed to Lotus. I cannot make heads or tails of her conversation, so I tell her I will be out soon.

I hang up. I flash a thought that I should have told Jewell where I have stashed my WIC coupons. I pick up the phone to call again. A nurse comes in, and I hang up before I finish dialing the numbers.

The sun fades quickly. It is the longest night of the year. I cannot sleep because breathing is my main fight. I am scared this night will never end for me. I want to leave my body at this point. I know if I do, then I take the baby with me. I am barely holding it together. My right lung is in so much pain, that I cannot lay on my right side anymore. I have made no noticeable improvements here in this hospital. It's becoming more apparent that there is no promise of tomorrow granted to my baby or me.

Beside water all I craved is prayer. Throughout this never-ending blackness I find the light and revel in it. I do not ask for help. I thank the One for all my blessings. I ask only for strength, as I embark on this voyage. I hold prayer and meditation all night long. The sunrise is the most intense beauty I have ever felt. It breaks over the trees and through my dusty window. I feel that whatever happens I have a hand to hold. If I cross over, I have loving arms. If I stay, I have strength.

With the sun strong in my window, I try to sleep. It doesn't last long. My nurse comes into the room happy and bright. At first sight I am annoyed at the sunshine he brings. Its blinding, and I retract.

I am surprised he doesn't want to wear a mask. He brings me breakfast, and the paper. I cannot believe he brought me the paper. I actually got the Sunday paper. It feels like a dozen roses. I read it happily, even though the weather is the least of my concerns.

His kindness is so intense that I really try to eat some of the rubbery eggs. He is watching me to see that I do. So, I try not to gag as some of them slide down my throat.

He chats with me like I am a human being. I am not a freak to him, or a patient. I am a human first. I can tell that he knows what it feels like to not to be treated like a human being. His mannerisms, and blunt flamboyant nature says it all.

He leaves me but not for long. He is back with a bucket of hot water, washcloths, a toothbrush, and a comb. He washes my feet. Then my legs, arms, and hands. I hadn't realized my lack in grooming. He gets up to get me a new gown and tells me to wash the "other parts" while he is gone.

I am clean. I cannot believe I have even brushed my teeth. I watch him as he comes back in with a shower cap. It is full of hot water and no rinse shampoo. He pulls up a chair. He sits beside me and massages my hair. Finally, he deals with the knots that have formed from the nightmarish sleeps I have dealt with over the weekend.

I want to snuggle into his chest and cry. I don't want him to leave me. Even if he isn't quiet for a second. I look up at him into his warm brown eyes. I smile. He touches my arm and smiles. He gets up and leaves me.

It is because someone else has come to take more blood. She stabs me numerous times. As she does, she tells me she is new at this and my veins keep moving. I swear I count ten good stab marks. Another person comes in with a cup. They want me to clean cough up one of those gray boogies. That means with as little spit as possible. It doesn't take long before I have a sample for them.

The main OB doctor comes in next and sits beside me. She chats with me about the flu and pneumonia. I ask her what her what would happen if I delivered now. She looked at me terrified. She said if I delivered right now the baby would die.

Her phone rings. She is called away to deliver a baby. A fat happy full-term baby. How I longed deep inside that I was up there ready to push out a healthy baby. I knew what to expect. I knew I would be home hours after that. With a healthy baby. This uncertainty has caused a wildfire of terror that is slowly consuming me.

They announce to me that I am going to be flown to Colorado Springs. Better facilities and newer medicine. They may be able to figure out what is going on with me. An hour later they say I have H1N1, and I am now going to Denver. The biggest most advanced hospital in the state.

I write Mom. I call Jewell. Jewell considers coming back in to give me things I may need. I tell her it's no use. I may leave before she gets here. I get a text back from Mom that she is on the way to be by my side. I feel some excitement that I can see her. I imagine spending Christmas with her and the girls. I will be weak or worse it may be delayed a few days, or even a week, but this is going to work out. I know it. I look at the clock.

My mom should take a day to get here. She will sneak me good things to snack on once I get hungry again. She will make me laugh. I won't be so alone. I am growing more and more scared. I am restless. I try to watch TV, but it is not distracting enough anymore. The white and black clock seems to hammer away the seconds. Seconds that I will never get back.

They give me something in my IV. I throw up everything but my birthday cake from three years ago, and my shoes. Thank goodness those are in the closet. I am instructed not to take much. What I chose to take must not be explosive. I ask about bullets. They say those have to go.

I dump out my small shiny black purse. Onto the table tumbles: hay, screws, nails, bullets, coins, crayons, crackers. I began sorting out .22 bullets from coins. I also take out my knife. When I am satisfied, I put my wallet in back in. I organize my clothes for Jewell to pick up later. They give me bags to put it all in. It's all on the bed ready to go.

After an eternity, a small cot finally comes in the room with three people. Two are guys and one is a lady. All dressed in thick canvas navy blue. The lady, with short hair, made me feel the most comfortable, because she had number of flight badges on her dark blue coat. I am guessing 40 safe flights from her badges.

I am naked under my hospital gown. There was no time for even clean underwear. Barefoot, and cold I climb on the cot. I was worried at first if I could even fit on the slim bed. They buckle me in tightly. Numerous buckles from the feet up to my chest. Being pinned down is scary. My skin crawls. I hate being at the mercy of these three, and a helicopter.

I have to pee again, but they won't let me out. They sit me up. They cover me with lots of blankets. Lastly, they put my purse, boots, and coat on my feet. It wasn't supposed to be like this. There is a momma right now holding a brand-new baby. Here I am on the top of the hospital being wheeled to a helicopter.

I can see from the third story rooftop that our town is a buzz with holiday rush hour traffic. How I wish I could be in a car driving away oblivious of mortality. How I wish my only care was about what to make for dinner.

The helicopter is amazing. It's shiny, and its bursting with deep orange and red color. There is a little red heart on its tail. The propellers look almost as long as the helicopter is. I think about doing a unit with the girls on helicopters. I can't even scratch my nose right now. In I go with a gentle nudge. They give me a helmet, so I can hear if they talk. Part of me is curious and excited. At any other time, I would have wanted to touch and ask questions about everything.

Part of me wants to scream and run away. Run away from my body. From this nightmare unfolding as a mix of horror, and lungs that won't work right. It's a reality that keeps turning, and turning, and its boxing me in, until I can't breathe anymore.

The captain is in. The other two, the lady and the other guy, sit in the back. I am in front. I can see everything. I feel like I am floating in a glass bubble. It's terrifying and exhilarating, as they lift off. Straight up we go with no lurch except for in my stomach. They act like it's a car ride. Nothing exciting. It's not like we are in a helicopter.

I stare at the panel. Brightly lit with all kinds of numbers and gages. The only ones I can read is the time, how far up we are, and the one that reads simply north, west, south, and east. Forty-five minutes, the captain announces, to get me to Denver. The sun has only got another thirty minutes of light max.

The helicopter sways as we come off the mountains. That was the only thing that terrified me. Climbing up the large mountains was breathtakingly beautiful. It moves so quietly, so gently. Dropping down the mountains, is a rocking terror ride.

I recognize where we are, but without the earthly bounds of gravity, and the confinement of roads that twist you where they want you. It is amazing the view. The tiny spider veins of roads. Mostly made of dirt leading to houses of all different kinds nestled in trees or hanging off cliffs.

That is until we hit Pueblo. Then all the houses clumped together with tight square roads. I got to see more than one angle of the poor orphan mountain.

The sun has finally given out its last rays. The last time I may ever see the sun again. It was gone. Without even a wink or a care. I want to claw my way out of here. People are dying all over the world. They will never see the sun rise again. There is no moon out for comfort. Just a silent beckoning of stars.

Below me, and in front of me is the glow of lights. Some moving. Some etching out roads. Some illuminating tall buildings. More and more lights come upon us now signifying Denver. Hundreds of little lights now. Some of them are moving on illuminated roads. They move and pause as the stoplights dictate brightly in the dark throwing colors of red, yellow, and green.

The captain of the ship announces that we are landing straight ahead. A big building unmistakable in the landscape of bright. It is by far the brightest thing there. It may be the largest building I have ever set foot in. There is no missing the huge helicopter pad.

They land without a single bump. Then they unload me in the dark and cold. Without hesitation they quickly push me through a door. I am quickly wheeled down a tight hallway. We go deeper, and deeper into a labyrinth. A labyrinth I will navigate for the next three months. Someone makes mention of bringing breadcrumbs, so they can find their way back. I am still fighting the urge to claw my way out.

I am amazed, and quickly just as lost as they are. I really don't understand where they are taking me. Big city ICU unit is all I know. I think it will be set up just like the small-town hospital. I don't know that they have it broken up into numerous little units all specialized. I hardly even know what ICU stands for.

All I know is I get dumped off in a small room. They place their bed next to my new one and push the brakes down. They want me to scoot into my new home. It isn't easy with baby, and the ability to flash anyone at any moment. As soon as I complete that feat they leave. I have hardly a moment to situate before they are out of sight.

The first thing that happens is that everyone on the ward at the time comes cramming themselves shoulder to shoulder in my room. There are roughly 10-15 curious new faces. They announce their names. They all smile and welcome me here.

They are so friendly. They are all wearing dark blue scrubs, and super shiny black shoes. I am surprised by such a simple warming welcoming gesture. I probably look like a classic doe in the headlights. They all leave except 4 or so nurses who set to work immediately.

I beg to get up and go pee. I look longing at the shiny toilet nestled away calling me. I had managed to hold it all the way up here. I instead get a yellow plastic tub handed to me. The nurse won't let me up. She turns on the water and pulls the curtain. I feel weird peeing on my bed, but I obviously have no choice in the matter.

The nurses are back in now. They hang my coat in the tiny little slit in the wall. My boots barely fit in at the bottom. My purse is placed on my bedside table. Then it is pushed aside.

The room is so small. It is bright white, and shiny. Everything looks top of the line modern. The wall toward the nurses is all glass. I have never seen anything like it. Even the door is a sliding glass one. I wonder if the whole hospital is like this.

They pull off my gown and throw it away. They cut off my old hospital band. I am naked. They do not care. They place patches all over my chest moving my breasts as needed. They listen to my lungs all the way down to my stomach with their stethoscope. I am gifted one of their gowns. They place a new band around my wrist, with my information. They are efficient fast machines working against a clock I refuse to hear tick. I can see their concern in their faces. Even as they look me in the eye on occasion. They smile at me, and I can tell they are trying to keep me as calm as possible.

Here comes the flu swab. I fell for this once. I thought they were going to swab my nostrils. Instead, they go all Egyptian and try to rip out your brain. My whole body clinches up, as I try not to move. Now it is them with needles in my wrist pulling blood and putting it in little bottles. I call it vampire soda. A nurse giggles. It feels weird, invasive, and painful. They do this four times on each wrist.

One lady says to me they have to put me in a coma for two weeks. They need to do this in order to save me. She goes on to say how this flu causes your white blood cells go crazy, and they make lots of extra fluid. A cytokine storm. She only gives me one tiny sip of water with two Tylenol.

The nurse looks at the arm that was jabbed numerous times. She carefully counts the jab marks shaking her head. The right one is bruised and bandaged from the last IV so, she places the new IV in the left.

Next, I am given a forced air mask to try to open my lungs. I feel like I am going to suffocate at first. If you have ever driven down the road at 80 miles an hour, and stuck your head out the window, that would be what it feels like I am sure. I figure out with my tongue or mouth how to stop it. I get in a rhythm of pausing it, so I can breathe out, then letting the wind fly as I breathe in. A nurse takes it away from me agitated thinking I am playing with it.

I am growing more and more frightened. It hits me like an iron ball. I have no clue really where I am. I am lost in a big city in the middle of a large hospital. I cannot just tear out my IV and leave any longer. Where would I go? I am truly alone. I look out in the hallway. I try to at least get a feel of my immediate surroundings. There is no turning around. No backing out. I am so disorientated, at this point, that I do not think to call my aunt and uncle who are only an hour away.

I want to ask them to wait for Mom before they put me in a coma. Feeling their concern made me quiet. I'm going to be 31 weeks pregnant when I wake up again. I think it is going to be a long nap. I think I will wake up and be groggy for a few days. At least that is what I force myself to think.

Christmas is no longer my concern. Something inside me is frightened, curious, and ready. This world, the earth, I know falls away out from under my feet. I feel for the first time the warm breeze of deaths door as it opens. I let everything go. This is my choice. This is my fight. If that is what I chose.

I am clutching a pillow tightly to my belly, desperately trying to stop the baby from bouncing, as I cough. I am facing the wall. The tiny windowless wall. The doctor comes. I feel his energy, before I even realize he has stepped in.

I roll over toward him. I sit up fully. He doesn't even need his white coat. I know by that educated somber look. He enters my room and quietly makes his way over to me. He sits on my bed next to my knees. He holds a clip board. He looks at me eye to eye. We don't speak for a moment. I know everything from his eyes. They hold sadness, and a true hint of sorrow. He may very well be blinking back tears.

Slowly, he finds words tackling the tough choice that I must make. In the case that I do not survive, while I am in the coma, he hopes that I will grant them the right to take my baby and give him/her a fighting chance. He hands the clipboard over to me. He pulls a pin out of his pocket and gives it a click before handing it over to me.

I know as I write my name, they are hoping to save one life. The one inside me. I'm fine with this. If she/he could have stronger chance of surviving. I know that Jewell and Mom will give my girls a great life. I sign the paper without hesitation. My name lay in ink with the curves and bumps that I practiced with for years. It is what moms do. They are supposed to die first.

I give myself to the powers that be. Yea, it wasn't supposed to be like this, but it is now. The nurse comes in. She puts something in my IV. My body relaxes. My eyes slide shut. My breathing slows. I have fully given myself over. My spirit to God. My body to the ICU. Soon my baby to the NICU. By Dec 23rd, in the early morning, I am well on my way in this adventure.

Mom has hours of driving ahead of her. She has no idea what she is speeding toward. The life changing adventure unraveling as the distance between us shrinks. She gets a call hours later from my nurse that it is time to gather the family. Anyone who wants to say their goodbyes has a chance. I am in a coma and started on life-support.

Jewell and my sick children are now a five-hour drive away. The kids are tucked away in their beds sleeping. Jewell tries to contact the hospital but cannot get through. She begins to pack and ready to drive up to me.

My aunt is there first. The middle child. My mother is the youngest. My uncle is the oldest. Cindy and I have had a special relationship. I always found her to be another mom to me. Cindy has always felt like I was more of a daughter than a niece. She navigates Denver, and the hospital. She has found me sleeping. I have a tube down my throat, and plastic over my eyes to keep them shut.

Everyone holds their breath and hopes silently this won't be the last time they see me. As a mess of tubes and wires. Chances are I will not wake up. Chances are the baby will make it okay here in this hospital, but I will not.

Invisible

My fingers cling to glass like rain in limbo.
I am the silence.
You don't know I'm there until you listen.
Stuck between echoes.

I am the silence.
Crawling up and through the cracks.
Stuck between echoes.
The creatures stirs.

I am crawling up and through the cracks.
I can see reality unravel.
The creature is stirring,
juxtaposed truth and lies.

I can see reality unravel.
Tediously rising from the dead,
juxtaposed truth and lies,
is the breath I thought I had lost.

I am tediously rising from the dead.
Feeling cinches my fingertips.
The breath I thought I had lost
takes hold as I grasp onto anything that will hold me.

The Hauntings

Aug. 14, 2014

I wrestle with creating this chapter. I have to write down the pieces. They are so fragmented that if I do not stitch them together on paper they will lay forever fragmented to poke and jab at me, as my mind stumbles around in the dark. This is an intense story, and it's a rare one. I do not want this story of hope to die with me. I want to pass the candle on.

I lean against the cold dry wall as I brace myself for the day. A moment alone means I can lay my guard down and come undone. The kids are out playing. My oxygen fills with a load hiss. My mind again struggles to put the fragments together.

The coma dreams are so real. I flash back to those strange days in the last week of December 2013. I am lying in bed rising and falling in the levels of consciousness.

Where am I?

Where am I?

In a brand-new land.

Where did I go?

Why can I not move?

Why am I being touched so much?

It feels cold, and vulnerable. I feel roughed around. I may be torn apart or dropped at any moment. I see nurses on occasion.

I begin to sense Mom's presence. I feel other familiar energies. They're in the back of my room. I feel the lights. They are so bright flickering off the white walls. I hear hushed voices, the rustling of clothing, and the movement of chairs.

The celling lights seem to pulsate all different colors. It's so bright. It's so new. I cannot make sense of my surroundings. I think there is a large house plant and create a large room in a mansion of some kind. It's clean and white. It's larger and lovelier, than anything I have ever experienced.

Maybe I am in Asia. I have nothing to grab a hold of. There is nothing I can recognize. I am drowning in a new land.

I cannot breathe. I cannot breathe. I cannot breathe.

There are noises everywhere. Loud screaming noises. Deep and earth shattering. I am pulled out of the coma just enough to see people everywhere. I am fully aware. The building could be burning down. I just don't care. Shoes squeak in the chaos. I feel the panic of others, but not in myself. Metal clanks. Voices hum all around me.

I'm being jostled. I know that I am being separated from Mom. I feel pain. Back in my coma I create a city where I am being pushed around and pulled farther and farther from her. I am alone and lost. I feel bruised. My lip bleeds. The pain I feel is beyond this world, beyond words.

I come fully awake. I know I am going to die. I fear only for my baby. For a second, my last second alive. I see that I am naked. I see people all around draped like a surgery. I see the blade digging down into my stomach. I see blood. The doctor stops for this flicker of a second. We make eye contact. I panic. I feel my heart tighten and stop. I know what is coming. That mortal fear is gone now. Death takes me in his arms. I fade to black.

It is not like walking away. It is being blown gently in a thousand pieces like a dandelion and coming together again like a wish that God materialized. I am.

There is no body to fret about anymore. I know no fear, no pain. No more fighting for breath. No cold. I am in a pool of thick liquid like honey. The peace. The light all around me is enormous, and warm, but not blinding or hot.

There are koi fish that come and nip playfully at my fingers. I feel myself laugh. It is not a laugh from a body. I feel immense joy, warmth, and peace. I want to be here forever. I know I am not dreaming. I know I am not on the earthly plane. I know I am without body. It is something I never want to leave.

It took ten days. Ten days for my body to go from the first sign of a cold to a wasteland. I lay dead as pneumonia, and H1N1 have turned into the monster ARDS (Acute Respiratory Distress Syndrome) and Sepsis. They have rendered my lungs useless shadows.

The trade was done. Two fragile pounds of a baby in exchange for my life. They still aren't giving up on me. Even if the odds are still higher that I will not pull through the hour. That I will not live through the night. That I will not survive a week. They are still going to try what they can to save this little nameless warrior's mother.

I suddenly feel like a thousand-pound weight. I hurt again. I am cold. This is the body. I have crashed back inside. I am drowning. I am paralyzed and full of fear. I don't want to come back in. That is out of my control.

Or is it? A part of me knows I can't leave them here like this. A part of me just can't walk away yet. I am not done. I need them. The tether was never completely severed, and I followed it back. It is no saunter back in. It is more of a rough yank.

I feel the gloves on my face. They are waking me up. I twitch. I try to fight. There is a light in my eyes, as a gloved finger and thumb pries my eyes open one at a time. The hand on my face has a strong grip. I try to pull away. I look up at the big blinding lights. Everything is so cold.

They move me onto another bed. My stomach lurches as the sheet lifts me up. It is a gentle and slow unfolding. Even if I am still dying, they do not forget I am still in body. Broken as I may be right now. It sends signals that I am safe, and as comfortable as I can be.

I see everything. I hear everything. Even if nothing is making sense. I think I am being rescued. Away from this pain. I do not fight. I cannot fight.

I see the doctors and nurses staring back at me. Can they see my eyes struggling to focus? There are so many of them all huddled around me. I think I made momentary eye contact with a doctor.

They are talking among each other. A humming between them. I see their faces full of emotions. Some hold happiness, and hope. Some hold concern mixed with concentration. Some faces hold sadness.

I focus in on a nurse. She looks a second away from crying, vomiting, or running away. I feel her touch my skin with the electric air of concern. That nurse I will see again. It will help begin the knitting of scattered memories together. Short black hair pulled into a pony. Her face a mix of different races, with the look of a new scared nurse buried deep in her brown eyes. She was all her own person.

I can finally tell coma, from death, from consciousness seeing her face again. It took me a while to sift out my death experience, but things kept coming up over and over again. No matter where I am in the levels of consciousness, I'm constantly looking for that pool again.

As I woke up; I thought at first maybe they have a special healing pool. Nothing could come anywhere close to what I had experienced. In my coma dreams I always know I am alive. I always try to protect my body. I know in coma that I can't talk or move. I understand I had a C-section, or at least I am no longer pregnant.

When I'm pulled into the edge of consciousness the heaviness that I'm nothing, but a shell of what I used to be, will only sink in deeper. The nurses wake me up every day that I am in a coma on the ECMO and ventilator. They want to make sure I haven't gone brain dead. If I did they would have pulled me off the machines. For that, I am forever grateful. These moments cause my coma dreams, and reality to become heavily blurred.

I always know I am not back on my farm in my warm house. I knew I was in the hospital. So, all dreams evolved around this new environment. There is no time for me to gather information about being in a big hospital. No time for me to get the feel of the ICU. I needed to be put under quickly.

I have been saved.

It's so quiet now.

So quiet.

We are safe, aren't we?

I clutch Mom's arm. That smell that is hers. She must have been in her thirties again. I can feel her warm clothes against my skin. I have her hand in mine. We are safe. I find us a boat and push us away. The boat rocks on away from everything: the people, the noises, the pain. It is cool and dark. Deep molasses dark, without a single star.

I feel immense sadness. I want nothing more than to be "There" again. I trail my fingers in the water crying. I thought I could find the pool. I know deep inside I won't be able to. Never have I been so torn. So joyful to be reunited with my family. Yet, down to the core I know I had found home. I had been home.

Not anymore.

Help me I'm fading.

Help me I'm falling

I'm in the helicopter again. It's pouring rain. Everything is soaked. They are rushing me into the hospital. It is slick this time and scary. I look out over the edge, and I see the fencing set to catch me. There is a ladder against another wall. In order to get out of the hospital I will have to find my way out and climb up this ladder in the rain.

In a coma dream you cannot escape your nightmares. I begin the climb. I slip. I catch myself. I pull up hard. I grab at the roof and try to hold on. The concrete is wet and slick. I am drenched and cold. The wind and the rain seem to beat against me. I am clawing my way up this time. I can feel my finger pads, and nails as they scrap against the hard concert. I am up. There is the hospital bed. There the nurses are waiting. It is like a loop.

Now I am being wheeled into the hospital. I think I am in Albuquerque, NM. The nurses are kind at first. I am toweled off and given a hospital gown. They move me through their elevator, and down into a new room.

Two nurses begin to fight. They knock my gurney over. From here things get worse. I can't talk. So, I try to make motions, but no one will listen to me. No one cares. Finally, I manage to get someone to listen to me. She vanishes. The only one who could understand me.

I am dying.

Slowly slipping away. A doctor looks at my scar. He sits beside me. My C-section scar is a small x next to my belly button. I need help. I cannot breathe. He, I realize, is going to let me die. He is trying to intentionally to kill me.

"We all die." He tells me coldly.

I am helpless, and without a voice. I can't move. I am bracing for the end.

I cannot breathe. I cannot breathe.

A nurse comes in. He is strong. He carries me away. He saves me. They watch me now and protect me.

I'm helpless.

I cannot move.

I cannot talk.

In the daytime the nurses will carry me and place me on a couch. People will watch over me. Two young boys, in particular, will take care of me as they go about their day. They are kind, and attentive. They are only 10 and 12 years old. I enjoy their company. Sometimes, Grandma and Mom will say hi and touch my face. This goes on for days.

Then Jewell calls. She must have made the doctors mad. They turn on me. Grandma, Mom, and the doctor all come in to tell me I'm probably going to die. They now put me in another weird area. The nurses leave me there like the trash. I am to wait there to die.

They say my liver is failing. They are cleaning me up now and talking to each other.

Please don't leave me.

Please don't give up on me.

Please, don't.

I am here.

I am here.

I reach out. I touch one of the nurses. I hurt her. She runs outs upset. I try to talk to a male nurse. I want to say I am sad, and I am sorry. I am ashamed and fearful. I ball my hands up on my chest.

I am left in the dark night. By morning they check on me. Seeing that I am still alive; they move me back up to my room where they hook me up to a new machine that goes all around the room. It feeds me. I see the white board has all the weekly lists of meals. It feels good. My belly is full.

I am still just carried around like a rag doll. I will go back, and forth as different people take care of me. I have different nurse's whose faces blurred, but their touches are very concrete in my consciousness.

The nurses are turning on me again. I am being jerked around. They are fighting. I am worried they are going to knock me over again. A strong, and angry woman comes in and sends them away.

She is caring and kind. I tell her my brother is coming in. He may kill me. The cops come in. They gave me a secret word to use. Then they hide.

I hear him coming down the hall. He comes in my room calm, and cold. His eyes are dark. His hair pulled back. He looks at me ready. I say the secret word.

"I hope you like your freedom."

He leaves, and a shot rings out from the hallway.

The nurses think I am too dangerous for their hospital now. They pack me up, and they move me to a new hospital. I am in the helicopter again. This one is white. Through the doors. Down again. Down into another labyrinth. I'm in Arizona now.

The doctor is in. He is talking to Mom and Grandma.

Grandma is complaining about all the medications I am on. She is demanding to know what everything is. I see I am hooked up to all different kinds of weird concoctions. There is a raw chicken on the windowsill sitting in the sun, and a tube directly to that fed to my arm. I am worried about how clean it is. I want to pull it out, but I cannot move.

They banter back and forth. Finally, the doctor manages to calm and reassure her. He smiles and his teeth show. He looks over to the nurse.

"Make sure she isn't cake batter, okay." He tells her.

Then he reaches out and touches my foot. I am awake. I felt it. I am awake.

I'm not cake batter!

I'm still here.

Please, please don't give up on me.

I have to prove that I am alive. If not, they may take out my organs, burn me alive, or freeze me. The only thing that will move is a twitch here and there. My eyes move. My brain is an explosion of chaos trying to sort through every new bombardment.

The tiles are dancing above me on the roof. They are twirling and moving like a calming dance.

Everyone in the ICU is now in a preschool situation. We are all grouped together to play as we please, and the nurses watch us. They want to take some people up to the top to look at the helicopter pad. I am terrified they are going to choose me. They pick five people to go up there. They say I'm still too weak to go. I breathe out a sigh of relief. I get to go play with a group of beautiful women learning how to hula hoop.

Jewell is here now. She wants to take us on a walk. It is a dark Tucson night. I am 18 again. Loose shirts, and a tiny body. A wonderful summer night in the desert. I am free. I want to run and scream in the dark night air. She smiles and hugs me tight. I slip through. I vanish.

Am I a ghost?

I'm gone now. Out of your arms. I am cold. I am in the hospital bed. I want to be back in your arms again. The nurse, and I lock eyes. I try to tell her I want to go back. She is typing on some odd contraption, but still looks over at me from time to time to smile.

She puts something in my IV. I fade. I am free for a moment from the hospital. I am in a beautiful countryside. I want to go home. I don't know where home is anymore. I want to find that pool again. I sit and bask in the sun. The grass is green, and it rustles under me. I run my hands through it.

I cannot smell the air. I wish I could. With all of this beauty I am lost. I don't know where to go and what to do. I realize I hardly know who I am anymore. I put my head on my knees and cry. I am crying on the most beautiful dress I have ever worn. Medieval looking, navy blue, and so velvety soft.

I hear laughter. It is my girls. They are all three playing in a sunny meadow. I get up to run to them. I run and run and run. I cannot reach them. I can only hear them giggle. I call for them. They cannot hear me. I am frustrated beyond words. They keep evading me.

I see something up ahead. It is dark, and hard to make out in this thick forest. I slowly inch forward. I come nose to nose with a black dragon. It looks at me threating, but only for a second. I reach out, and I pet it. I snuggle up against it. Its warmth envelopes me. I drift off to sleep.

My baby is walking the halls. She must be 2-3 years old now. She is following Mom around. Skipping happily behind her in a black dress with a big pink bow in the back. Her hair is thick. My coffee brown color, but curly, and pulled into pig tails. She comes into my room and sits on my chest. She tells me I cannot die. I hold her tightly. I am slipping away again. I am dying. She bites me hard on the hand, and then she hides under the bed.

Mom comes in my room. She sits by me. I point under the bed. I cannot talk now. She looks at me puzzled. The baby is under the bed. She doesn't understand.

Mom is with me now. I feel safe. She rubs my arms, and head. I want her to stay with me. I cannot communicate. I know she sees me. She looks right into my eyes.

I watch as she fades away into the hall. She is living in the hospital somewhere, and I will find out. That way I can see my baby again. I get up. The wires come off of me easily. I sneak past the nurses, and out into the hall.

I find her room quickly. It is big and nice. Just a fancier version of a hospital room. There are bookshelves from floor to ceiling. I look in the closet, and all around for my baby. I don't want to get caught.

I hear the door creak open. I have nowhere to run or hide. It's too late they found me. Six of them come charging into the room.

The nurses pin me down. They pull of my hospital gown. I have wet myself. I am ashamed and scared. I need them to survive. They bathe me. I am shivering cold. I cannot breathe. I feel like I am going to die. The doctor is mad at me because I have contaminated the room. Mom and the baby have to move now. They have to burn everything in the room.

I'm sorry.

I want my baby.

I want my freedom.

I wake up. I am in a wheelchair. I must have had another surgery. I feel my neck. I cannot talk. They took my voice. I want to escape. I cannot even move. I am in a dark waiting room. Someone will come and bring me back to my bed. Back to a nurses warm touch.

The doctor pushes me into an elevator. They send me up to the top floor. They push me out onto the roof. I am freezing. I can't breathe. I am helpless in this wheelchair. I am too weak to move, and I have no voice to cry out with. I know I am going to die right there. I am beyond that. I just want to cross over again.

Please, let me cross over. Please God, please release me. I can't do this. I am drowning from the inside. I cannot breathe. I cannot breathe.

I want the pain to cease. I need those horrible alarms to stop screaming.

I wake. The nurse is typing her chart by the end of my bed. I kick her in a desperate move to get her attention. She scowls at me.

I can't breathe. I reach over and begin to whack at the machines. The nurse runs over to me and ties me down. She tells me the machines are too expensive to be knocking over.

I fight it. I pull. I rip and jerk at my bindings. The pain finally ceases. I can breathe again. I am not cold anymore.

I'm tied down.

I'm tied down.

I pull and pull. If I can get them to my face; I will chew them off. I try. Sometimes, I can jerk enough, that an arm escapes momentarily. Sometimes, I will spend what feels like hours exhausting myself jerking on my wrist bindings. If I feel myself about to poop, then I really pull on them. I know it's wrong, and weird to let myself go like this. I know I'm completely at their mercy.

I can't talk. I am tied down. I am in a dark room. I am completely helpless. I desperately need to get someone's attention. Please understand that I'm still alive. I see a nurse lean over me. My eyes struggle to focus on the dark blue, and the name tag.

I try to show her I'm alive. I am here. I think she notices. She pulls the blankets up on me.

Pure terror, and confusion envelops me, as an understanding comes to me that I am on deaths door. I don't want to die. I don't understand how I can still be here.

She tucks me in. Her hands are soothing and warm. I try to relax. I find some solstice in her eyes. She looks right into my eyes. She sees me. She sees that I am fully present. She puts a hand on my head, and she strokes my hair. Tears fall from my face onto the pillow. She pulls hair out of my eyes and rubs my checks. I ease into her touch. So light, and so full of love. She stays with me, until I am able to sleep again.

I am ready for the court to judge me. It doesn't feel like a normal court room. It is just a place out of body; where I am being held. They discuss my life and my choices. They show pictures of me dressed in sexy lingerie and heavy makeup. I have never dressed like this, and never have I taken pictures like this. Its startling to see, yet empowering.

We flick through my memories together as one unit that I am and yet am not. I give reasons for my choices, and my actions. I am nervous, but not scared. I never see or hear a voice during this. Information flow between us is done through emotions, memories, and thoughts. At the end of it I feel released from everything. I am cleansed.

I awake back the hospital. The nurse turns on the T.V. for me. It is my life up to this point. I watch my starry night sky. The house we built. My kids. I watch with amazement. I watch me like I can't see me in the living. I am above me, and around me. I'm a spectator watching what I had created. What I had left behind.

I am overall proud. It isn't much. It isn't even great. It is positive, and full of light, and love. It is mine. It is my dusty fingerprint. The tiny mark I have left behind. It will last as long as my kids, wife, and mom are alive.

I hear mumbling in my room. I struggle to open my eyes. Mom is talking to Jewell on her cell phone. I watch her over at the window. She's pacing back and forth facing the window, the wall, and casting quick glances at me. I see her tears. I see her crying. I can't yell out. I can't say what is bursting forth. I want to cry too. If only I could lift an arm.

I'm right here Mom.

I'm still here.

I'm still here.

Now, I am bracing for death. I am bracing for my end. I wait and wait. No end comes to me. I close my eyes and try to die. No end comes to me. Finally, after hours of trying to die naturally, a nurse decides she will just shoot me, and be done with it.

She is trying to be secretive, so I am not scared. She doesn't have it in her to pull the trigger. I wait and wait for her to just get it over with. Once she does fire the gun off it only nicks my head sending a blood stain on the wall.

The head nurse comes in mad that she has fired a gun. He kicks her out. He is watching me now. He sees that I am fine. He removes all the tubes and wires with simple yanks.

I find Mom. We get our brand-new baby. We find a nice place in the hospital to stay. We need milk for the baby. My breasts don't work. I also want to get snacks as a celebration. I leave our secret safe spot to get what we need. When I come back, they are gone.

I open my eyes. I swear I see my ex-partner standing there looking at me. I want to reach for him. Is it him? He leaves me without saying a word. Is it really him? Not long after I hear a horrible noise. There is a helicopter crash in our building killing him. Mom and the baby have to leave to avoid getting hurt.

I lay in my hospital bed and cry. I have lost them once again. I am alone once again. I am lost. I am trapped. I am bound down, as I continue to rock back and forth through consciousness. The doctors are terrifying enemies. I rely only on the nurses who seem to be in an entirely different dimension holding onto me by a thread.

Nameless

I crashed into another dimension.
You were thrown through the window of worlds.
No one could have warned you about this upcoming collision.
No one could have warned you how fast this warm cocoon would fall open,
leaving you tumbling free,
before your wings were ready.
No one could have warned you how fast this connection,
between us would be severed.
As my last breath faded.
As agile gloved fingers found you,
lodged in my ribs dying slowly.
You are delicate and starved for oxygen.
Most babies come in screaming.
You came in as quiet as an angel feather,
as the snowflakes that brushed against my window clinging to life.
An early present on Christmas morning.
You fight for your space, and your time in this world.
On the coldest days of the year.
With little weight and little breath.
Your mother's arms did not await you.
No warm soft breast for comfort.
I wait instead for you on the other side.
We can dance together.
Without the burden of our heavy bodies.
Yet, the arms of a mother are there, always eager,
 always waiting.
For you to open your eyes and meet this new world.
Her tears may fall on you as she holds
the tangled mess of wires and tubes that are your new cocoon.
Even if her baby is dying.
She still has a love for you like she birthed you herself.
You have a belly full of warm breast milk as

moms reach out for you.
They weave a net,
interlocking arms and hands to keep you from falling with your tissue
paper wings.
You don't need a name to fight.
You have the fire of a thousand suns burning in your eyes.
You don't give up on you.
My snowflake.
Nameless weightless little fighter.
Angel feather.

The Gnashing of Teeth and Claw

The weirdest thing is how the whole world never stops. The strange lurch, that is caused by the sudden jamming, the stick lodged in your wheel, causes dementia. Life stops for no one. It goes on and on.

The few people that survive this belly of the best quickly move away to other places in the hospital. One day I won't be here. The sun should still rise and fall. Ashes to ashes. On time will spin, as the merciless devil it is. I am pushed farther and farther, into this never-ending forward spiraling motion.

All around me everyone carries on. At 7am/pm the nurses change shift. The lights in the hall flicker on brighter to signal 6am, and they tone down at 10pm. I use the outside window to get an idea of what time of day or night it is. I can't read the clock very well.

People come and go, as I lay here unable to even move to my side. Most people that are in and out of my room are alive. Some are dead. There is an older couple in my room; that are very much not of the living world. They stand there watching me, smiling, and chattering between themselves. I know they are trying to impart some hope onto me. I get fed up with them staring at me, so I chase them out.

The gloves. They are my main connection to reality. They often jerk me to the edge of waking. The gloves are such a strange feeling against my skin. I am being handled as gently as a baby.

The strong surgical lights above me often make it hard for me to open my eyes. I open them enough to focus in on the new swarm of blue scrubs. There are people talking either to me or about me. I can't tell you. Hardly any of my native tongue makes sense.

My gown is off. I am naked. There are numerous people inspecting and washing my body. One lady points to my all over rash. I look down with groggy eyes to see my splotchy skin.

They rub me down with a cold soothing cream. It is heaven. It instantly cooled a fire; I hadn't realized was there. A female nurse checks my breasts, moving them around, and giving a slight poke here and there. She packs ice bags on them. It is cold as well. I don't understand why she cares about my breasts so much that they need ice packs. There is a sign taped on my T.V. printed in big thick letters demanding a new icepack to them every two hours.

Why?

Did I break them?

I get a new gown, and warm blankets. I feel myself being moved, and pillows being shoved under one side of me. Most of the nurses leave. My nurse walks over, and fiddles with some tubes on the left side of me. She pushes some buttons. I pull one of my arms, heavy as lead, slowly up on my chest. Then the typing on the computer. The incessant tap, tap, tap.

I'm no better than a newborn. I can imagine their worlds still shifting and changing like mine. Our bodies so useless and limp. I need to be changed, turned, and bathed. It is scary relying on people I don't know.

I wake quite a bit in response to being cleaned. The nurses chatter on happily. I pick up on all kinds of interesting conversations when I can understand them. Some of them are probably blurred by the strong medications they still have me on.

Once, I heard them break out into a new song. They stop for a moment to dance, and then they erupt into laughter. I know I smiled. I like it when I hear giggling, and happy chatter.

One night I hear a nurse say, "Watch this. When we turn her she will do something funny."

They move me, and I give a strange automated response to the slight lurch. The nurses all laugh. I try to open my eyes. For a moment, the lights blind me. I see about 6 people in a blur of dark blue covered in name tags and pens, all leaned over me. They are chatting away like usual. I feel a hot rag against my bare skin.

I have come to feel a comfort in this now. Trust is not something I hand out for free. I can relax in this moment. They know I am alive. They don't mind me being so helpless. I smile trying to tell them the best I can that I am here. I fade out again.

The first days of January. They began to more forcefully pull me out of the coma. Slowly, a little more each day. I still struggle to find the dividing line between dream and reality. I can't piece together: who I am, where I am, or how I have come to this point in my life.

I am transfixed and terrified at the black dogs in the parking garage. Large and looming like death. They run around snarling and snapping. They are out to get me.

So is the guy trying to brush my teeth. I believe he has Novocain on the brush. I fight him and bite at it the best I can. I believe he is trying to take away my voice. Somehow, they are all after me, and don't want me to tell Mom. I'm tied down. I fight as a panic wells up in me. I pull and jerk as hard as I can. The nurse is in rather quickly, and before I know it, I am asleep again.

That night I wake in a nightmare, but quickly realize it is reality instead. I am really here. Wherever that is. The lights are all off in my room, except one small one, over the sink. I can also see the hall lights. I can't speak. So, I begin banging on everything in terror. Someone comes in slightly grumpy that I am making such a racket. He holds a laminated sheet up to me. He tells me to point out what I need.

I am too confused. It may have been my native tongue, but it is not registering with me at all. I point to the house a couple of times. I want to go home.

I stare at it stupidly, until he takes it away. He gives me the nurse button to push. I do repeatedly, until I hear him groan with pure frustration. I am hearing the Disney tune when I push the button. I like it.

I slowly come around so pumped of drugs that I dream of eating the blue gloves. The nurse is leaning against the sink and chattering away with Mom and Grandma. I am laid out flat without a blanket. I have my gown on at least. I don't care about anything. I want to try the flavor of them. I imagine them packed with nuts, and chocolate. This is a good day as I come off the coma meds. I am docile, and I don't think anyone is going to kill me. I am just wanting to eat.

There is a time I'm certain that Mom is the one out to get me. I'm convinced she is running some kind of scam infomercial, and she's out for me because I know the truth. I think she took a picture of me. Something had startled me. I dreamed that I'm watching her trying to sell some heavily chemical laden powder to kids that is disguised as a health drink. There's a couple of days that I feared her.

Fear is my main go-to. No one gave me anything to fear. I created it in my mind. Would they give up on me? Would they leave me here and let me die? I couldn't allow it. I had to fight it. I did fight just about anyone, and anything. It didn't matter what stunt I tried to pull. The nurses are always there for me. They are stern for my safety; yet kind and loving.

Jan 2nd, I think it is. I am more awake than ever. I think I can just shake these wires off grab my coat and leave. Yes, fresh air I think to myself. I am lying there staring at what I think to be the exit. There are probably vending machines full of food just waiting for me. It reminds me of my middle school. I will load up on food, and then I am going to find my baby. I am so ready to be out of here.

I shimmy to the left side of my bed. My mom vanishes quickly. I will catch up with her. We will be all together soon. My left booted foot slides off the bed and dangles. It hangs there scraping across the floor. I stick my tongue out in extra effort. This snail needs all the help she can get to execute the brilliant plan.

Nurses are running in my room now. Four strong guys. I swear that they keep a box of strong men hidden away somewhere. They don't share my enthusiasm for escaping. My body is slow, heavy, and uncoordinated.

They surround me. I am engulfed in blue. They rudely lift my leg up and shove me back on the bed. They pull the side railings up with a harsh snap. Then they leave. They probably go back to their box. Just like that. I am tempted to try again, but I don't want to be drugged.

I want to be with Mom. She fixes my gown and blanket. She pulls a chair up to sit with me. I reach out with my heavy uncoordinated hand. She is always responsive and warm. She squeezes it. She is firm and strong yet loving and gentle. I fade away wrapped in her warmth and safety.

I think they are putting me in the morgue at night to watch the kids. It's scary and dark in there. I need to prove to the nurse, who is typing out my chart in my room tonight, that I am still alive. I raise my fist in the air like a victory.

"You startled me." She says. "What you are so excited about."

"I survived." I tell her.

She gives a loud laugh and agrees it is exciting.

I wake again. I can move a little bit more. I don't know what has happened to me. Who is alive and dead? Mom is by my side. It is daytime.

The nurse is leaning against the sink talking to Mom. She smiles at me as I come to life.

"Well hi there!" She says smiling brightly. "Touch your throat for me."

I do. I run my finger over a plastic tube sticking out of my throat. This is my ventilator, and it is breathing for me. The reason I can't talk.

Next, she instructs me to touch the right side of my head.

I run my fingers around my neck and head. There are two garden hoses sticking out of somewhere in my neck. I am not to pull on them or touch. They are circulating my blood. They are warm. I can hear a constant rushing noise. I can see that they are red. I run my fingers up to my head. I am wearing a head band that has the tubes connected to it. I shudder.

My turn to ask a question. My belly is now deflated and empty. I know I am no longer pregnant. I tap at my belly. Then I make an exaggerated rocking motion. Hand to elbow, hand to elbow, like I am rocking a baby. I stare at my feet. I want to cry. My heart is hammering away in my chest. I am scared to make any eye contact. What if I had lost my baby?

The nurse claps her hands together happily. I chance to look at her. The nurse smiles at me.

"Congrats." Her smile broadens until I can see her teeth. "You had a little girl. She's up in the NICU."

"She looks just like you." Mom says reaching for her ancient iPad.

She wants to show me pictures. I am so relieved that she survived this madness. That doesn't mean I am ready for pictures. I push her away. They look at me funny. I don't care. I don't give a flying fuck right now. I am too confused to be over the moon. My birth has been stolen. Someone else is touching my baby and loving on my baby. Someone else gets to bathe her first, touch her first, and feed her first. I am strapped here.

She survived. She survived.

Thank you, God.

I blink out.

I am wide awake on January 3rd, 2014. I run my hand over the table that is resting over my bed. Who am I? How old am I? I try to bring up memories. The first ones I can grab a hold of are Dad's funeral.

Mommy. Mom is here, isn't she? Did I see Grandma too? Is she here? Where am I? What has happened to me? Wasn't I pregnant? Where is my baby?

My eyes wander to my left side. There is the window. It looks like a large parking garage is the only thing I can see. By the left side of my bed is a large number of poles. They have all kinds of medications dangling in bags, controlled by these funny button things. I can hear my ventilator, and other strange small noises.

On the right side of me I can see my little sink. I remember the nurse from yesterday. I touch my throat. Everything comes back to me in a flood. This is worse than a nightmare. This is reality. I freak for a moment. I'm in too deep. How do I undo this?

The room is small. The walls are bright white. There are chairs by the window. That is probably where Mom and Grandma spend most of their time guarding and advocating for me. The bathroom is spotless and tiny. I cannot see it completely.

The right side of my bed. Above the sink is a window. I see my nurse at her computer. Beyond the sink is the sliding glass door and glass wall. It is the side where my ECMO machine is attached. My largest and most watched machine sits right where it can be accessed quickly.

Looking straight ahead is the white board. This is the first time it made any sense to me. I am appalled at the long list of names needed to keep me alive. There is a main nurse, a nursing assistant, a perfusionist nurse, and a respiratory nurse. There is one main doctor. Moms number is on the bottom right. I am curious how Mom can stay here?

The clock barely made any sense to me. It is perched perfectly center hammering away seconds, minutes, hours. It is something I hardly give a care of anymore.

My coat. A bit of me comes to life. A spark in a seemly dead fire. A spark that leaps and grabs hold of a dry piece of grass to hide in and smolder. Hopefully, it will grow, and my fire will catch again.

Tattered green is my spark. Thick canvas and nothing fancy. Just a simple warm man's coat. There it is. Hanging limp and lifeless to all but me. It is my totem. My lifeline to the world. The first thing I can focus on, because it is mine. The only thing I have here in this sterile environment.

It whispers my name. It tells me old stories. It is something I look forward to touching again. I want to need that ugly thing, with the tears from fence lines and tools. I want so bad to wrap it around me and leave.

It made my room stink of farm. A mix of wood smoke, hay, live earth, and farm animals. I couldn't smell it. That simple coat. Without it I am lost in this sea of confusion. It is my gulp of air. My focus.

I still don't know where I am. Just a big hospital. I have come to an understanding now, that I am truly helpless, and completely in their care. The hospital, the nurses, the doctors, I need them in order to survive. I am starting to realize that I have missed Christmas.

I have a new baby girl. I haven't seen her. I haven't touched her. I didn't get a chance to go into labor like normal. Nothing is shaved. My nails are not painted. I didn't get to freak out like I usually do at 8cm.

I haven't bought anything for the baby. I didn't have time to go to the thrift stores and buy clothes. There is nothing washed. I have no: blankets, diapers, wipes, sucky bulb, diaper bag, or even a car seat. No breasts that work, and no bottles. I know nothing of formula.

No cutesy first baby pics with momma. No social media status updates. No nursing and cuddling. No first baths. No name. This little fighter had no official name. Did she?

There are two mothers now watching over her. They are there for her. They are there for me too by taking lots of pictures, and videos. That way if I make it out, I can be there again. I have never seen a NICU, but it seems like everything is under control.

I have to put that aside. Or, they will be drugging me again as I try to escape. I have to focus on me. I have two nurses. The nurse that I had seen right after my death experience, and her teacher/fellow nurse. A rough guy. They get a new nurse in my room. She does physical therapy. She checks my feet, and notices one is drooping a little.

They want me to get up. They pull the moon boots off me, and the pinchy leg things. They put yellow socks with rubber padded bottoms on my feet. I have five people in the room now. They want me to get up.

The whole world spins as I sit up. I want to dry heave. I swing my feet over the bed and sit there with a walker ready for me. The physical therapy nurse wraps a belt around my waist. The world still swam and spun as though I had never gotten up in my life. First, they want me to make motions with my feet like I'm driving a car. Next, they want me to pull myself up. I am scared with the buzzing dizziness.

The room sways. I have to push past this. I have a new baby that needs me. I grip the walker with white knuckles and pull myself up to standing. Everyone is extremely pleased. I feel Grandma and Mom watching me, but I dare not turn my head to find them. The nurse has me make walking motions with my hips and knees without actually stepping. I repeat this ten times. I finally sit and lay back in bed.

I sleep and wake that night. I have a young scared male CNA. He is instructed to pull something out of my nose. I didn't know I had giant tampons shoved up there. I realize by now that nurses don't just use the space that we do to pick our noses. They go way up there. He dislodges one.

We both look at it. We both understand without words, that it looks like a giant bloody tampon. I brace, and he pulls the second. Well this guy is so uncomfortable about it, that my ornery streak comes on full force. I decide to flirt with him all night long. Every time he comes in my room, I give him the "come hither" eyes. By the end of his shift I think he is utterly creeped out.

The coma and paralyzing meds start wearing off slowly. They drug me less and less. One night the top half of my body slowly wakes up. It burns and tingles. I am hot and cold. I have lots of blankets piled on me, and my teeth chatter. Then I kick them all off and am sweating. The next day the bottom half wakes up. Same pains shoot through me like pins and needles from hell.

I am freezing and sweating in the same moment. I throw my blanket off angrily, as I shiver. It's getting maddening. There is an older nurse who comes in. She sits with me. She holds my hand, as my teeth chatter, and I shake. Yet, I am sweating. She just holds my hand and rubs my shoulder on occasion. They think I am kicking the last of the flu.

"I wouldn't wish this on anyone." She says. "Just keep fighting. You can do this!"

During the day I lay there now fully awake. I just stare at the wall. I do this for a long time. Two days it could have been. I am getting depressed. This path is too hard. I don't know if I am really strong enough to make it through.

The CNA comes in and gives me a wet sponge to suck on. These cute little star shaped pink minty sponges of heavily bliss on a stick. They cool my dry mouth. She comes in again the next day and reaches over to turn on my TV. I think it makes her very uncomfortable, that I am just staring at the wall.

I fight with the controller. My clumsy uncoordinated fingers finally figure out how to turn it off. I am alone now. I think it is about 12:30pm. Mom has gone up to be with the baby. I still stare lost at the wall ahead. The clock, the white board, the dark TV.

The nurse comes in. She sits next to me. Her words would echo through me. They are at the time when I'm at a crux. I could have gone any which way. I could have given up just as easy, as I decided to push myself forward. Her words, and her confidence in me is what gave me the strength to move forward no matter how painful, scary, and uncertain things may be. She sits on my bed and turns to me. She smiles at me and takes my hand in her gloved ones.

"You got this." She begins. "You're young and strong. It's going to be a long hard road, but you have kids waiting for you. Don't lose hope. You will beat this."

She squeezes my hand and rubs my shoulder. She fixes my

headband. She fiddles with my feeding bag, and then she fades back to her spot by the computer.

When Mom comes back; I am ready. I poke her as she sits next me. I point to the laminated sheet. The ECMO nurse has snuck in behind her, and she knows what I want. She hands it to me. She seems thoroughly happy that I am trying to communicate.

With a finger I slowly and deliberately spell out "THANJ". It's as far as I get. I want to say thank you to Mom. I can't spell it. My brain is too fuzzy. They put it back.

I make the rocking motion again. I point to her iPad. I want to see my baby. She excitedly shows me pictures.

I weep. Mom wipes the tears and snot off me. I try to escape again. I want her in my arms. I want to go see her and touch her. This beautiful being. My baby. My baby.

I get mad at Mom who can't explain to my drug-soaked mind why we can't be united. I shimmy again to the edge of the bed. I need to be with my baby. I want to hold her. I need to be with her. Mom leaves, and eventually they have to drug me to keep me from being so combative.

Grandma comes in by herself the next day. I am slightly scared that maybe Mom is mad at me. I know I can be a real pain. I look to Grandma who has pulled a chair up to sit next to me. I smile as I reach out my hand for her.

She tells me that Mom has gotten sick. I feel immediately guilty, and also worried about the baby.

Grandma continues, "She needs rest. She's burned out, and her immune system has suffered. Both you, and the baby are finally stabilizing and getting stronger. No worries, you will probably see her tomorrow."

The nurses have a surprise for me. They have taken advantage of such a rare day. It probably won't come around again. They have set up a private meet and-greet with the one person I need to see the most.

The nurse comes in and tries to get me in the chair. I refuse. It is hard enough standing up. So, they put my bed in chair mode. I think I am going to fall off the face of the earth, or dry heave to death. Everything shifts and moves. I cannot complain or fix any discomforts. I am growing extremely frustrated. They give me fresh warm blankets to pacify me. I sit unwillingly and unable to escape. I hear a commotion in the hall. My surprise has arrived.

I glance over to the door. A large white machine is being maneuvered into my room. I have never seen such a contraption in my life. By now, I am getting used to strange contraptions. The ICU is a whole new world.

This contraption is being pushed by two young beautiful female nurses. They manage to get it through the door, and around my machines. At first, I don't know if I should be intrigued or scared. Then they turn it sideways.

It is an isolate. I have never seen one before. Inside is my baby girl. She is wearing nothing but: her diaper, oxygen, feeding tube, and leads. She is good in color, but so tiny. I want to touch her warm skin. I want to tickle her little feet.

The two proud female nurses that are driving the crazy plastic container move to the back side of it. They open the door and reach in. They pick the baby up and turn her more toward me. She cries out with strong lungs. Her cries are music to my ears. I want so bad to touch her, and hold her, and nurse her.

She stops crying almost as quickly as she started. She just wanted to announce she didn't want to be messed with. She turns her head toward me. She crams a fist in her mouth. Her and I lock eyes.

"Well here I am." She seemed to say.

We hold eye contact for the longest time. Here is this little baby who can't hear, smell, see, or touch me. Yet, she knows who I am and where I am. Her eyes refuse to leave mine.

I whisper how sorry I am that we are in this mess. Tears stream down my cheeks. I tell her I love her, and we will be together soon. I tell her of how I will be there in her dreams. I would have given anything to be able to touch her. It is almost unbearably madding that I can't caress her face. Hard as it is, I understand that.

The nurses' then show me all of her stuff. Her first diapers, and blood pressure cuffs. Next, they pull out a camera that they are using to document all of the baby's firsts for me. Right before they leave, they give me a little pink knitted hat and a tiny diaper. The ICU nurses tape it to my bathroom door, so I can see it.

They want me to remember to fight and remember who I am fighting for. I am crying. For once, it is a happy cry. They wipe the snot and tears off my face. They place my bed back to where I like it to be. Angled, so that I'm not drowning in my own fluid, about 45 degrees.

Grandma is thrilled with our little visit. She scoots a chair beside me. She shares stories of the baby. What a fighter she is! She tells me of being able to hold her, and how small she is. She tells me of the huge poop explosion that covered the isolate and got into places that seemed impossible. She gave a laugh, as her bright blue eyes twinkled.

Then she tells me of a book she is reading on her e-reader. She asks if I would like it if she read to me. I smile and nod. She explains the story leading up to where she is going to begin reading. Her voice is calming. I feel like a little kid.

I was in her apartment again. I was enjoying her company, and her laughter. We always shared a love of reading. Her house was always a place I was respected. I always loved the quiet. For once, it wasn't hard to come by.

She was my summer safety from the chaos of my everyday life. One of my favorite things about her was her lack of TV. The constant drone of the idiot box that never ceased at home drove me crazy. Even when I locked my bedroom door, I could still hear it day and night. It is no surprise that ten years into my adulthood I still refuse a TV in my house.

As she reads on, I think about the art store she would take me to. I would pick out little porcelain animals to paint. I remembered the blue bear with the black paws that I did at seven years old. Mom still had it somewhere wrapped in newspaper and tucked away now with a chipped ear.

I fall asleep more at peace than ever before. Grandma says goodbye, and she fades down the hallway. Now I am madly in love with a three-pound little girl. It is a dreamy and trance like sleep. Not like the heavy drugged sleeps I had fought.

I am awoken in the middle of the night. I must have slept through my bath. It is my name rudely spoken that jerks me awake. She's barking at me. This must be my night nurse. She angrily demands that I tell her the date and time. I look up at her dazed, and then at the clock. It is 1am. I mouth it to her.

This nurse is extremely pissed at me. I'm having trouble figuring out why. She then preceded to tell me I have pulled my feeding tube. Four other nurses come in. She tells them how I had done it on purpose. She says she came in and seen it on my gown. I was smiling. I know I didn't pull it maliciously on purpose. I could only conclude that I had hooked a finger on it or something?

I don't have much time before they are holding me down. She forces it down my nose, and down my stomach. It is fast, but it is still shocking. They all unceremoniously leave.

I am pissed and hurt. I stare out into the hall for a long time daring her to come back in. At daybreak, I finally try to sleep. I know it won't be long before the change of nurses. So, I close my eyes.

When the sun gets too bright to ignore Mom is coming in again. She sits next to me. She is saying how much better she is now. She says that she is all healed thanks to garlic, and other all-natural herbs. I can still see red puffy eyes, a runny nose, and more tired movements. She is still fighting a cold. I'm a little bit worried for my baby, as well as myself.

I make motions to my breasts that I want to breastfeed. I am surprised I get through as easy as I do. I use the rocking motion and touching my breasts. They explain to me they had to dry me up for my own safety. Mom and Grandma leave the room to talk to the ICU nurses who then call for a lactation consultant.

A lady appears quickly. She is kind, and although has spent many years here she has never dealt with someone on ECMO. She thinks it may be worth a shot. Mom and Grandma are worried about my medication levels. The consultant gets a list of my medications. It seems that all are okay for nursing. She pulls the curtain. Then she takes the gown off my chest. She leans over and examines my breasts. She rolls and pinches a nipple.

She happily lets out a cry of surprise, when my breasts respond with small drops of milk. She finds the right cup sizes for me. Then she hooks it all up with tubes. She asks how hard to put the suction. I motion for all the way up. Mom brags on how I had nursed all my babies for two years.

They hold the cups on my breasts for 15 mins, as the suction moves from strong to weak; just like a preemie. She pulls them off and then collects 1ml of milk. She tags it, and says she is going to freeze it for me. Then she promises to return in two hours to try again.

I have numerous people in and out of my room all morning long. So many people. So many questions and poking and prodding. It is an insanity for someone with Asperger's who has not slept for most of the night. When the lactation nurse comes back in, I'm cramping, and hurting, and taxed out. I yell, or should I say my mute mouth and face made all the motions I needed to state. I am done.

The nurse left. I know she is shocked and upset. I have given up too soon. I hurt too bad to continue. Mom and Grandma leave. The nurses come in and check me. The stimulation has caused me to pass blood clots the size of baseballs. I shiver and stare at the wall ignoring Mom and Grandma watching from the window, as they clean me up.

I pushed them away again. I can't cry out I am sorry. I lay there all alone. The nurse comes back in. She wipes my face and nose from crying. I can't believe I have just given up like that. I hope Mom will come back.

After they had cared for the baby, they come back in to check on me. I try to apologize. Mom hugs me. She pulls up a chair. She puts some Vaseline on a q-tip, and she wipes my lips down. She tries to fix my head band and pulls my blanket up.

I know she understands. She may not have got it all the time, but she does a great job. She understands me better than anyone here. Sometimes, the miscommunications could get weird. She would come up with crazy things like there is a horse in the room, or I want pie.

Sometimes I would get mad at her and make exaggerated motions to ignore her. I would scoot to the left side of the bed, or just stare into space. For someone that couldn't escape, I could wall myself off, or at least pretend too.

I thought I had been shot in the beginning. I tried to show Mom the "bloodstain" on the wall. I think I tried to show her for three days. Finally, she just agreed.

One time I swore a nurse had written that I'm now HIV positive on the curtain. I try to get Mom to look at the curtain. She walks over and closes it. I shake my head. She opens the curtain. I give her the death look. She walks around the curtain, and finally gives up.

I am getting strong enough now to hold a pen. I'm starting to cognitively comeback together. I'm slowly able to push hard enough to write, and I'm getting the paper to cooperate. I am also starting to remember how to spell simple words. It is a huge breakthrough. Even if it is practically illegible.

I also begin to click with my tongue. That is my new go to for attention in the room, because banging aggravates everyone around. If the nurse is in my room, but their backs are turned to me; I can touch my tongue across the roof of my mouth and click. She/he would respond, and Mom would look up at me. I can then ask for a pen by using one hand as paper and acting like I'm writing with the other. I can sometimes form words slowly and exaggeratedly for them to understand. Surprisingly, most of the nurses can understand me this way. We are all getting the hang of the new communication game.

Nevertheless, I am nowhere near halfway through the woods yet. I have simply survived longer than anyone has expected. It seems at first glance like a straight path out. Hard work with a few bumps. Little did I know; how much I am still teetering. I am still standing, with deaths door wide open, and simply peering in.

Something has gone wrong. I don't know what, but I am standing by my bed. Nurses of all kinds are rushing in. My body is being bagged by my nurse. Four people press against the white board. They are ready to spring into action. Someone is giving me medication through my line.

I stare at the two people pressed against my sink. My skin crawls. I know they are doctors. They are dressed like businesspeople with ties. They hold clipboards. They cast eyes back and forth from my numbers to the clock. I know what they are waiting for. They are waiting for me to die.

I am finally back in my body. I open my eyes. The pain is back. There is a nurse at the foot of my bed, and he smiles at me.

"Feeling better!" he says with a grin.

I want to punch him very hard. I look toward the sink. The two men look on at my numbers, until they shove their pens back in their pockets and leave. The four nurses leave after them. Now it is just me, and my nurse. She is still bagging me but stops for a moment.

"Do you hear that?" she says quietly, almost in a whisper.

I look at her funny, but I do hear a small noise like a scratching of a mouse.

She bags me a couple of times more.

"It's you." She says, pausing. "You're trying to breathe."

I look at her shocked. She stops for a moment, and the slight noise is there again. It could a butterfly's wings fluttering around in there.

I release one of my hands, that is white knuckled gripping a new baby blanket, I reach out and touch her. I mouth thank you. She smiles. She pushes the hair out of my face. She reconnects my ventilator. I am given something to relax and sleep.

They don't know if my body is going to hold out. I'm showing problems. I'm bleeding from somewhere I shouldn't, and those clots I passed are raising concern. They decide to run a battery of tests.

First things first, they need to address the bleeding issues. I wake up in the middle of one of many surgeries. A colonoscopy. I hear people in the room, as one person announces that this is my colon. Someone else pipes up that the blood is old. Thankfully, it is only coming from my stomach. I don't realize that all the people in the room breathed a sigh of relief that I wouldn't be battling NEC.

I want to giggle at the thought of a bunch of medical professionals staring deep into my butt. Yes, the medication they give me helps make light of everything. I think I fell back to sleep, or they knocked me back out, with the giggles. If I could giggle. That night they give me a thick white substance for my stomach. It is heavenly. I want more for the full cooling feeling. It is amazing.

They aren't done there. The ultra-sound tech comes in two nights in a row. First, she gives me an ultra-sound to check my uterus. To see that I am healing, and there isn't anything of concern leftover from my crash C-section. She uses new, and rather rude technology. It had to be inserted inside me, and then wiggled around to take the necessary pictures.

She comes in the next night to check all of my insides. This time with the old school technology and gel. I get to see my liver, and my poor lungs. They look like a pair of frozen butterfly wings. The left is trying its hardest, but the right refuses any movement.

The next night, they clean my lungs out. They have put me under, but again I wake up and gaze at their monitor. They give me a few moments, before I'm forced back to sleep. All of this work coupled with all the chaos every morning brought with its slew of doctors and nurses leaves me exhausted.

I wake up at roughly 18-hour intervals. I lay there and think about my baby girl, and struggle to figure out if it is day or night. I imagine my chakras turning back on one by one. I began at my feet. Alongside the chakras turning on, I go through all the colors starting with black and move through the spectrum to white. This takes me days.

I wake to a perfusionist screaming as loud as he can, at every nurse available, that a dial had been bumped. I feel as if my head is going to explode. As soon as the dial is fixed, I go back to sleep.

I wake to Grandma telling me to calm down. Gloved nurses stand around me ready to spring into action. They flick their eyes between me, and my numbers on the screen. Everyone in the room seems to be holding their breath. I feel like my heart is going to give out at any moment.

I stare at the blinds on the nurse's window. They are purple from the setting sun. I think about nature. I imagine my kids running rampant in a field. I see snowflakes, and deer. I recite a poem I know over and over again. I think about the crunch of snow underfoot. The cold sharp biting winds. I think of a horse and his hot breath cutting through the cold. It is not time for me to go deep into the forest yet. Finally, everyone takes a deep breath for me, as I finally calm my heart.

Never knowing what I will wake up too made me not want to close my eyes. I'm afraid Mom might leave me. I'm afraid the nurses would give up on me. I'm afraid my baby will be gone. I'm always afraid that I might not wake up again, and my girls will grow up motherless.

My day nurse comes in on the tenth. She bolts straight for the window. She forces my curtain open. I'm groggy and struggle against the bright January sunlight screaming at me. It is morning. I'm going to see Mom soon.

The nurse tells me they are going to try to get me back on a day/night schedule. They have decided to curb some of my medication in order to give me more daytime energy.

I squirm around in bed excited. The nurse gives me a cap to wash my hair. There is non-rinse shampoo in it. She got it perfectly enticingly warm. I sit with it and rub my head. Time is still so blurry that I don't really know when the last time this was done. It feels so good. I feel human. Then she gifts me a washcloth to wash my face and hands. I love it. I even put a corner in my mouth to savor something wet.

I soon spot Mom coming down the hall. I want to jump up and hug her. She smiles big to see me awake. She loses no time in finding a pen and paper. She tells me they are screaming at her to name the baby. Social Security is having a fit. The baby is 3 weeks old now.

She gives me three options. She hands me the pen to circle or write out the baby's name. I read the first one, and I know immediately that is her name. Meadow Dawn. It's perfect. I circle it. I try to make a star by it to show my enthusiasm.

Underneath it as best as I could coordinate the pen and the paper I sloppily write "Still not in body 100%".

As, I still fight off sleep, Mom sits beside me, and fills in the birth certificate. I can't remember my birth date, or my phone number. My social security number is out of the question. She doesn't have to ask. She knows. Most of the information she didn't know already she gets from Jewell.

She then hands it to me for approval and signing. I check it over carefully. Double check the spelling. I notice for the first time the day she was born.

I poke Mom and click. I point to the date. It's Christmas morning. Mom nods and goes back to her phone. I am sure she either isn't ready to go into detail, or she doesn't exactly know why I'm clicking.

I take my time. I savor this tiny bit of proof that I did in fact have a baby. I didn't even know or care about looking at my C-section scar. All I have is a vague memory of them messing with it when I was in the coma. With a weak hand I push the pen down on the paper. I sign it.

Now she is no longer little G.G. (Girl Gasson), or Pumpkin, or Missy. She is no longer The Baby. She has a real name. Nobody wanted to name her Noel or some Christmassy thing. Some of the nurses are hoping for a name like that. For those nurses, and family that experienced the birth it was too traumatic. We didn't want it haunting her every time she signs her name, and every time she looks in the mirror.

I told everyone when I was pregnant that this is my baby, and its middle name would be Don, or Dawn. Nobody knew if I was going to survive this. If I die it is silently agreed on that we want her to carry my memory, but not the hauntings.

Mom tells me of how miss Meadow Dawn is doing. She is now four pounds. They have her on low flow; whatever that is. I guess she has even graduated out of her isolate.

I make motions that I want to hold her. Mom tells me soon enough. I start to get upset because it is almost a month now. Instead I take a deep breath and hold out my hand. She squeezes it in her strong way. When she squeezes it, it is like she is pulling me back into this world. Like she would grab ahold of me when I would chance at crossing a road by myself. Mom looks a lot better. She digs around in my bedside table and pulls out the Vaseline to swab my peeling lips. Then she goes after my nose with a tissue.

She seems more relaxed into a routine, and things seem to be mellowing out. My heart hurt, as I thought of all she must have gone through these past three weeks. She works slow, proud, and full of diligence.

She begins to tell me that Grandma and her are now living in the Ronald McDonald House. I have no clue what that is. Maybe a free motel for people helping people in the hospital? She says they can shuttle here in about 15-30 mins. She also tells me they have awesome quarter vending machines, and they offer at least one free meal a day usually at dinner. They have all the amenities.

She shows me the yellow laminated card held by the black rope around her neck. I had seen it on her as I woke, but never was able to figure out why it was there. I thought it was how she got into the hospital. I raise a shaky hand and hold it.

I rack my brain to think back right before this mess happened. Mom had barely settled in with Grandma before I got sick. She had no time to house or job hunt. To think she had taken care of Dad during his last, and now she is taking care of me.

I feel horrible waves of guilt. I want to chase her off and make her forget about me. I also know as a mother that nothing can keep me from my kids. Well nothing, except my need for the ECMO machine, and those strong male nurses.

My concentration comes in waves. She must have known I'm spacing out. She gives my hand another squeeze. I turn my gaze back to her, and I smile my loopy smile.

She tells me she got me a late Christmas present. A Galaxy Tab. She says it should be perfect for my situation. I can communicate with her when she is out of the hospital. I just have to hang tight for the case to be delivered. As weak as I still am; I am bound to drop it.

I'm thrilled to still be able to get a Christmas present. I wonder if my girls had celebrated Christmas. My stomach lurches thinking about them. I promised them I would be home soon. I promised them I was ok. Promises that are now empty and shattered. Time moves so oddly in here. It feels like moments ago that I was pregnant.

I wonder how my girls are doing at home. When you are a kid, I know that time can crawl by painfully slow. I want them to come through my door and hug me. I want to get up go home and cook them dinner. I want more than anything to snuggle in bed and read them a story. I wish I could call them and tell them I love them. I want to tell them I am sorry. Times like this made the clock slow down agonizingly for me. I wonder about Jewell. How is time is moving for her? It feels as though an eternity will pass before everyone will be reunited.

Kids in the Morgue

They want me to watch the kids in the morgue again.
It's cold in there and dark.
No one wants to talk.
They all just want to lay there,
with their white sheets.
How could you miss me?
They have scrubbed my teeth tell they shine.
I am shivering and scared.
He comes to me.
His little body gave up the fight.
He's so sweet showing me how he died.
It's over now come and snuggle.
Let me watch over you,
until you're ready for that one last leap.
As long as I lay an outstretched bridge between worlds
swinging my legs back and forth on the fence,
with my veil lifted, and all ties cut,
you can snuggle with me.
I walk the halls with my father whom I never thought I would see so
soon.
He stands every night at my bed by my feet
By the coat that smells like my earthly world:
full of hay, dirt, and wood smoke.
You cannot wash it clean.
It is one of the few things left of me.
That reminds me.
That pulls me back.
An old poem, and a new blanket for the baby,
I clutch tightly as they try to save me once again.
Yes, I have promises to keep.

I clutch the blanket to my chest.
I look toward my angel standing beside me.
She is whispering in my ear.
She is in the NICU now.
She clipped her wings to save me.
My baby girl who pushed me back.
She forced the veil back over, retied my chains,
and pushed me down.
Back into scattered reality.
Away from the simple peace.
I have promises, three little promises, to keep.

Sucking it Up

This is the way things had fallen. Apart or into place is yet to be determined. This is a brand-new life that I am clawing myself up and into. I told God that I would fight this battle with all my strength, and dedication, and focus. I only asked that He be my net, my bandage, my guiding hand. This is my battle. This is going to be the hardest thing I have ever done. I'm not afraid to face it. The only reason I fear failure is because my children are still so young.

I imagine climbing up a tall jagged mountain. At the top of this mountain I will shake off my wires, and tubes, and throw my bed pan over the edge. I think this came from the January commercials. I imagine every day, that I am getting closer to the summit. I am on a mountain, and it is dangerous. I have the harness of the ICU that is helping me pull myself up, and hopefully out of deaths hands.

I could still fall, and I did. Death still has me cradled in his hands. They hand Mom the funeral pamphlets. They instruct her to give me the faith, but also brace for it. Any day, any night Mom may have to deal with my body. I slip one more time. One last fall. One last tumble down through the dimensions before the gates would close. One last walk in the halls with Dad.

I don't remember the last time I died. I know I was having a terrible nightmare, and I was drowning. I remember the Doctor in my room. All of them are chatting about my lungs. I might have been unresponsive to them, but my mind is very much aware and alive. Anything that is said fades away. I am only looking for negatives.

I am still fighting as hard as I can to stay awake in the day. The nurses are still winding down on the medications. The bags that hang on my left side dwindle down slowly. One of the things I can do to pass time is watch the monitors that feed the stuff into my tubes drop down to zero. It will beep for a nurse to come in. She will refigure buttons, or pull that particular one, or change the bag above. There are so many tubes.

They put me on a pain pump in my very beginning of waking up. The button is lovely at first. Every two hours you can feel heavenly bliss with just a click. Sometimes the nurses will come in and assess how I am feeling. If I'm getting antsy or hurting, they will poke it for me.

Now they give me Tylenol. I can usually smell and guess the flavor through my feeding tube. The water they use gives me a full feeling. It is the closest thing I have to real eating.

One night as the nurse tries to rearrange me, I wake with my tongue out. I make motions like I'm licking a Popsicle. I tell the nurse I want a grape popsicle. She laughs and tells me ventilator pneumonia would be no fun, so I will have to wait.

My face is so dry. I crave anything wet. They give me wet sponges on occasion or let me suck on a wet rag. Nurses or my Mom will rub Vaseline on my lips as they are constantly peeling. Sometimes they will come over, and wipe boogers off my face. That is weird for a mom who had spent years wiping other's noses. I always forget that there is no air coming in or out of my nose and mouth. I can't really tell what is going on in these areas.

I am getting strong and cognitive enough that I learn to work the TV. At first, it is news or infomercials. It's boring, but I need to find ways, besides sleeping, to pass the time. Normal life seems so far away.

One day as I lay here Mom and Grandma come in. This time they are followed by my aunt, my two cousins, and my uncle. They are all standing around my bed.

One of my cousins has friends here, and she doesn't really care to be here. I don't blame her. For one, we don't get along. For another, I am kind of embarrassed to be so helpless, and dependent. So, I am rather glad that she leaves.

The other cousin, her brother, two years older, and one year younger than me, also fades quickly back into the hall. We used to be close. When we were young, we always got in some kind of trouble. We fake smoked cigarette butts and peed on the lawn. I mean we were babies. I too can understand his discomfort with me.

It's just the two sisters, brother, and mother. They talk mostly with each other, because I am still so hard to understand. I don't really mind. I am glad to have the company. I'm blessed to hear them laugh.

My uncle comes in a few more times over my ICU stay. He taught me to call him Uncle Marty Great when I was just a baby. It stuck. Here at the hospital I would say he earned that title. He is stealth and comes in early in the mornings. I realize he doesn't always want to deal with Grandma and Mom. I love to wake to feel him stroking my hair and rubbing my arms. He is so kind, just like a dad should be.

"Poor, thing." He tells me. "It must be awful for you to wake up here strapped down with all these wires, and that awful feeding tube. So young and strong and then poof it's all pulled away from you."

I look up at him. I'm still swimming in medications that make me loopy. I try to communicate my thanks. I feel tears cooling on my cheeks. I try to ask him a simple question of how his kids are doing. It is a little misconstrued and turns awkward for a second. He laughs it off. I decide it is probably best to keep quiet. He fades into the hall, and unbeknown to me for another two weeks, up to the NICU, to hold his great niece.

I am getting stronger now. More of pieces of me are coming together. My favorite game becomes pull the pulse oximeter off. I will rip it off anywhere it is. They have a fun time re-taping it to my fingers. Then it is re-clamping when it is on my ear. Finally, they give up and tape it to my toe. I hate it there. It takes me three days, but I finally work it off. I demand it back on my finger. There I decide to make truce and leave it alone. Most of the time.

I now actually have something to put my mind to. Mom has brought my new tablet in. I'm glad it is the smaller one. She gives me a big white bear that helps to hold it. I'm so weak, and still my brain is cloudy. It is hard to work at first.

Mom hands it to me turned on. The weather is set to Aurora Colorado. I wonder if that is in the Denver area. I am in the Denver area, right? The date is January 15th, 2014. Where has the time passed? It's a shock to see that many days have slipped by me. It is almost a month now since I have been originally hospitalized. Not only have I woken up in a new month. I have woken up in a new year. A wave of guilt washes over me as my girls come to mind.

Mom has put lots of pictures of Meadow on, and some of where she is living now. I'm not ready to look at them. There is lots of music. I am happy to see books. I have always been an avid reader.

I pick it up and open a new book. It is heavy. So, horribly heavy. I should have known. A pen is still a struggle. I am too weak to read for long, and comprehension is a struggle. It is disheartening. My favorite thing in the whole world, and all the time in the world to indulge, and yet I can hardly make out the simplest of words.

Mom puts on a song called "Aurora". I leave it on and let it run constantly. It's a low-grade music, that is supposed to repair your DNA. The perfusionist's at night find it extremely calming. I even watch TV with it on. I sleep with it on. I tuck it underneath me or place it on my chest. I don't have to worry about rolling over on top of it. I just have to watch the nurses, so they don't forget to move it before they turn me.

I use the bear at night to cuddle with. It is almost too big for me to keep control of, but I love the comfort. I snuggle with it just like a little kid. I want it to be one of my kids, so I close my eyes, and think about the times I have had with them. I work hard to hold onto this big bear, and to pull memories back together.

I no longer care that my wall facing the hall is all glass. The door is a sliding glass one. I don't care anymore about the nurses who sit at the window typing and always watching me. I have no privacy left. I don't care. I'm too busy struggling to survive.

The nurses all spend so much time typing away on my chart. They are probably writing down exactly how many calories I am getting. The exact balance of fluids in my system. They will come in, and measure exactly how much I peed. My medications. My moods.

Now that I'm awake they will start figuring out who I am. My personality. My temperament will start showing more and more. At 6:30am and pm nurses will sit around, and they will chat about me as they stare through the window.

Sometimes it makes me feel like a zoo experiment. Once a whole gaggle of medical people came in, not looking so much at me as my machines. They have clipboards they scratch at with their pens. They are led by a perfusionist that I knew I had irked many times. He smiles at me genuinely. I return the gesture. He stops to show them every little button.

I spot a hot new Perfusionist for the first time. I didn't know then that I would see him many times after this. We would come to call him the Jesus ECMO guy. I want to look good. The only thing I can do is pull the blanket up to my shoulders and pat down my matted hair. Now, I just stare at the wall and try to blend into the bed as much as I can.

They walk around my bed and check the hoses that are clamped to the head of my bed. He is there checking how it is connected to my neck, and how its looped to the machine. He takes careful notes of everything about my external iron lung.

Then they leave still chatting away. I would have breathed out if I could. I look out in the hall for the cutie. He is still there. I fight with the controllers hard to press buttons. Finally, I manage to turn on the TV. I become engrossed in the news.

I feel a fart. I need a moment to see if it is safe to pass or not. I'm not given the gift of time, and instead I explode. I am very thankful for the mattress pad. I look out in the hall. He is still there. I glance up at the clock. Mom won't come in for a while. I can wait for him to leave before I call in the nurse for help. I go on watching the news, and hope he leaves soon.

Time passes and the show ends. I try to change the channel, but my weak hands drop the controller over the side of the bed. I cast a quick glance around hoping no one heard the loud thud the controller made as it hit. I try to play cool, but my ever-attentive nurse is already winding her way around the bed. She bends to pick it up. I bite my lip, as my faces flushes bright red. She pauses to look at me from the position of picking up my controller. I want to hide. She hands it to me, and then lifts my blanket. She rubs my shoulder, as I try to look away. My face burns. I fight back tears.

"It's okay." She whispers.

She goes out to the main desk to round up help. Before I know it there are four nurses gloving up. To my horror Jesus ECMO guy is at the head of my bed watching my hoses. First, they lower the head of my bed. I usually freak at this because I feel like I am drowning. I try to keep still, pretending I am invisible, or anywhere but here. They strip me naked.

On command I grab the side railing, and I roll onto my side to face the window. I count the pillars of the parking garage. They have to put thick cream on my butt from waiting so long. It's a relief from the burning. On command I roll the other way grabbing the side bed rail with all my strength over the hump of all the dirty laundry I had made. I want to die. I am so embarrassed. I try not to let it show. There is nothing I can do or say.

The nurse makes me comfortable when everyone leaves. She tells me to page if I have time, and she will get me a bed pan. I nod, and mouth thank you.

I wake up with an ice pack around my left hand. By now, I am getting used to sleeping through things that would have been impossible before. It is unnerving for a moment to be reminded how I am so far off from where I used to be. I lift up my left hand and wiggle my fingers. Maybe I bumped it. I wave it at the nurse.

"Do you need paper?" She asks.

No, I want to say, what happened? I want to say how did I not know. I am now convinced the anesthesiologist is probably a ninja. Maybe he or she is hiding under my bed. I just guess that maybe I hit it, and I leave it as that. The ice is cold, but it feels so good that I decide not to rip it off to investigate further.

Mom comes in, and she doesn't seem to be at all surprised at my bound up left wrist and hand. The nurse is still checking me out. Cold stethoscope, and quick a reattachment of leads. She looks at my feeding tube. Then she messes around with the feeding bag. She begins to speak about how I should get up and go sit in the chair. She looks at me for a response.

I nod. She smiles and finishes what she is doing. It's time for me to start facing this fight head on. If I don't begin now I may never. Courage is hard. It doesn't mean you're not afraid. It means you suck it up and push on.

I have a physical therapy nurse in my room. She checks my feet, and then puts on the yellow socks with the rubber padded bottoms. The nurses pull off what is not needed. The pinchy leg things for once come off. There are more people in the room now. A perfusionist and a respiratory nurse have joined in alongside my nurse and nurse assistant for the day. The physical therapist wraps her belt around my waist and cinches it tight.

I sit up, and let the world go out of whack for five minutes. The room spins, and sways. Everyone is telling me that I can walk. I can do this. They puff me up, until I am sure I can. I am on the left side of my bed so as not to tangle wires or pinch my ventilator. There is a chair waiting for me less than three steps away.

I put my hands down on the bed. I push off like I am instructed. With the physical therapy nurse right there for me; I stand. I step. My legs give way. For a fraction of a second, I'm hanging in the air like the ghost that I have become. I collapse into the arms of this strong woman who pulls me forward and sits me in the chair. I did it. I am so proud. I took a step. I am out of bed. I have slayed a new dragon.

Everybody cheers for me. Mom pulls up a chair right by me and takes my hand. She is beaming. She hands me my tablet. Most people fade back out into the hall. The main nurse rewards me with a warm blanket, and a pat on the back.

The nurses' assistant checks out my hair. She tries to comb it. It's too matted and thick. She puts in a special order, and has a brush sent up here. For two days, she works on the rats nest my hair has become. Finally, she gets my hair contained, and puts in an 80's style ponytail. I am so relived. I thought I would have to get a pixy cut. It's not a big deal. I had one done last year, so my hair barely touched my shoulders.

I feel like more of me is coming together. I get Mom to cut my nails, because they do not have nail cutters up here, and I trust her only. I clean my ears. All of these simple things, that I haven't done in a month or more.

I find the movie versions of coming out of a coma laughable. This is no movie. I sure as hell don't have blown out hair, and a manicure. I have greasy dandruff ridden hair. Mom did a good job cutting down my daggers for me. I probably seem less dangerous to the nurses now.

I have also been given the good to go on the flu. They no longer need masks, and gowns to deal with me. The only way they could find it was to clean out my lungs one more time. Then the samples taken had to sit for a week, while they tested it periodically.

I woke in this bronchoscopy and watched as they worked around my pink lungs. I'm so glad I don't smoke. They are almost all clear now of those gray boogies.

"Doctor she's awake." I hear the nurse say.

"Let her watch she is strong." The Doctor responds.

I am content that they let me watch. I hear the doctor talking as he cleans, and picks samples to be tested. He's quiet in concentration. He is also strong, clear, and concise. They move around to the back side. I watch for a few more minutes, before I fall back to sleep.

After a week it is official. The nurses tell me happily that I have slayed another dragon. The biggest one. I have beat H1N1. Now, I am left with trying to heal from the effects of pneumonia, and ARDS. I'm struggling to survive life support.

What a funny term "life support". Ten years ago, I would be dead. Simple as that. The advancements in the medical field are amazing. I hope that they learn a lot from me. I hope that they can reunite even more mothers with babies.

These men and women in their bright black clogs, sneakers, and dark blue uniforms. They unnerve me at times. They deal with people every day. They are okay with people. I have Asperger's. I tried, but I missed the boat socially. I watch them. I have always watched people. I love seeing the different personalities.

I learn quickly how different personalities affect my care. If you are mean or too weak, I will suffer. I will be uncomfortable and ready to tear my cannula out, by the end of the shift. If you have the right balance of strength and caring its perfect. To know when to just pull the trigger and get it over with care. I guess it's what they all work for.

Major bonus if your candid and funny. All but a rare few are amazing and strong.

I try to socialize despite my current and past blocks. I know it's not all on them. It's also me, and my personality. My personality has already proven that it can be hard to handle at times. The way I see the world, and experience it too also has a huge effect on the nurses. I have had a hard time learning to trust and let go. Vulnerability has always been terrifying to me. I have never had to experience it to this degree.

I have no choice, but to trust. Mom and Grandma are my advocates. Jewell holds my medical decisions in her hands. I lay here in bed as the chess game carries on. I am unaware of who holds the power. It never crosses my mind, and if it does, I don't care at this point. I only worry about making through the day, and then surviving through the night. Everything else seems to prove that I am very much alive.

I have tactical issues, and the blankets feel almost painful at times. The sound they make alone, and my pillow drives me nuts too. I can look the other way. I know I am alive. I will try not to grind my teeth, or squirm too much. I have also been a finger sucker since birth. When I was younger my dad broke me of the thumb sucking. When Mom left him, I picked it back up. This time using my first and pinky finger instead. My partners and friends all know it's just me. Just my own glitch. I am afraid of the chemicals, and the new environment. I take to just twirling my hair and tongue sucking. It is probably harder than not being able to roll over onto my side. Thankfully, they have me so heavily medicated, or I'm still so sick, that I am too lethargic to even care.

The sound of the gloves. The squeaking, and the stretching. It's like balloons. I am almost terrified of balloons. I also don't necessarily like being touched that much. Their blue gloved hands all over me is something that takes a while to adjust to. The fact that they are checking my machine every hour. They touch knobs, and I want to jump out of my skin. The tubes they check. The drips. I feel like I have blasted completely off earth and landed on a whole new planet. If I had a voice, I would be asking a ton of questions.

The people who work here are human beings just like me. These humans in the medical field are of a different energy, than I have ever been around. I have managed to keep on the fringes of human interaction. Now, here I am right smack in the middle of it all. I am amazed. Here they are with their books and hand sanitizer. They have taken me into this strange world. With such a determination, skill, and kindness they care for me. They too know I am human. They smile at me. Most treat me with respect and compassion.

I wonder how these nurses live their lives. What do they do when they are not staring, at monitors, and giving medications? What do they think about as they tend to me? What is it like to be on the other side of the glass?

A few tell me stories of how I crossed their minds while shopping. One is brave enough to tell me she couldn't take care of me in the early ECMO days, because she just had a baby. She had too much empathy that Meadow would be soon become motherless. She admitted that she passed me on to another nurse when I was in a coma.

I am fully conscious now. The safety net of being in a coma has faded. I am truly aware of my peril. Without being heavily sedated, I begin to wake and sleep in a semi normal fashion. This place is always buzzing with life, and it has pulled me in. I am now apart pulsing with its energy.

Sleep can be hard. I am learning the art of sleeping on my back. It has always been a taboo for me to have my belly exposed like this. It's creepy how I sleep with my arms down at my side or folded over my chest. If I die it will be a perfect pose to roll me to the morgue with. I try to not let that thought in much. But, it's there.

I wake first at about 4-5am. Sometimes I get restless at 3am. Radiology somehow knows. Even if I play dead. Playing dead in an Intensive Care Unit is probably not a good idea to begin with. It never works.

They come in with their little machine. They shove a cold board under my back and snap a picture. The board is like ice under me, and its hard as a rock. Then they jerk it out. They leave without a word. They push their machine out the door, and down the hall for the next victim. They leave me in a mess. The weaker they are at pushing the board under me, or out from under me, meant the more disarrayed I would end up. I have a few that are so impressive, they could probably pull tablecloths out from under dishes.

Most of the time, I need to call the nurse to help me fix my blankets and pillows. Sometimes, I need to put back on my head band. I just don't want to move very much. I'm so weak. I'm always scared of dislodging my ECMO hoses.

The nurses will use that time to lift me up and tilt me the other way. I like to go to sleep facing the window. The lights of the parking garage are interesting to look at. The cars. The lights of the cars. I imagine all those lives. Most are shinny and newish looking. I come from a rural area. If you weren't covered in dirt and still driving 90's or early '00 then you weren't from there.

I will watch in the early morning. I become adept at telling when the nurses shift is about to take place. Car traffic will pick up. Then a flood of people will file into the elevator or use the stairs. I will watch all the busy bees chose one or the other and disappear down or up.

Going to sleep facing the wall and window means I will be tilted toward the door in the early morning. I am front and center of the nurse's desk. Their white board, the phones. I can watch them working. My nurse is usually positioned at a smaller desk, right against the glass. She can see me, all of me, and my stats. I like being tilted toward my door. I feel ready for the barrage of people that are going to start coming in soon. I prefer to see them, before they invade my space.

Usually after radiology has ravaged me, and I have been straightened out again I turn on the TV. I can't go right back to sleep. If it is before 4:30am I usually go to my infomercials.

One of my favorites is a fancy juicer. I wish someone would make me an exotic juice and push it through my feeding tube. I drool over fresh fruit and veggies way more than the fast food chain commercials. All I fantasize about is watermelon ripe and red. I wanted one slightly over ripe. No seeds just lots of juice. I dream about the day I will be able to eat again.

I avoid the commercials as much as possible. Most of them are so annoying. It is January, so it is all about taxes, and low-calorie snacks. Car insurance companies are never ending. If not those then it is about a new horror movie. There is one about a girl in a coma that gets eaten by a clown. There is another one about an evil unborn baby.

That is a big hell fucking no!

Eventually the news will come on. I'm not going outside for a while, but the weather is a good way to pass time and see outside my new little world. I'm always glad that I am in here with my heated blankets when the snow flies. Then there is the news. I just listen and watch for fun. The mainstream news is not something I want anything to do with.

I wait for Mom and grandma starting at 6am when they flick the lights on brighter in the hallway. The next person in my room is the cleaning lady. Sometimes, if I seem really intrigued by her, or click at her she will talk to me. I love her accent. I love it when she hums and sings. I can't place it, but I love the full warm happy voice. Other times she will just smile at me in acknowledgment, and busy around. She slides her mop under my bed. She collects hair and blood, and God only know what else. She also takes out my trash and laundry. She cleans the toilet I never get to use, and the sinks.

I go back to the news or try to sleep in order to pass the time. I ignore the nurses that have grouped up outside talking and looking at me. This became impossible at 7am as the nurses are now in and out of my room. The nursing assistant stocks my room with supplies. I have my temperature taken, blood drawn, teeth brushed, and my catheter cup dumped.

I request a bed pan for my usual clockwork early morning movements. I want it over before Mom, and Grandma come in. The nurse of course will measure, and borderline creepily study it as well. Then she will dump it and rinse my pan for later.

A respiratory doctor comes in next. He gives me tests with my ventilator and checks my tubing. A respiratory nurse gives me albuterol treatments and checks my trach collar. They will be in every four hours to repeat this process. They deep suction me. I hate this. I don't want them doing it too much, but if they don't do it enough; I will be coughing and choking. So, I give in knowing I will feel better once the painful coughing it causes is over.

I eventually became aware of rounds. That is when all the doctors on the unit come around to each room. They discuss the patient, the plan, and the progress if there is any. I quickly try to look better, with my quick hair pat, blanket pull method. I think it means little here. I'm alive. I think that impresses them more than anything. I will strain to hear anything. Most of it is a hushed gibberish.

The main nurse for the day will be back in to give me my medications through my feeding tube. I look forward to it so much. My belly feels full. I watch as they crush some things and mix them with water. I usually click to announce I'm watching. They will usually explain to me what they are doing and what they are going to give me.

They change my feeding bag and fill it up. They look over my IV, change solutions, and make adjustments. Sometimes they will take off my blood pressure cuff. Sometimes they check it, or not even notice it. They pull off my gown to see my scar and check all my leads. I can get fresh warm blankets out of them after this.

I snuggle in the best I can. I try to watch TV again. By now, it is repeating the 4-5am news. Mom and Grandma come in around 10am. I hang with Mom or Grandma next to me. Often, I can get Mom to chat about Meadow. I talk back with pen on paper.

The nurses can coax me out of bed with Mom's support. It takes time, and about 5 people minimum to help me move. I sit up and let the world spin. It takes a while to reorient myself. I have a belt wrapped around my middle, so if I fall there is something to grab a hold of.

They move my old bed out of the room. They want to give me a new one. I think the weight isn't working. They also want a slightly different one since I'm a functional human being again. I watch as they shove the dark blue bed out. Soon, a new one lighter blue, takes its place. Their eyes and movements tell me I should be proud to have graduated to this new bed.

So, from 10-12am I sit in a chair. I have the nurse button in my lap, and Mom beside me. Mainly for comfort and encouragement. I fidget on my Tablet or watch TV to ignore the fact that I'm tired, and dizzy. I quickly build myself up to sitting for an hour. As I sit, they come in and fix my bed. They fluff my pillows, check my sheets, and anything that may need changing. I am still purging from the birth, so a mattress pad has to be with me everywhere I go.

I eventually get strong enough to sit on a bedside commode, which I am very proud of. Even if I still am not in charge of wiping myself yet. It bugs me terribly, but I understand that I can't just get up and wash my hands. So, I relent.

I get to rest for a while after I have sat for as long as I can. I sleep for a couple of hours. They give me my first blood transfusion for the day while I sleep. Mom leaves to go care for Meadow. I won't see her again until 2pm. Grandma will stay with me. I'm still nervous about falling asleep. I close my eyes, with the fresh warm blankets coxing me to relax.

It only feels like moments before I hear noises. I open my eyes and glance toward my door. It can be frustrating to try to sleep in a place that is so alive all the time. This is one of those times. It is just not easy for me to let go.

They have a funny looking walker in my room now. They want me to practice real walking. The nurse looks at me and asks how tall I am. I raised a hand to show 5 feet. Then I lift three fingers on the other hand for the extra inches.

"I thought you were taller." He says looking at me.

I smile my response, and he turns back to readjusting it. I know what is coming next. I can't hide from it. I want to. They set me up on all moveable machines. Here is everyone in my room now trying to get me up. There is the belt around me, and those yellow socks. I sit up. I swing my legs over almost too quickly. It is hard at first to be up as usual. They help me.

Respiratory is watching my trach and ventilator. A perfusionist is watching my ECMO machine tubes, while pushing that crazy contraption around. I have physical therapy showing me how to lean my weight against this big walker, and how to hold onto the handles. I guess it uses your upper body strength. I still have that.

I just need to get my feet to go in some kind of order. My main nurse is in front of me. He is a kind male almost ready to retire. There is someone behind me pushing a wheelchair in case I need to sit. It is a parade. The onlooker's Mom and Grandma watch cheering me on, and they take lots of pictures.

I am too busy, at the moment, to notice. I am scared as soon as I push out of my room and bump into the nurse's desk. I am on life support just hanging here. Terror almost overtakes me. I want to run back into my room. My nurse tells me to be calm. He wants to tell me a joke. As I follow him, he says something funny. Then to keep me distracted he shows me a picture of his cute doggy. Before I know it, I have walked to the end of the small ECMO unit.

There is another ICU unit connected to it. To my right is doors I think you can go through. The door I thought existed is just another room. I wonder where in this mess my baby is. I want to keep walking and go see her. I am so exhausted. Fear is creeping up inside me again.

This is now my afternoon activity. They will have to coax me out of bed. It's not easy. I don't want to move much on these scary machines. I'm tired, and I'm actually starting to get hungry again.

Back in my room I lay back in my bed. I want to sleep and am drowsy. I try to give my attention to Grandma and Mom. I try to write to them or let them read to me. They usually call it a day around 4ish. Then I am on my own.

They are not that far away. Anytime, I need them I can just write a nurse who will make the call. I am scared at first being alone. I always bite the bullet and put on my best face. I also start to communicate by messages online. I don't want to bother Mom too much. I know she needs her rest. I'm always okay. I have my dad standing on the edge of the bed. He is watching over me.

After a while I look forward to it. The night routine is much more my speed. It is quiet and calm.

I can get more one on one with the nurses. The perfusionists are very interesting to communicate with. They come in every hour and write numbers down. They tinker with it. They are there not just for my machine. They also help pull me up when I have slid down. They help clean me up. They talk to me and encourage me.

I watch the popular sitcoms that are silly and simple, while listening to "Aurora". After one last quick cleanup of my room people will finally stop coming around to bug me so much. The day nurses are busy changing hands to the night nurses. Then I get another full stomach of water and medications. The last hurdle for the night is my bath.

They give me the option of early in the morning, or late at night. I want the late night one. I am never a friendly creature in the morning. Also, if the rare opportunity of me getting a chance to sleep in happens, I don't want it interrupted by them bathing me.

So, they prepare my bath. They let the water run tell its hot. Each nurse has his or her own way of preparing the washcloths. They all feel good and are hot all the way through. It's nice, because I feel like I am always fighting to keep warm.

They drop my bed down flat. I am drowning. I panic. They tell me to relax. It is hard. I react by coughing and sputtering. They give me the little sucky stick thing. I can suck things out as they come up. I try to stay calm. I try to be calm.

They pull my gown off. I am exposed. They always make sure the curtain is closed first. I let them spray me down, and then rub me clean. Then I grab the side rail and roll toward the parking garage. This is over a small hump of sheets. I still have a lot of upper body strength, and they are grateful for it. They rub my back and make a huge lump of laundry. When they tell me to, I roll over to the other side of the bed. If I am really tired, they will have to help me. They finish fixing my sheets. I find it neat how they can give me a bath and change my sheets at the same time.

I can't speak. But I am awake. I am still bursting with life on the inside. The nurses are almost always kind. It is rare that I feel like they just do their job, and I feel like a computer, or some unhuman piece of their work. They chatter on about their lives while wiping down my body. I don't mind. I sometimes cherish being alone, but not lonely.

On an even rarer occasion, they can even make remarks about me without thinking about it. One nurse mentions the fact that I have restraints under my bed. She tells my nurse for the night that there would be no way she would put up with me. A part of me wells with anger. I want to show her why they put me in restraints. Sadly, I restrain myself.

I found it rather funny once when I accidentally had a coughing fit, while they were cleaning me up. The girls screamed as I spurted blood.

'I'm in ICU ladies.' I thought to myself mentally rolling my eyes.

I reach out to apologize. The nurse just smiles at me. They are all laughing off their strange girly response. I smile with them.

The bath out of the way I can watch TV uninterrupted until I'm sleepy. It is hard to deep sleep for long here. There are too many noises, and bright lights. The leg massagers are constantly on. Sometimes I can pretend I am running. Most of the time I wished for the strength to rip them off.

They have a fun weekend of movies that I enjoy. The sad thing is that Mom and Grandma are watching them too from the Ronald McDonald House. They come in and start talking about them. I want to talk too. Especially about my favorite ones. I thought about clicking and pointing to the TV. I figure that will be as far as I get. Any deep conversation would never happen. I feel so left out.

The CNA comes in and writes the names of my night nurse, and nursing assistant on my white board. They are both guys. I usually have one female on board. This I'm not happy about. Eh, its night, and I should sleep through most of it.

As soon as the nurses finish their usually change of hands ceremony the main nurse for the night comes in. With a smile on his face, he says hi, and who he is. He starts to prepare my night medications. He is tall and intimidating. Did he make a mistake, and join med. school instead of NFL tryouts? My ICU room seems to dwarf.

He turns around and studies me for a long time. Is it because I am staring? He stops what he's doing and leaves. Maybe it is my facial expressions. I am not upset, just shocked. He is healthy as horse, at least 6ft tall, and muscular enough to bench press a small car.

He comes back a moment later with a kit. He walks over to my left side, and he places the small package on my body. I don't move. I'm intrigued. He opens the tiny package.

Inside are sterile gloves that he wrestles with. He complains about how they never have gloves in there that fit right for his big hands. His big hands have more fine motor coordination, than I could even dream of despite my advanced sewing experience.

He's not quiet, but also not annoying. He treats me like a human being. I can have a conversation with him easily with my eyes, my facial and body expressions, and occasionally mouthing something. It is amazing how attentive he is to me.

Gently he peels off the layers of tape, the nurse's past, have stacked over each other without much thought. He cleans my nose and apologizes for the strong-smelling cleaner. He notices that my feeding tube may have also slipped too far into my stomach. He calls radiology down. They snap a picture. With his pinky he guesses it is 4mm too far.

He pulls it gently out. After another picture, it is no longer curled. He tapes it back down.

He takes off my blood pressure cuff. The relief is enormous. He makes note of the tightness and redness. Then he gives me my meds. Afterward, he lets me watch TV until about bedtime. He has two female nurses, along with my nursing assistant. They work together to give me my bath. He reattaches leads and checks my scar when the female nurses are there.

The male nursing assistant also takes gentle care of me. My vent pops off, and I am holding it too my neck. He quickly runs to reattach it. I am surprised and humored, at how fast he can move in his round short body. He fluffs my pillows, makes sure the hair is out of my eyes, and my headband is on right.

I can forgive him. I can. I know he wanted to wash my breasts on purpose. The main male nurse was not there at the moment. He went to get my blankets. The female nurses eyed him angrily, but sighed, and handed him the washcloth. I know he took careful attention making my nipples stand, all the while humming about boobs to himself.

I am awake, alive, with feelings and emotions. I am not paralyzed anymore. I cannot speak, and the medications have made me drowsy. I am still right here trying my best to hold on. Drowning in my fluids. I am exposed to you. To your touch, however you chose to touch me. I have resigned myself to you entirely.

I get my two warm blankets. They tilt me toward the window. My main nurse does something so shocking that it almost puts me to sleep instantly. The blankets are not just thrown over me, or around me. First, he sees to it that my gown is actually over my shoulders and snapped in.

Then he tucks me in very tightly. Just like I would do with my kids. I know we are the same age. He told me so when he was taking care of me. Any other time this would be awkward. I am in need of this small and monumental comfort. In the middle of the night nearing morning they tilt me the other way. They are so strong, and I feel so safe that I hardly wake.

Dancing Dead

Corpses in the hall,
full of hope,
that cannot stall.

We've seen them mope.
We've heard them scream.
They pass time on all machines.

They pump and hiss,
and ring their bells,
with deaths sweet kiss.

Take my hand.
I'll pull you through.
Rise up and stand.
       Dance with corpses in the hall.

Breathing it Out

I have now mastered new forms of communication. I'm sitting and even walking, with a walker. I am now a toddler. A toddler that is still stuck in limbo. I am still in between breathing in and breathing out. My lungs hang like shadows in my cage. The clock is ticking. Life support is just a bandage. A very temporary bandage.

I'm told that I have six to eight weeks' maximum, before my body will fully give out. Four weeks are now looming around the corner. I'm growing nervous. I try not to think about it, but it is constantly there. It's a spot on a lens. I don't pull or move my right side much. I am not sure how deep the ECMO is inside me. The horror of it pulling out keeps me very still.

Mom, Grandma, Jewell, nurses, doctors: everyone has worked so hard to get me here. They keep me comfortable and calm. They rub my lips down when they dry out. They take note of what makes me happy. Even the little things like having my sucker thing at hand when my bed is lowered. The relaxation that two heavy warm blankets spark in me. The things that cause pain and irritation they try to keep at a minimum.

The nurses though paid for their work seem more than happy to go above and beyond. They watch me all the time. They watch my heartbeat. They are always on the ready. They always seem eager to give me strength when they come into my room. I rely on it. The small smiles, and conversations. Their ability to stay calm here in this harsh landscape never ceases to amaze me.

I am not the only one lost right now. I am not the only one strapped here to this bed. The whole family is right here with me strapped down and holding their breath. I am not the only one dying. Everyone I love is dying with me. If I heal, we will heal together. If I die, I take a bit of everyone with me.

I am so sorry to my babies. I am so sorry I left Jewell like this. I am so sorry to see Mom and Grandma chatting beside me despite being hungry, and tired.

I am trying every moment. I don't want to let them down. I don't want to let my kids down. My lungs need to work. I don't want to start reliving the bumps that I suffered in the beginning. I'm glad I got to touch and taste the peace of being out of body. I deeply want to go back There. I know I am not done here, and we all eventually die. My turn will come again. Until then, I need to push myself.

I finally scream out to God that I want to live. I ask The One for help. I feel tears in my eyes. I silently cry out. I pray for help.

"Please, help me push through. Please help me heal. I want to live!" The words scream in my mind. "Please, God, please."

I can't think of any bible verses. The bible is a new thing to me. It is a large vast sea that I swim in unable to cling to anything. I have studied it alone. I read the Psalms, and Proverbs to my kids. That is the extent of all I know.

Through blurry eyes I stare at a perfusionists cross that hangs daintily around his neck. It is Sunday, I think. He notices me staring at it. He asks me if I have taken Jesus into my heart. I nod. I had long ago, but I never felt the right time/place to be baptized. If I knew then what a clergy was, I would have had him/her in here to read to me, pray with me, and maybe even baptize me, while I was in the hospital.

Early Monday morning I jolt awake. Something has changed in me. I see an angel. Above me. Wings and eyes fully open. I have no fear. I'm enamored with her. She is gone. Before my mind can wonder or race. I reach up and touch the air that she occupied. I want to cry.

A moment later my ventilator makes a loud pop. I startle. I look over at it. What has changed? I glance at an unalarmed nurse typing away and enjoying coffee. It is calm and bright. I don't need to look at the clock to know the nurse shift has already happened.

The sun is streaming in. I know I'm not going to have my eyes closed for very long. I manage to let go, and doze gently. A doctor comes marching into my room. I keep my eyes as closed as possible. I know awake he will test me on the vent.

A moment later I here screaming. From the doctor. Not bad screaming, but pure joy. Like my ventilator had spit out the winning lotto tickets. From his heavy Asian accent, I can finally tell that he is screaming in joy about my lungs. They are working now. They have relaxed. I am breathing.

"Your lungs are finally healing!" He almost screams. "Your lungs are healing!"

I open my eyes, and I give him a smile. His joy overfills my tiny room. He touches my feet with both hands. He almost skips out of the room.

I want to ask a thousand questions. I want to get up, and dance too. Does this mean I am getting off ECMO soon? How long before I have my face back? Oh water, and eating, how I crave it.

Mom comes in later on. I want to tell her all about it. I want to scream how happy I am. I can't even begin to describe my joy on paper. I want to scream in frustration. I want to touch her and replay my morning telepathically. I need to ask my hundreds of questions. I know pointing and clicking won't work.

They get me up, and in the chair. I am pushing 30-60ccs of air in me. I only have to reach 400cc and hold it for three days. It seems like an impossible feat. I mean I have been doing this simple task from the start of my life earth side. Now, I have to do it again. It is almost four weeks now into the ECMO. How long will this task take?

I have a physical therapist nurse that is gentle and kind. She explains to me that I need to open my thoracic area then try to breathe. I follow her instructions slow and deliberate. It sets off alarms. They fix it, and I begin again. More alarms. She instructs me to sit up tall and open. She helps me lift my arms up over my head and stretch. She says that when I lay back in the bed to bring my arms over my head and breathe as deep as possible.

"You were damaged in the thoracic area, and you have a bad habit of balling up and closing off. You are protecting yourself which is understandable. You need to open up. That is why we have you sit in the chair every day. We need you to open this area back up. Stretch as much as possible."

She ties bands around my bedside railing. She demands that I practice arm exercises. She also demands more practice with my feet. Just like I am driving a car. They give me different boots now. They are lined with a fluff that is unbelievably comfortable but get hot quick. They are meant to correct some of my drop foot issues. The doctors also demand that the nurses get me up and walking twice a day.

I fight this. I fight this tooth and nail. I want my warm blankets, and my good medications. It is so hard dealing with the fact that I have to learn everything all over again. It is so overwhelming. Me at 28 years old needs a walker, and 5 nurses to move. That I, a mother, can't wipe my own butt, or nose. I can't eat or drink water.

"Don't worry so much." My older male nurse tells me as he lays my bed down flat.

He was the one who had started me walking out in the hall. I am coming to understand that he must be one of my main nurses. I see him quite a bit. I enjoy his company.

"If you make it out of here, you'll be at the pub drinking some beer, and telling this crazy story." He says.

Who says pub? I thought and smiled. The smile isn't so much the strange use of language, but the fact that time may heal this. I will one day, "if" I get out of here, look back, and say yes, I did this.

I make a look back date. The middle of June. That will be when the watermelons are ripe, and the sun is warm. Meadow and I should be out of here. I think about my imaginary June date, so I won't freak out on the drowning feeling. They pull me up. I fix my knees, so they will catch me, and keep me from sliding down the bed again. At least for a few hours. Then, I move my bed up where I like it.

The hurtles out of here, and to June are becoming clearer. I need: to breathe, get off ECMO, learn to walk, get off the ventilator, drop the trach size, learn to talk, move to rehab, get out, rescue baby, and reunite family. It feels like I am prepping for the Olympics more than just trying to live a normal life again. Everything is still so out of whack.

Encouragement comes in the form of two new doctors. They introduce themselves as the heads of the rehabilitation unit. They think I am an excellent candidate. They tell me it will be hard work. Three hours of therapy a day. I have to be able to scoot at least 150 steps in my walker. They smile touch my feet and leave. 150 steps seems like a mile. Like I always say one step at a time.

My catheter moves that night as I watch TV. I poke the nurse's button. When she comes in, I make motions to my belly. I am still too confused to put words to what is going on. I tap my stomach. The nurse tries to figure out what is wrong. She looks carefully at my scar. I internally sigh and wave her on. I ignore it until morning. When the nurse goes to change my catheter bag, I can tell she is appalled by the color of my pee.

I remember one time reading an article using different color beers to demonstrate what each color meant. Mine is the darkest one, a horrible brown color. It said go to hospital right now if you see this. Well here I am. I almost want to giggle at that. I am in the ICU. If anyone can fix it, they can.

The nurse has it observed by numerous people and even tested. The catheter has moved, and now needs to come out. No problem. I am potty trained.

The night comes around. I am staring at the parking garage, and the painting on my wall by the window. Something isn't right. I think I am wandering around the library of my childhood lost. Where am I?

The nurse wakes me. With her semi grumpy tone, I know I must have done something. I realize I am cold. I realize at the moment she tells me that I have wet myself. Everything is soaked. I know I'm going to get another bath. I grumble about it as much as she does. I'm surprised that she knew before I did. Was it a rise and dip in heart rate?

The next night sadly repeats itself. Deep dream state leads to grumpy nurse, and grumpy me having to be bathed again. I decide I need to pee right before I fall off to sleep for the night. Even if I don't think I need to go.

I use the nighttime to really practice breathing. All the nurses know it, and they don't jump like Grandma or Mom do when the bells start. The nurses come in and encourage me.

Breathing is my focus. In and out as much as I possibly can, while I am alone. I hold Meadows little pink loose knitted hat. I run my fingernail along the ridges. I struggle to remember all the things they have told me. Open up the thoracic area. I pull my shoulders back. My nostrils flair as I puff in air and out again. I am getting closer and closer.

The doctors come in one night. My main doctor is a tall, dark, with very intense eyes. I like him. I can tell he really cares for me as a person. I do try to seem lively and smile when he comes in the room.

The other doctor is a smaller guy with glasses. I call him the Bill Gates looking guy. He is ready to take me off ECMO sighting that I'm now at 200ccs.

"Come on." He tells my main doctor. "She's so small like a two-banger car. I don't think she's a four banger. I don't think she can breathe 400ccs."

He thinks about it looking at me. Eye to eye. I feel he can read everything about me. There are so many things I want to say.

"No." He says sternly. "She can make the 400 mark just wait and see." He touches my feet and returns the smile.

In the morning I lay there debating on whether I should stare at the wall, or the nurses. Should I play with my tablet, or watch TV? Maybe I should tear off my pulse oximeter or loosen a lead wire. My day is so packed and busy. Let's see, if I give the bulletin board too much attention, the wonderful view of the parking garage will get jealous. I go to lift my tablet, but there are people in the hallway. Is someone new being swallowed by the beast?

I watch as the chaos party stops at my door. Of course it does; after all who doesn't love a chaos party. After a moment they come barging in. I finally see what they are wheeling in. My heart must have jumped out of my chest and danced all around my room. It is Meadow. Meadow! My baby!

That little pink hat is all I have of this mythical creature. It's my unicorn hair. Proof she exists. Mom tried to run off with it, and I smacked her hand away. I run my fingers over the tiny diaper they gave me. I named her. I got to see her once.

I know she is somewhere in this hospital. I lay sometimes staring at the door imagining simply getting up and going to see her. I would thumb through the pictures of her. I get information from Mom about how she is doing. I fall asleep at night imagining all three kids playing together. It is January 20th, 2014. She is going on 4 weeks old.

They have her in an open container. It is beyond words. Threads of terror and immense joy surge through me. This unicorn. My mythical creature. My mouth is dryer than normal as she is tightly bundled and placed right into my arms. It seems like a dream. My baby has survived. I praise God.

She is two floors up from me fighting her fight. She is on oxygen, has a feeding tube, and leads. She has weak lungs just like me. She is cared for by people also in dark blue scrubs. It is frightening, and yet relieving that she is so tiny. Her main nurse leans over me. She begins to tell me about the mythical creature they call the preemie baby.

They are not like normal babies. Not at all. I am told how she loves to be swaddled. It looks like she is being strangled. I want to rip the tight blanket off. She says it helps her to build muscle and feel more comfortable. I'm also not supposed to touch her feet. I make a mental note to break that rule as soon as possible.

From the moment that she is placed into my arms I felt a huge rush of emotions. This baby looks more like me than Rayne or Lotus. I'm glad. The birth is so empty. There is no linking memory of her leaving my body. I have the scar to prove it. The nurses look at it every shift change. I avoid looking at. Nobody talks to me about C-section care. I don't know if they used staples, or if they just stitched it up. The scar was on the mend by the time I had come to the realization that it was there.

I used the birth certificate to find out when she was born, and at what time. I never thought I would have a Christmas baby. I haven't yet connected the memories together. So, I don't know why just yet that this birth is so shrouded in mystery.

There is my most important link in this whole mess. The one who keeps it all together: Mom. She leans over the other side of my bed when Meadow begins to fuss. She places a hand on Meadow's head, and she quiets.

I have to open the blanket up. I have to see her. I unfold it the best I can coordinate my hands too. She is wearing a cute little girly onesie. I wonder how they get it over her oxygen cord. It is fastened behind her head instead of under her chin. She has big stickers on each side of her face holding it in place. Her skin is so warm. I count fingers, and toes. Such tiny, tiny fingers.

I want to weep. I want to scream and throw dishes against a wall. I feel so at peace. I'm so exhausted. I try to fix the wrap and Mom reaches over to finish my wish. I clutch her. I want to know that the worst of the storm is over. I want to know that it's okay to let her go. I want to know I will wake up when I go back to sleep. I don't want her to grow up without me to protect her. I have already failed in protecting her.

I want her near me. I am exhausted. I want to get up and go with her. I want to boss people around and change her diaper. I want to bathe her and smell that new baby smell. I want to fall asleep with her in my arms alone. The nurses give me time.

The NICU nurses and SICU nurses don't converse normally, so they are chatting, and acting like they are not hawk eyeing my every move. They watch the stats and Meadow's oxygen tank. The tank and the time finally gang up on me.

They quietly pull her out of my arms. She's supposed to be in my belly, growing and pushing against me for space, while I gripe and moan. I cry as they pull her out of my arms. In her cart she goes. I see for a moment an escaped foot. I can't get up and tuck her in. I can't whisper to her. I have to be content with the little clicks I can make. As soon as she wheeled away my arms feel cold and alone. I hug my bear, but I am lonely.

They hang blood for me. I am given time to rest, sleep, and quietly mourn alone. I finally am ready to walk again. I push harder. The goals are now tangible. My biggest one is to go to rehab no matter how hard it may be. It is the key to being able to be at least half of who I was before. Someone who could at least care for a baby.

My breathing is getting better and better. I am breathing 200ccs now. Sometimes I jump all the way to 300ccs. The bags that hang by my bed with all kinds of medications are dwindling even faster. The days are still crawling by slowly. Changes are happening at a recognizable rate.

They change my oxygenator in the machine. I am in my chair practicing breathing. The nurses are in with all their tools. Swift as they can they pull it out. I am not paying much attention.

Then I grow uncomfortable. I feel something almost touching my heart. I put down my tablet. Something is wrong. I'm edging toward panic. I'm suffocating. The nurse outside peering in I realize is fully focused in on me. No half assed eyeballing while typing. Both eyes are watching me frozen, like a cat ready to spring into action. They all know what is going on. Except me. They quickly snap in the piece, and it starts up again. Things are normal. I watch as they replace four tiny screws.

That night the nurses tell the doctor, who has come in to see my progress, that they managed to change it without much problem from me. (Yea, you're lucky I don't want to be put back in restraints I thought.) It probably won't be long now. The doctor is surprised and happy.

I have a speech therapist come in my room the next day.

"I'm the light at the end of the tunnel." She says. "When you see me, it means your almost out of here."

I'm delighted. She explains to me I am on c-pap now. She explains that I breathe the best I can, and the machine makes up the difference. She makes me aware that there is a balloon in my throat. I swallow or at least try. I can feel it.

She says she will see me again. Once I get off the ventilator, and have my trach downsized. She will give me a test to see if I can eat. She said eat. Oh, my goodness how bad I want to taste food. To know how close, I am. I work even harder, and I fight the nurses even less.

Not just for me. Grandma is saying that as soon as I am off ECMO she is going to leave and head on home. I'm up around 350-400cc's now. I know she needs to go home. She is tired. I can see it in her eyes. She needs to be done with this. To be back in her big warm chair with her coffee cup in her sanctuary of a home.

Every morning now since my first breaths Grandma will storm in and check my breathing level. She will also rub my feet. I love and hate it. They never fully woke up. They hurt constantly. I'm worried this is new normal. That my feet will never stop hurting and tingling.

She is a powerhouse that makes sure, short as she is, that everyone on that ward knew she is a force not to be reckoned with. She can pry information out of anyone, and just as quickly chase anyone out of the room. Because of her there are now two nurses who know better than to step into my room.

Mom on the other hand understands that I still need someone day and night. Most importantly I am a new mother with a 5-pound weight wrapped in a towel trying to build up the muscle just to hold her safely. To care for her by myself is a long way off. I still can't even walk without help.

I am slowly starting to talk to Jewell again online. It's only a few lines a day, but I try. I update my social media status for the first time in over a month. Everyone in my immediate circle was posting for me. Posting pictures of the baby, and of my progress. They were keeping everyone else informed. I'm surprised to see this.

I have a new perfusionist. She is a short and strong. I sit there trying to breathe. She looks over her clipboard at me. I think she can tell that I am about to cry again. She pauses, and then tells me it's okay. It's going to hurt like hell for a while, but I have to do this. I can do this. I am holding now 400cc's.

Two respiratory nurses come into my room. Its mid-day, and I am alone. They take their positions one on either side of my bed. The male nurse on my left side does something to my trach. The balloon in my throat is collapsed. They give me a small round green thing that snaps onto my trach.

This little device, called a Passy Muir valve, changes the way that I breathe. It is going to train me to breathe back out of my nose. They say that the way I am breathing now is through my neck. Not freaky at all.

They try to get me to talk. It doesn't work. I try to sound out some letters. It doesn't work. Every time I try to talk it pops off. I can't do it. I can't even say a letter of the alphabet. I will breathe in through my neck but trying to breathe out through my nose is too hard. I, disheartened, put it back in its case, and place it next to the hat, and the diaper.

Night bath as usual. The six nurses are rubbing me down again. Somethings different. It's rude. I realize I can smell. For the first time I breathe in a mix and mash of bubble gum and coffee. I want to retch. I can smell again. I can smell everything. I never even realized I had lost this talent until this moment. It is horrible, and its wonderful all at the same time.

After everyone is gone and the lights are out, I realize I can smell my coat. It makes me happy to inhale the farm, wood smoke smell that now permeated the whole room. I now understand why some nurses crinkle their noses up when they first walk in or walk past it. It is completely out of place in this super sterile environment that otherwise reeks of cleaning chemicals.

No one was allowed to touch it under Moms watchful eye. She washed it to rid of the flu but put it back. She understood that it is my totem. I don't know how, but she understood, and therefore advocated that it stay right where it is, right where I could see it.

They turned my ECMO off after three days of consistent 400ccs. I of course didn't know it at first, but the perfusionist is messing with the nobs more and more. They started doing it slowly as I began my breathing. Casting quick glance at me. I can't hear the rushing noises I have become so accustom to. I know I must be doing it on my own. It is four weeks now. When are they going to pull it out completely, and would my lungs collapse?

I want this machine out of me. I want to go see my baby. They are bringing her to me. It's hard sometimes. It's breaking all kinds of hospital rules to bring her to me. The nurses would see, even if they had to put their own job on the line, that I could hold her. A few nurses "went rouge" with Meadow secretly bringing her to me.

Meadow is still overwhelmingly exhausting. Always so well worth it. I have learned to turn out the lights in my room. She will open her eyes and look at me. Sometimes she will suck on a finger while snuggling into me. I click to her. I'm strong enough to now touch her beautiful scarce hair. I touch her little toes. I know she will be gone from sight in a blink of an eye.

Hopefully, I will survive this next leap. I don't want all of this struggle and work to melt away like a winter with no spring. They are ready now. I have to be ready too.

I have now gone three days without the ECMO to support me. I am fully on c-pap. They are going to pull my ECMO out the next morning. I wake without opening my eyes. It is early morning. I listen to a prayer. I chance a look through my tiny slits.

"Lord Jesus Christ, please help this child to heal and continue on her path. Please stay with her on this journey and bring her back to her children. Amen."

It is the perfusionist that had asked me if I had taken Jesus into my heart. I feel like my heart is going to explode out my chest with love. Everything I had put this poor guy through. Yet here he is standing over me praying. I fall back to sleep.

I have a nurse call Mom as soon as 6am rolls around. It is January 26th, 2014. I hardly slept past 4am in my nervousness. Mom is here early and alone. She is trying her best poker face. I can see past it. The changing tide of nervousness, and excitement. I have her sign the surgery papers. She is my good luck charm.

After that they ask me if I want to be knocked out or fully functional. I tell them to loop me out, but I want to be awake for most of it. They set up a tray by my bed. I grow nervous, but the nurses are quick to give me a medication that does just what I said. I am here, but calm and giggly.

The doctor is in. He tucks in his tie. He washes his hands. Then he explains what he is going to do. He is touching my neck where the ECMO is. I feel him pull it out. I feel myself slipping out of consciousness. When I wake Mom is sitting beside me. She is beaming with happiness. If I can keep this forward momentum going, she won't have to plan my funeral.

I get up this time for my daily walk. I only need a few nurses' help. I know how to turn so I won't pinch the ventilator. I sit in my chair afterward. My nursing assistant brushes my hair and puts it in a pretty bun on top of my head.

They bring me the baby later in the day. It truly is magical seeing my progress. I can see what I need to tackle next. I am accomplishing things. I am healing.

I think everyone is a little nervous that anything can still go wrong again. Grandma stays for three days to make sure I am not going to relapse. During her last day she finally steals my coat and says loudly to everyone that she is going to wash it. Mom promises me she will keep an eye on it and make sure it is with her when I am ready to leave.

I roll my eyes and let her abscond with it. I guess she doesn't enjoy the farm smell like I do. She hugs me and leaves. She is heading back to Arizona. I don't know when I will see her again. I am glad she can find some normality in her life again.

The nurses tell me my next step is to get off the ventilator completely. Then I will be moved to a step-down unit. They say they want to make sure I am completely stable before being whisked off to their rehab unit. I ask how long I may be in the hospital.

They think I am still a month away from walking out the door. I am almost in a panic. What about the baby? When would she be released? Mom tells me not to worry. They are not going to let Meadow out until her due date in March. I have plenty of time to rest and heal before worrying about the baby. Maybe we will be released together. That still doesn't solve the fact that I lack everything for her. One step at a time is all I can do.

I click to Mom. I point to the phone. I want to call Jewell and hear my kids' voices. I can't remember my phone number. Mom understands and makes the call. She puts it on speaker before placing it on my table. Mom leads the talk with Jewell. I click letting her know I'm here. Sometimes I nod or shake my head and Mom translates for me on the phone. I click for my kids to hear me. I don't think they understand why I'm not yet talking.

They have me on a trach collar now. It is a load clear vacuum like tube that pushes air around my new breathing hole. Now just 24 hours on the trach collar alone, and they can call me vent free. For the first night they want me to sleep with the full vent giving my lungs a rest. I watch TV trying to ignore the obnoxious pressure, and the fact that it doesn't want to breathe with me. I try to coordinate with the machine. I try to sleep. By midnight I call a nurse in. I point to the machine and my chest.

She finds a respiratory nurse. The respiratory nurse goes over to the ventilator. She messes with the controls.

"Do you want your old settings?" she asks.

I nod.

"Okay fine."

She sets it. I finally take a deep breath. A long deep breath. Back on c-pap I can sleep now.

"I've never seen someone come off the vent so fast." She says smiling and shaking her head as she walks out of my room

The next night I try to stay up all night, because I am scared to go to sleep without c-pap. Finally, the third night I decide to leave on my trach collar, while I try to sleep. I stay awake until 4am and sleep until 7am.

I did it. I went 24 hours on trach collar alone.

That morning the nurse for the day pushes the last of the life support machines out the door. My ECMO machine is still there. I think because it is so big and complex.

The nurse comes back in later in the morning. She asks me if I would like to go and see the baby. Could I leave my room right now? She has a wheelchair. She hooks my trach up to a bottle of oxygen. Mom and my nurse help me into the wheelchair. The nurse tucks a blanket around me like an old lady. She has a portable monitor for my leads, and places it in my lap.

She pushes me out of the tiny unit that I am gradually walking more and more of. I'm in the hall that Grandma and Mom traveled every day to see me. Mom has been traveling between here and the

NICU four times a day. It is a walk that is for sure.

I can feel a breeze in my hair, and I can smell my nurses grape bubble gum. Fresh air was something lost to me for too long. The sunlight. The change of scenery. Even if it is just an elevator and a new floor. I'm finally getting to see what the hospital looks like.

The nurse isn't sure that her badge is going to scan her into the NICU. She places it up to the scanner. The little light flashes red. So, she calls a NICU nurse to come, and let us in. Mom takes this time to proudly tell me the security here is heavy.

They push me into a room. I think they are still worried I may be carrying something. They make me put a face mask on, and hair net. I am having terrible dandruff problems. They bring her to me. With a pillow. I sit exhausted as usual. I click for her. I hug her, and rock her feebly.

January is ending quietly. I have spent over 5 weeks in the ICU. This is my first time out. I point to the outside window when the nurse brings me back. She smiles and says they can't take me outside. It is too cold, and it may cause my lungs to collapse again. I sigh. I actually sigh. Not just from the inside.

That night dad reaches out and touches my feet. Then he smiles at me, and finally walks out. I feel a sadness. A deep happiness that maybe he will cross over finally, but the impending sadness that he is really gone.

By the end of the week, they drop my trach size. Another small surgery. I ask again to be looped out and use my mom as the lucky charm. The doctor forgoes dropping from 8 to 6 to 4. Instead, he goes straight to 4. The 8 gage is so big I hardly even needed the balloon to cut off my airway.

The speech therapist is in later that day. I get the okay for ice chips. She places the green Passy Muir valve on me, and I try to talk. Something comes out. Its horse, cracking, and jumping.

"Hi, Mom."

Mom gasps and giggles. She is just as amazed as I am. There I am again. I can speak again. It is rough and hard to do. Pneumonia still has a residual cough. I still am spitting and coughing phlegm. It makes this new task harder. I use my stick to suck it out of my throat.

They give me cough medicine to curb it. All of my medications are given to me through my PICC line or my feeding tube. They draw blood through my PICC line. There are three odd things that hang out of the side of my upper left arm. The nurse tells me one goes to my heart, one is for my vein, and the other is to draw blood. I wonder how they do not mix them up.

I have a new focus now. Talking. In the evening when Mom is gone. I practice and practice. I cough sending it against a wall. I call in my nurse.

"What do you want?" He says.

I point.

"What do you want?" He repeats slowly.

I give him my death look. He responds by taking one finger and placing it to his throat.

"Do this and tell me what you need."

I take a lovely deep breath. I feel my lungs expand. Then I place a finger over my trach and send out a choppy raspy voice saying that my valve had flown over there.

He goes and fetches it.

"I'm surprised the speech therapist didn't teach you that trick." He hands it back to me after a good rinsing.

I place it on my trach. I curse up a storm. I pop it off, so I can breathe new normal. I place it back on, and I begin to make farm animal noises. I let out one loud long moo. I bleat like a goat. Finally, I make my favorite chicken noises. I pop it off to catch my breath. Place it back on again to curse like a sailor. I do try to be somewhat quiet, because I do not know how far out noises can travel.

This is the ICU. I hear alarms and have watched nurses run panicked. Sometimes they all but a couple vanish after I hear a hushed whisper about a new helicopter landing. I hear no screams or voices beyond the alarms. The nurses are not quiet when they come into my room. There has been a fair share of screaming and crying in here. That must mean the walls are pretty thick.

When I am well on my way to making clear sentences, I tell Mom to record me. My voice cracks and jumps as I tell the kids how much I love and miss them. She puts it on the social media for the kids to watch. Jewell sees it and calls me happily to say that the kids are thrilled. They have watched it numerous times.

The Speech therapist said I could have three ice chips over the weekend. Now that my balloon is down, I am given spongy sticks as much as I want. Only one nurse dares to balk. Someone must have shut her down because she eyed me then finally gave up. Mom snuck me a large handful to hide in my bedside table beside the diaper and the hat. There is a film over the roof of my mouth. I don't know when it will go away.

I wet my mouth slowly. Then I suck out the extra liquid. I let ice cubes melt in my hot parched mouth. Then I suck all the water out. I suck and chew sponges to pieces. I do this for three days. The first ice chip I let melt and go down my throat is a surprise. My throat had become a place that didn't exist. Now it feels like someone turned on a light in a hallway. I can tell my swallow is weak, so I don't chance much.

I guess I am still at 10 liters of oxygen. I can't leave ICU until I'm down to 7 liters. They still want to deep suction me. At least twice a day. Its rude and causes violent coughing fits. They also bag me at least once a day now to make sure my lungs stay popped open. I get so mad at a nurse that will not breathe with me that I take the bag and do it myself. They laugh.

They are tough on me. I'm counting down in a way of baths. I know one night will eventually be my last bath. I'm not going to miss it. The end is so close.

The nurses are coming in less and less during the day. No more vent and ECMO means just my nurse and nursing assistant watch me. It is quiet and peaceful for once. X-ray is someone I still cannot escape, but at least now I can fix myself after they shove their cold board under my back. Now they are telling me to take a big deep breath in. I am so proud to be able to do that. It makes it worth the trouble.

I'm restless and ready to move on. My body is moving at its own pace which is much slower than my mind. I am learning more of my medications. I have figured out that one better have Zofran on hand before giving me potassium. I learned this through a nightmare.

Mom, and I are venturing into this old abandoned house we found on the side of the road. Something is wrong. Butterflies are coming out of her mouth. I wake suddenly. I am throwing up. The nurse of course knows before me. She is at my side trying to clean me up as I jolt awake.

They have to change my sheets and bathe me before I can finally go back to sleep. Sleep here is hard. I am nervous about dozing off. I spook awake easy. They are trying medications to get me to sleep as naturally as possible. Maybe it's because I am a night owl by nature, and this place is so unnatural to me.

"You're weaning down on oxygen quite nicely." My main nurse tells me the next day.

I click at him. My way of saying good morning to you, too.

"I don't speak squirrel, but I do speak ground hog. I have an excellent ground hog puppet, and I do shows."

That's it. His new name is officially Gopher Guy.

He asks if I have seen the video of the fox.

I look at him oddly.

He smiles. "I guess you were in a coma then, about the only excuse not to have seen the video. Here check it out online. It's funny, and everyone's been raving about it."

He gives me a slip of paper for what to look for. I stick it in my tablet case.

He helps me up for my mid-day walk. Mom is up with the baby. I am going to push myself to the next unit or row of rooms. This unit is about 5 rooms and then another unit. I make it there proudly. I turn myself around hunched over my walker.

My walker is a neat one not at all like the grandma ones. They said my balance is too off for one of those. We all learned that the hard way. This one has a seat, brakes and four wheels.

I'm almost back to my room when I start coughing. I place the brakes down. I'm having a horrible coughing fit.

"Don't you dare twerk."

What is twerking? This guy is weird. One moment he is all old school pub, and now he is all twerking. Now, I am de-stating. I sit on my walker struggling to catch my breath. He runs to get a deep suction kit. I must have dislodged some nasty left-over phlegm.

He helps suck out whatever I have dislodged. As soon as I can I am up and pushing myself back to my room. I am exhausted. I sheepishly smile at him. I feel guilty I almost gave him a heart attack in the hall just trying to push myself a little harder.

Mom is back in and sits next to me. She tells me that Kyron (my brother) has to move in with her at the Ronald McDonald house. I look shocked at her, but I try not to look sad. She explains to me that he has been here the whole time just living at Uncle Marty's. I was hoping for more private time once I got out of the hospital.

I reach for my walker. I want to get closer to the window. Mom has told me there are shops down there. Food shops. She helps me up, and steadies me. I creep close, and sure enough five little food shops are down there. I touch the cold window. My breath forms small clouds on the glass.

Mom has moved a chair for me to sit down. I watch as a few people come in and out. I want to go outside again. I want fresh air. The doctor is still scared the cold air may collapse my lungs or put them into shock. It's understandable.

My nurse has a better idea. When the sun is setting, she hooks me up to my necessary gadgets, and helps me in the wheelchair. She tucks a warm blanket around me. We aren't going to the NICU. Instead we go to an all glass hallway. It links the parking garage to the hospital. It is beautiful. The rays of the sun are fading fast. The moon is up with what stars can be seen in a city. I stare for a long time quiet as a mouse. I am memorizing streetlamps, and the dark uninhabited street down below. This is amazing.

The next day everyone that can sneak a little orange into their daily wear does. It seems the CNAs have an ability to get by with more. There is orange fingernail paint, and hair ties. Everyone wants to wear the team's colors. Dark blue scrubs work perfectly. I ask the CNA if everyone has their TV on. She says everyone that is conscious at the moment.

Even if I can't eat, I tell Mom to go get something special and come back. They never once ate in front of me. I know that Mom is still a little uncomfortable chowing down on something awesome. I try not to stare. Not because I want it, but because it has been so long since I have even seen food.

Kyron even comes around to say hi. He doesn't stay long. Sports is not his thing. He does stay long enough to go down with Mom and get food. He brings me a Sprite. I am still not allowed to eat or drink. Sometimes though, now that it has been a week that I have been practicing with ice chips, I will have Mom scout for any watching nurses. When I get an all clear I will take a tiny sip of water.

I take the Sprite from Kyron and hide it in my blankets. Mom nonchalantly gets me a cup of ice. I pour it in when I get an all clear. I will put some in my mouth when Mom gives a clear sign. Then I will suck it out. I do it again and again. Then my sucky stick stops working. I call the nurse. She goes to the wall where I didn't know it is attached to a cup. The cup is full. Thank goodness it is clear, and it looks like water. I just hope she can't smell lemon lime. She empty's the cup and eyes me. I smile up at her like I am innocent. She casts a death glance at Mom. She pretends not to notice. So, the nurse hooks it back up and leaves.

They bring me the baby. I have been wanting to go see her, but the nurse was busy. They said they would bring her yesterday, and they never did. By 4pm yesterday Mom was once again wiping tears and snot off my face, because I was crying with frustration. Out of all the pain I am in. Out of all the uncertainty. I only cry for one main reason. Being separated from my kids.

I think this time it's compounded on the promise that Jewell made to me that she would be up here around the Super Bowl. I wanted her to be with me so many times. She does have the kids, and a farm, and a shaky car situation. But the last time that it fell through it turned into a large fight, on the phone, between Mom and Jewell. Now they aren't speaking.

The baby is finally brought to me. It's day later than I'm hoping for, but I take anything I can get. I prop up a pillow on my right side and tap it so they know where to put her. I take her into my arms. I snuggle in hoping they will let me keep her a little longer. My TV for once is left on. Off I hear everyone else's, so it doesn't matter. Mom does turn out the lights.

I touch her face and hair. There isn't much else I can do except cuddle her. I realize that I can use my valve now. I reach for it while Mom helps steady the baby. I place it on.

"Hello Miss Meadow." I say.

She opens her eyes. Her eyes smile at me. She sticks a fist in her mouth, and she snuggles in deeper. I don't know what else to say or even do. Babies are so much work. I know. Now, I have taken a backseat. I pluck and play with her little outfit. I trace the seams with my fingernails. I try to memorize all the cute designs.

Meadow is always wearing the cutest outfits. I know it's the NICU. Mom said they won't let me bring in my outfits; if I had them. She said it is flu season and nothing is allowed in. No stuffties, no blankets, nothing. It relieves the pressure. I feel like a horrible mother being so unprepared.

In the beginning my aunt wanted me to have a baby shower. They talked about it. Now, it seems like it isn't going to happen. I am healing so slowly. It is looking like I may be on oxygen, and in need of help with walking for a long time.

The respiratory nurses are in every day still. Their main job now is to look at my trach. One of them has a newbie with her. She explains to me that they have a new batch of babies, and she got to name hers.

Enrique is his new name. I smile at him. She tells him to change my trach gauze. If he had any confidence at this, I might have left him alone. He is terrified. I mean he is just changing my gauze. What would happen to him in a high stake's situation?

When his gloved hand finally gets brave enough to touch my trach, I lick him. On his gloved hand of course. He retracts. The older nurse laughs. He tries for my gauze again, and I attempt to playfully bite him. Just the threat freaks him out.

Finally, he goes for it and gets the gauze under my trach. She shows him how to change the gauze, and all the when's and why's. She points to my trach and shows him how to tighten my collar, and somethings to watch out for.

I don't think I'm ever going to get out of the ICU. I have managed to trick a few of the nurses into believing that I had already had my bath. It worked it for about four days. I knew if I didn't get out of here soon, I would be back to bath-ville.

The doctors come inside my room for their nightly rounds. I regret my decision in tricking the nurses into believing I am still being bathed. I sit up and smile. They usually don't come into see me directly. This is a really rare treat. Four of my hero's right here.

I wish I knew all of their names, but the only one that I know strongly is Dr. Babu. He is written across my whiteboard. The other doctor the one I called "Bill Gates" was right alongside him. There are two others beside them I recognize, but not as strongly.

I waste no time in this once in a lifetime occurrence. They are all looking at me fondly and smiling. I place my finger on my trach.

"Thank you!" I say as strongly as I can.

Tears well up inside me. I let them fall freely.

"Thank you, so much. You saved me."

They touch my feet. They ask me a few questions and leave. What they have done is beyond amazing. I couldn't emphasize it. They saved me. I'm going to make it home. I have an opportunity to raise my children. I would have never had that chance even ten years ago. There are no words that can explain the amazement and wonder, that these simple human beings could do such things with their knowledge and technology.

The nurses are also calling everyone around to get me checked out, so I could get the ok to begin eating again. I started this pregnancy at 160. Despite holding back and living on dried cereal to see that the kids made it through the month okay; I still was hospitalized at 190. I'm now 150 lbs. How many people dream to lose that kind of weight a month after having a child? It's my nightmare.

Yes, they feed me feeding tube style, but it isn't the same. I want food. I want a watermelon. I want chocolate pudding, and applesauce. I want my lingering pregnancy craving, dark grape juice. When I get bored, I write Mom all kinds of crazy food dream lists.

I am also using Mom now as a bearer of news for a couple of people I have become aware of around here. One is a girl three years younger than me that ended up on ECMO. She came in a week after me but only spent one week on ECMO and is now two weeks ahead of me in the rehab unit. I know I might see her there if I ever get my oxygen levels down.

I want to see another person who has been on this unit longer than me. She was in a car accident and lost both of her lungs. I watched her and her husband (who had lost a leg in the accident) walk the halls every day.

The day after the Super Bowl brought her a pair of lungs. They used only a fourth of it to create her new lungs. It is amazing what they can do.

The alarms went off. They are screaming loud. I hate that noise. It always makes my stomach drop, and my heart rate soar. All the nurses run at full speed. It isn't me this time. It's her. Had it failed? Would she die?

I watch as they run with her bed, and gadgets past my window and down the hall. I pray she would make it. I wait a half hour until I'm sure it has all cooled down. I poke the nurse's button.

When she arrived, I asked if the patient had died? She smiled at me and said she had a setback but should pull through. Mom kept me updated from there. Happily, just days after that she is off all machines and readying for rehab herself.

As a new day dawned, I watch the usual mopping and stocking of my room. The nurse for the day is on the rector scale for most bubbly. It doesn't take me long to come up for a name for her: Bubbles. She is almost frighteningly optimistic and happy. How has she survived in this environment? She tells me I am her only patient today. She spends the day spoiling me like an only child.

First, she takes me to see Meadow early in the morning. I reach out in my wheelchair for the sink. I wash in hot soapy water and grab a mask. Mom say's hi to the desk worker as we pass.

I am trying to soak it all in. This time we aren't going to the room. We are going to go where Mom goes twice a day. Into the pod where Meadow has been since being classified a "feeder and grower".

I beg to feed her. Mom told me she got to try it, and I want to also. I want to be a part. I need to do more than simply hold her. I am not so shyly jealous.

I have never seen her without clothes, or a blanket. I don't know if she has an inny or an outie bellybutton. I can't stand up long enough to change her diaper, or clothes. I can't last the minute it takes to take her temperature.

I can move from the wheelchair into a chair to hold her. That is the big feat of the week. To be plopped into the chair, and have my monitor situated beside me, and my oxygen pumping 7 liters on the other side.

"Don't de-stat in here." Meadow's nurse tells me smiling. "We don't know how to care for anything over ten pounds."

My nurse seems to take that as a que to check my oxygen tank and try to cast a casual glance at my stats.

They hand me a pillow. My scar still hurts, so it's a good cover. I watch Mom as she finishes care and gives the nurse all her stats. She wraps her up tightly in her blanket. Carefully watching wires, and her feeding tube Mom hands her to me. The nurse hands me a bottle.

This gets super complicated quickly. I have hardly ever held a bottle and fed a baby. To make matters worse I'm instructed into the ways of preemie feeding.

First, I have to stimulate her gums with my finger. Next, I have to hold her at sixty-degree angle, and in my hand not in the crook of my arm. Folded blankets help me. Now, I have to get her to latch. I rub her gums with the nipple. I stick it on her tongue. I poke her cheek. I try over and over, and no latch.

She gives a weak suck. It is sporadic, but I get two sucks from her. Now I am instructed to tip her up, so the milk stops flowing. She loses suction. I can't get any interest back in her. She's done and exhausted. I feel the same. The whole experience is very much bonding. I need to act the part. Even if it is just a few shaky moments. I hand her back. I watch as they set up the rest to be fed through her tube.

I'm on so much oxygen that these trips are quick. I feel empty leaving. I love Meadow with every fiber of my being, but I am just unattached, and empty. I am too ashamed to even look Mom in the eyes. What if she sees what's going through my mind? The jealousy. The anger. The love mixed with healthy dose of pure exhaustion. I feel Mom squeeze my shoulder in the elevator.

"You tired honey?" She asks.

I smile and nod.

After I had rested some Bubbles then takes me to the windowed hallway. I watch the moon rise in silence. The streetlights twinkle invitingly, but the road is deserted.

She spends lots of time in my room chatting with Mom and I. I'm sad when 6pm comes around. I know she is going to be leaving. I might be able to beg a grape Popsicle out of her.

They let me eat ice. That is my argument. I pulled a stunt that one of my kids would have with whining and puppy dog eyes. Bubbles doesn't say anything. She leaves, and I hear lots of talking around the nurse's station.

The doctor comes in. He is bundled up for an expedition.

"What's so funny?" He says. "It's like 6 degrees out there."

"Can I have a Popsicle?" I ask.

"Take a drink of that water." He says

I do. I almost choke, but I pretend that it is no problem.

"Okay." He says. "Yes, you can."

Then he waddles his stuffed penguin self out of my room. I hope he can drive safely in that outfit. I choke back giggles.

I am so happy I feel like I have won the lottery. The waning day is getting even better. First of all, Bubbles is still here. She demands that I get a bath. The glint in her eye tells me I have been caught. I'm willing to do anything for this firecracker. As she and her fellow nurses clean me, I smell coffee on her.

"What kind of coffee do you drink?" I ask.

She has been in overdrive energy since early this morning, and now we are hitting 8pm. She was buzzing before the sun, and now the sun had run out of energy before she had even started hitting up the coffee.

She sits in a chair next to me. She shampoos my hair. She brushes out my impossible mess. She Dutch braids it into cute pigtails.

She breaks the news that in just moments she is going to wheel me away to the Step-Down unit. I ask that she call Mom. She nods as she steps out to finish some paperwork. She drops back in to tell me that Mom is on her way.

Then she begins to prep me for leaving. I have been here for 6 full weeks. The few items I had collected here are: Meadow's diaper, and hat. My paper and pen. My tablet, Chapstick, my new brush, Passy Muir valve, and a few sucky spongy sticks. Then she hooks me up to an oxygen tank. I'm down to 7 liters. She gently tears off all my leads.

She leaves me once again. When she comes back, she has discharge papers that she places in my lap. Then she hands me small cup full of grape juice and ice. A moment later she is pushing me, and my bed right out the door. I don't even look back. I am enjoying the ability to swallow and taste, to breathe, and to feel the air as we are moving along.

ICU TLC

Roses are red.
Violets are blue.
There is nothing scarier then waking up in ICU.
I thought you were trying to kill me.
Instead, you worked night and day to heal me.
Thanks so much for all that you do.
Your patience.
Your kindness.
Your feeding tube stew.
The catheter draining felt good too.
Thanks for warm blankets,
and your kind and gentle baths.
You were the hand I grabbed
as I skidded toward death.
You gave me strength to take that first step.
There are three little girls you see.
Who now have a mom now,
and not just her memory.

Truth and Dares

The energy is different. It isn't a somber energy. It isn't tense. There is no more walking on eggshells. I have won this fight. It took everything I had. Soon I will be in rehabilitation rebuilding and readying for new fights.

Death seems to go off center stage. He waits now quietly. When will he make his grand entrance again? I don't know. I hope I have grandkids, maybe even great grandkids, before my final act.

In the elevator we lurch up. I don't have any clue of where I am in this large labyrinth. I only vaguely now know how to get to my little girl. The door pings open, and she shoves me out into a new hall.

New nurses. They replace my leads. They have a new way of monitoring me. The leads are the same. Now, I have the monitor in my pocket. I suppose they will watch me with the same intensity, but without sitting there next to the clear glass.

The door is now wooden. I am in a private room. There is a bathroom, but a sign saying I cannot walk without assistance. I have a new foe: the bed alarm. The new bed massages and moves me all around. It's unnerving, but it feels good. No more pinchy leg things. I ask for warm blankets. The nurse laughs at me.

"Only in ICU honey." She replies as she wraps a new band around my wrist.

The TV looks brand new. It's a flat screen, and not the 90's dinosaurs bolted to the wall in my old room. There are lots more channels. I guess people cannot enjoy this in a coma or dead, so I can understand.

Mom and Kyron are not far behind me. They come barging in only 30min after I had arrived. It must be near 10pm now. I smile. Mom hugs me tightly. She comments on my cute hair touching it softly. She stands tall and takes in the new room. She smiles as her eyes fall on the new soft couch and nods approvingly. Instead of stiff chairs in a tiny room full of machines; there is now comfort and space. Mom is in love with the couch. Kyron is in love with the big TV.

I am so enamored with my grape juice that I'm hardly paying attention to anyone right now. Dark grape juice was something I hated, until my last pregnancy. Now it's a craving that I just can't get enough of.

I realize I need to go to the bathroom. The nurse is now tapping away at her chart. I plug my trach hole with my finger.

"Can I go to the bathroom." I ask her.

It's been over a month since I sat on a real one. She goes over to see what my oxygen setting is.

"7 liters." She mumbles to herself, and then turns to me. "Well, let's see if we can get you up without it, okay?"

I am more than okay about this. I am dying of excitement. She unfastens my trach oxygen hose. I gently get ready to stand. She helps to support me as I walk like a drunk dinosaur to the bathroom.

I use the bars to steady me. I sit on the cold toilet. I'm so happy. I feel as though I have been crowned queen of Denver. I'm just sitting and spacing out. I hear alarms. I look up slowly. The room is moving and swaying. A heard of nurses come racing in. I find humor, as the seven spooked nurses take over my bathroom. They pull me off and drag me back to bed. I am quickly reattached to my oxygen.

Mom gawks at me.

"Your blue." She says. "Your lips, fingers, and your face."

"It's okay we will just make sure we have more oxygen leads for you later. I'm so sorry, Hun."

I smile at the nurse to let her know there are no hard feelings. My fingertips are blue. I wonder what my face looks like. Mom still looks spooked.

Mom offers to stay the night, until I feel secure. I let her know that I am very worn out, and I will be asleep in no time. I thank her for coming. I know it is cold, and she has that Jeep. Kyron and Mom decide to leave. I watch as they leave out of the smaller wooden door. There is a click as it shuts, instead of the rushing sound the sliding glass one makes.

I sleep very well. It is almost pitch black in here for once. Just a light above a tiny sink by the door. The nurses are very quiet when they come to check on me. No more x-ray machines at 3am. I lay in the dark waiting for them, and they don't come. Next, I realize I'm still laying on my back. I'm still up at my required 35-45-degree angle, so complete comfort is still a long way off, but I chance to roll over on my side.

I am up early as usual with the nurses who come in. They give me my medication through my feeding tube and PICC line. They check my feeding bag, but don't seem too quick to fill it.

Mom is in early too. She smiles at me and takes her new place on the couch. She doesn't get too comfy before another person comes in. He's not dressed like a doctor or a nurse would be in the hospital, but obviously he is from the hospital. The ICU nurses have been driving everyone crazy about finding someone who could clear me, so I can eat again. This nice man has come in on his day off it seems.

There is a female nurse beside him. She is holding lots of goodies. I see chocolate pudding, graham crackers, milk, and applesauce. She places it on my table. Then she pulls a plastic spoon, and a straw out of her pocket. I am liking how this test is shaping up.

I finally pry my eyes away from the treasures on my table, and look at the person, sitting patiently waiting for my attention. I notice he has something in his hand. It looks like a small cassette player with a long wire, and a tube at the end. He tells me he is going to shove this lovely little camera up my nose, and then down my throat. My job is to talk while eating.

I'm not going to fight it. That's all it's going to take, and he's here when he could be sleeping in. In a moment he is gloved and ready to go. The nurse readies the treats by opening them all for me. He, in a flash shoves the camera up my nose. I gag once as it hits my stomach opening. Then he pulls back and instructs me to try some applesauce. I chance to try some.

"Now say E." He says watching his little monitor.

"EEEEEE." I repeat back.

On down the list. I am scared of the graham crackers. They are so thick and sticky. I bite some off chew slowly then swallow. Then I am aloud to drink the milk.

I pass the test with flying colors. No aspiration. I do have a weak swallow. They instruct me to use a straw at all times and to take things slowly.

The nurse for the day says I may be here in this step-down unit a week. I think I might die of boredom just sitting around doing nothing. Wasn't it already proven that I'm stable? I flip through the channels and sigh. I nibble on my pudding, and drink a coconut water, that Mom has brought for me. I am not ready for any big meals yet.

Thankfully, the next night after nurse's shift change, I'm again moved. This time it seems as if we are traveling forever. Through corridors, and at least 2 different elevators. I wonder if Mom will ever find me again. I wonder if I will ever see the front door.

I am dumped off in the rehabilitation unit. This time no leads at all. They pull all the sticky patches off me. No more wires. Just my hospital band, PICC line, trach, and still my feeding tube. The kind nurse must have seen on the chart that I had an affinity for dark grape juice, because she brings me a large cup of it with lots of ice and a straw.

She explains to me that they will pull all of these crazy things out of me quickly. As soon as I can prove that I can orally take most of my medications I will get the feeding tube pulled. Eventually, they will pull the PICC line. Finally, the trach can go after I prove that I can breathe and speak normally.

"Its 7pm did you have dinner yet?" The nurse asks once she replaces my band.

I shake my head.

"Oh, well what would you like? I'll make a special order for you."

"Watermelon." I quickly say.

She leaves when she is done typing. She is back within the hour with a small bowl of watermelon and a small bowl of strawberries. I eat slowly. This fresh fruit meal has been my dream since I came out of the coma. I know it is February 4th, not the time for watermelons, but it's what I crave more than anything.

I watch TV and finally fall off to sleep. I wake at 3am. I sit there with my trach hose gurgling and hissing. I look to the door. I realize the nurse has crept in to take all my vitals. She smiles while she does her thing quickly. She asks if I need water. I shake my head. Seeing its 4am I flick the TV on.

At 6am I am given my first round of medications. At 7am I am brought breakfast, and a menu. They explain to me that because of the trach everything has to be soft and cut up. I see that quickly as my pancakes are cut into tiny pieces. To have a menu is really neat. I just need to call in what I want by 8pm (for the next day), and it will come piping hot to me.

I am surprised I can order so much food. And the protein shakes. One of the nurses tell me to order a shake right before going to work out, and it will finally be soft enough to eat when I come back in. I haven't been able to eat this good in so long. Now, they are encouraging me to eat, and order as many protein shakes as I want.

When I was at home, I was eating lots of dry cereal to push down cravings. I was leaving all of the fruit for the kids. I was skipping breakfast, skimming minimally for lunch, and cutting what I could eat in half at dinner. I wanted to be sure the kids got their fills first. Jewell and I did everything to make sure they had full bellies.

I had gone from pushing back hunger craving for my kids' sake to this heaven. The pancakes they gave me are huge, and fully cut up. Two fluffy eggs. Fresh fruit. Orange juice.

I ate some pancakes and eggs. The coffee, though I let it thoroughly cool, burned me like I had stupidly gulped battery acid. No amount of milk and sugar stopped the pain as it sat there eating away at my stomach. I didn't need reminding that it is tea from here on. Orange juice has the same horrible effect.

The nurse has brought most of my medications in pill form. I am scared with the trach intruding on my throat. She tricks me into it with applesauce. They are pleased. A few more times and the feeding tube can go.

Mom has come in now. She never fusses with her hair. It takes her half the time to make the trip here. I know she is always eager to see Meadow, because of the intense and rocky bond she formed with her. I can now offer her the comfortable couch, and a nice view of more than cars and concrete pillars. She plops her big black backpack on the couch.

The nurse has brought me a pair of starchy light blue scrub bottoms. New ward new rules. I came here naked. I spent over a month in ICU with a gown lazily thrown over me. They want me to dress, and groom everyday here. With their help and three hours of therapy a day. They are going to retrain me to live as normal a life as possible.

She turns off the bed alarm. She makes sure that the rubber padded socks are on right. She fiddles with them turning the seam right. I'm a little kid in my first day of life Kindergarten. Then she tries to tie my gown better around the back.

"I don't think any guy is going to worry if I give him one last jolly." I utter as she cinches it up tightly.

She stifles a giggle that sounds like she is choking.

She hands me the scrub bottoms. Sitting on the edge of the bed I lift one heavy leg after another fighting with starchy thin fabric. She cinches the belt around my middle right below my breasts. I know I can get up now. I rock slightly heavily relying on the nurse who is tying the scrubs around me. I have officially dressed for the first time in almost 2 months.

The two nurses steady me on my walker. Mom has taken up the responsibility of carrying my oxygen tank. They all follow me and point me toward the right way. Nurses and weak patients abound. I see a different kind of rounds going on. Just the nurses and doctors have relaxed chats. I wander down the hall past the doctor/nurse's station. Not far from here they direct me into a gym.

It is rather large with all kinds of equipment. Not like a normal gym. This one just has a few bikes, a treadmill, wooden stairs, mats, bars, balls, and little arm weights.

There are two bars about waist high with a mat on the floor, that I am directed to. I practice walking. My legs feel like lead weights are attached. Lefty wants to drag and turn. The muscles are atrophied. The coordination and balance that I have is horrible. I am used to walking on the balls of my feet. They want me to put my heel down first which is throwing me off more.

I am gifted my fourth child. A 6-pound soft weight like you would use to wrap around a leg. They wrap it in a towel, and hand it to me. I am now in charge of carrying "fake baby" with me everywhere.

Lunch is waiting for me. I lay utterly exhausted. I have my third and final therapy. It is speech therapy. She will watch me eat. I am thoroughly irritated with her. She has these obnoxious cognitive tests, and lots of papers that tell me how to regulate thought and breath. I know she means well. I know she is the last of the over exuberance of people. She has an air about her that keeps me on guard at all times.

As soon as she has gone Mom tells me she has to leave as well. She isn't going to care for the baby like normal. She is going to the store. I need clothes. She asks me if I have any requests.

I shake my head. I am still not into to talking that much yet. I smile at her as she slowly packs. Then she leans over my bed and hugs me. The bed alarm goes off. The nurse comes in and quickly fixes it. Mom asks more in detail of the things that I will need. Then she bows out leaving me.

I ask the nurse to help me sit in the chair. The nurse guides me over to the chair. I pass the rest of the day fiddling around on my tablet and watching TV. My cognition is coming back more and more, yet I am still easily lost.

I rub at the sticky glue left over on my skin. I wish I could go and be with my baby. I can't think of a way to sneak away, and I am terribly lost now in the hospital.

The next day dawns as a nurse grabs my shoulder and pulls my face off the side railing. Spit and hair are stuck to my face that is red in places from my sleeping position. I am rather aggravated. I lift my eyebrows high to signify that I want answers.

"You can't breathe with your face smashed against there like that."

She says worried

I place a finger over my trach. "I'm not breathing with my face." I retort.

She looks at me speechless. She huffs and takes my vitals.

"Still it's a bad habit." She says, after so much time has passed, I did not think she would respond at all.

I yawn, and finally close my eyes again. Its 6am before I know it. I am given my pills orally this time. Then they are back in an hour later with more pills. I take them all to their delight. I cannot sleep now. I am too excited. I graze through the TV channels thoroughly enjoying all of the new options.

Mom is in earlier than usual. She places a large plastic bag stuffed to the breaking point, full of clothes, on her couch. She takes all the items out and places them on my bed for approval. I am so grateful I feel tears swell up in my eyes. I had no money, no means for these things and yet she bats away my thank you.

Inside the bag is: socks, undies, bras, two pairs of soft sweatpants, one zipper hoodie (bright pink), and three t-shirts (low cut to accommodate my trach).

She also bought me a pretty new pair of shoes that are black with lime green laces. The shoes turn out to be too painful. After a couple of days Mom ends up taking them back in exchange for a pair of soft cotton slippers. They are pretty white with two pretty pink poms on each one. I can wear those, barely.

I want a shower. The occupational therapist arranges it. She gathers a shower chair, a towel, washcloth, toothbrush, deodorant, soap and shampoo. She works to get the water hot. My main nurse covers my PICC line as well as she can with tight plastic.

I wheel my walker into the bathroom. The thought of a wet floor terrifies me. I always seem to have a pair of steadier hands on me as I make this transition. It eases my fear as I have to let go of my safety. They help me slowly into the shower, and down on the seat. The water is hot.

I want to be in here forever. I let it run over my hair. The first time I had washed it this way since the day I got the cough. The nurse the whole time is watching my every move. I don't give a shit. As shaky as I still am, I am kind of grateful. I reach over and turn off the shower. They hand me a towel and help me up.

Over to the sink I shuffle slowly. I lean against the wall as I brush my teeth. This is the first time I have seen myself in a mirror since I was pregnant. I'm scared to look at myself. I take a quick glance to see how sunk in I have become. A quick look at my scars, and my trach. This is the body. This is what I have chosen. This is what I have become.

I reach my hand out for a nurse who steadies me on my walker. I sit on my bed dizzy. She gives me a few minutes to recuperate from the exhausting excuser. The nurse gently helps fill in where I need help getting dressed. Socks are impossible still. Too much bending. I get dizzy so easy. What used to take me 20 min took an hour and two others to accomplish, but I did it.

I grab Fake Baby. I am so tired, and yet I am not ready to give up. They tell me it's time to start walking without the walker. I have a belt wrapped around me. Then I am pulled up to standing. I stagger relying heavy on the wall and the railings. All the time I am trying not to kill Fake Baby. Mom follows silently with my oxygen tank.

In the gym there is more practice without the walker. The nurse giggles at me and tells me to drop my arms and walk normal. I'm afraid if I do, I will lose balance. I let my arms down. I rock back and forth. I manage to walk the line without any support at all.

I notice people in there. Some of them are missing limbs. A couple look as emancipated as I am with trach's in. I wonder if they got hit like I did.

There is one girl younger than me. I suspect she has gone through a major car wreck. I watch as she cries while they put her in a harness on a slow-moving treadmill.

She is always smiling when I pass her by in the hall. I had glared at her a couple of times for it. Despite my cold nature I cannot help the motherly love I feel as I hear her crying as they go one more time.

I know how hard the nurses push and shove us along. One guy squeals and cry's loudly as he is worked. I don't blame him he's missing his foot. The next day his girlfriend is there with him, and he is turning purple trying not to make a whimper.

As I get stronger, I manage stairs. I accomplish stepping in and out of a bathtub. I quickly evolve from walking like a T-rex, to an awesome rendition of Thriller, to just being wonky.

I drop my oxygen to 2 liters despite wanting to barf and pass out. I am pushing to get out of here without oxygen and without a walker. Of course, fake baby is in my arms at all times, as I manage these feats that were once done by me thoughtlessly.

One day instead of going to the gym PT decides to take me outside. I can have my walker this time seeing the distance I need to cover. The belt around me, and Mom having a hold of my tank, I gingerly step onto the elevator. It lurches down as I am on the 8th floor. The nurse pulls on my belt helping me keep balance.

It pings open to the magical first floor. It is busy. So full of life and normal people. I feel nobody looking at me. Everyone seems to be in their own worlds somehow existing together at this moment. I push right out the front door.

It's a warm February day made just for me. The thin coat is just fine for this day. The breeze rustles my hair. I breathe in as deep as I can. The nurse directs me onto a path winding around the front. I stop to rest on a bench under a tree. I know that I need to get back to my room soon. Exhaustion is creeping around my already wobbly legs.

They make me find my way back to my room. My short-term memory is still rather terrible. I will wander into anyone's room. Sometimes I am almost jealous at the amounts of pictures and flowers others have on their walls. I wonder what kind of stories these others have, and how long they have been here. Finally, I manage to find my bed. There is a frozen ice-cream protein shake waiting for me.

Mom takes Fake Baby out of my arms. She gifts it some hair; dried grass that she picked. I try to give it a face by marking tiny eyes and a mouth on the towel the weight is wrapped in. I hold the thing at night, I carry it around everywhere.

I beg for oxycodone. I deal with the obnoxious speech therapist hawking me as I eat my lunch. She occasionally interjects on how I should look down while drinking, and always use a straw. Then she makes me practice talking with my valve. One thing I learned from her is that I can still easily make change, and figure math out. I can't figure out where the hell I'm going, but math is okay? I answer her cognitive questions with ease. Finally, she leaves me alone.

By the new start of the week my PICC line and feeding tube have been removed. I am shocked at the length of my PICC line. When they said it came close to touching my heart, I know they weren't kidding. I wondered how they threaded it through my vein. These nurses are amazing. I'm more than glad to see all of this go. Even if it now means that I need two shots a day of blood thinner. The piercing of skin doesn't hurt that bad, but the medication burns like a hornet's sting.

As soon as the nurse is done with my shot and leaves, I surprise Mom with the fox video making her laugh. It's probably the third or fourth time I have played it. The unexpected stupid lyrics never fail me. I know it won't be long, and I will go see Meadow.

"I talked to Grandma the other day. She has gotten into the Christmas presents we left there." She says almost giggling. "She promised she wouldn't, but she is all of a sudden talking highly about Himalayan salt lamps. I got her one for Christmas."

My mouth fell open. I know she genuinely found it funny. I had not thought for one second since I woke up on how close I had been to Christmas. It hurt too much to do more than graze over it.

Mom breathes in deep and continues. "I guess she earned it having to clean the fridge of all the old food. You know how we eat. How many salad things had probably turned to soup, or evolved enough to bite? She told me that she has just been dumping tubs. I don't blame her for not wanting to open anything that scary." She laughs.

"You didn't open any presents?" I wide eye look at her.

The presents aren't a big deal, so much as I am just picking up more puzzle pieces and putting them together. I didn't know when they had come into this mess. I thought about laundry and dishes being undone. The house that was probably left in disarray as they thundered through it hastily packing. My world had stopped abruptly before holiday season. I awoke in a new year. An odd sort of shock.

Her mood darkens. She is finally talking about it. Healing something in her and in me. I lock eyes with her for a moment to let her know she has my full attention.

"I packed. I threw in some useful Christmas presents. Kyron's new phone for instance, a warm blanket, a sweater that my mom got me. I grabbed Kyron and left." She drew a deep jagged breath, fighting tears now.

"I called when I got to Pueblo. Jewell said she couldn't get through to the hospital. So, I called." She choked.

"They told me that they put you on life support. You were not expected to live. The nurse wanted me to call the family in, and anyone that wanted to say goodbye might have that chance."

She is crying now. I feel sick and dizzy. I watch as her face reddens as she is struggling through trying to hold it all at bay. The pain that everyone must have gone through. I can't imagine. I am only seeing a tiny flash of it.

"I called my mom, your grandma, and she took off as fast as she could. You know how much of a speed demon she is. Well by Christmas Eve we had everyone: all your cousins, your aunt, uncle, your brother, me, and grandma. They all went in two by two to say goodbye to you."

"What about the kids and Jewell?" I interrupted.

"They were there too. I took the girls in to see you." She drew a breath as she debated what to say next.

"There were others just like you. Well no one pregnant like that.

But there were a lot of people in their late twenties, and early thirties who got hit just as hard. There was one who had two little girls almost the same age as Rayne, and Lotus. She was 33, I think. Well, she died from a blood clot. The nurse rudely came into the waiting room and told the little girls right in front of them. The two little girls started screaming and crying. I don't blame them. It freaked Rayne and Lotus out. Lotus kept asking me if you were dead. I told her you were just sleeping. Rayne was in shock."

"When they did see you, you were still pregnant. You really just looked like you were sleeping. You had a breathing tube, a couple of tubes down your nose, wires and IV's it seemed everywhere. There was plastic to cover your eyes, so they wouldn't dry out. It wasn't too traumatic for them to see you. Except there was blood on the floor, nothing more than a few drops, but it really bothered Lotus."

"Jewell left. She just left. I don't know where the hell she went, but she was gone almost an hour. Maybe the cafeteria?"

She is crying. I don't want to press any more I am crying too. Jewell escaping to the cafeteria to eat in such a stressful situation is not in her personality. I have a feeling there is another story there.

"Everyone went home. Lotus was sick, so Jewell took the five-hour trek home. Grandma went back to Uncle Marty's to spend Christmas morning there. The nurses and doctors thought that you might have stabilized. I stayed though. I wanted to spend Christmas Eve with you. The nurse made me a bed next to the window. I hadn't slept much. I read you stories and talked to you. Then I drifted off to sleep."

"I awoke to bells screaming, and so many people were packed in the room trying desperately to save Meadow. You were dead KaDawna. You had completely flat lined."

"They set up a room right next to yours with an incubator, and everything ready and waiting for this moment. They showed me before I settled in for the night. Anyway, I looked up, and the doctor looked at me as he was ready to cut you open or had already began. I grabbed my shit and ran for it."

"After a few minutes they took off with the baby at a full run down the hall. I ran after them screaming that was my baby. One nurse stopped for a moment to tell me it was a little girl."

"I called everyone freaking out. Grandma was speeding back here. She ended up lost in a field somewhere. I went back to your room, and it was empty. There were wires thrown everywhere. Someone was mopping up the floor. It was covered in blood. They said they were trying a heart and lung bypass machine. If your survived they would move you to the second floor."

"They had a nurse take me to see the baby. She was so tiny. Just 3.3 pounds with life support, and 2.5 ponds without."

"Plus, Lotus was spiraling down. She was sick too. I heard word from Jewell that she was desperately doing everything she could to keep her from the E.R. She had spent two nights awake watching her to make sure she kept breathing."

"I couldn't see you until almost 5pm that day. You flat lined at 7:15am. I don't know what happed after that. No one expected you to survive the night. They gave me a room in the NICU that night. Then the NICU nurses got me a room at the Ronald McDonald house."

"Grandma and I moved in. You survived 5 days on the ECMO machine, so they trached you on New Year's Eve. The next day they started to wake you slowly. Everyone was holding their breath. People thought that if we lost the baby, we would lose you, and the other way around. It was like walking on eggshells. Every time my phone rang. Every morning I woke up. I just prayed that I wouldn't have to bury you, Meadow, or Lotus."

"I had to walk by a family of mourners who had lost someone due to not getting the ECMO in in time. Early thirties again. They just left her body there, with a box of tissue on her chest. They blocked my way to you crying and screaming. It was horrible. Absolutely gut wrenching."

"They couldn't find the H1N1 in you until they did biopsy's cleaning out your lungs. They ran like forty tests on you. Even looking for poisons."

"Lotus pulled out of her nosedive. Meadow stabilized. You hit a few hard bumps in the beginning. They woke you up too soon. You died on us again, and they had to put you back under."

"I am sorry for what I put you and Grandma through." I whisper. "I could tell I really upset her."

"Don't apologize. You had no control over what happened. As for Grandma, the great grandpa you are named after, Don, he died of pneumonia. Something went wrong. They put his bed down, and he drowned in his own fluid. Every time they lay you flat you would freak out. That hit too close to home for her. She had to leave."

"Anyway, I think I can finally breathe again. It was so hard."

She shakes her head as if trying to empty her mind of the ache. We sat in silence for a while just looking at one another. This is too big, and too out of my control for I am sorry. It is beyond words.

The door creaks open, and the nurse comes in to wrap the belt around me. My oxygen tank is set up and held proudly by Mom. Her eyes are still puffy and reddened. We head down to the NICU. We catch the tea cart that comes through. We load up with goodies and sip tea. Meadow is against my chest.

"Thank you." I whisper to Mom.

Meadow clutches my finger with her tiny hand. The nurse hands me the small tube that contained the 1ml of my breast milk. I warm it in my fingers as I pretend to nurse her. I slip it in her mouth as soon as I have it warmed, and she greedily sucks it down like it is a golden love. She nudges me for more, but I am completely dried up.

I don't give up. I try to pump again. I'm in my room with my gown off setting up the cup sizes trying to get it going on my own. Mom had left for the night. The nurse comes in. He is a tall and skinny older male.

"I'm sorry I walked in on you." He says turning around. I grab my gown for his comfort, not mine.

"Seriously." I playfully scoff. "I have just spent 6 weeks up in the ICU where I couldn't even wipe my butt by myself."

He cracks a smile. He gives me my blood thinner shot for the night, and my medications. My arms are bruised from the shots, so he has to give it to me in my stomach. It hurts less than I thought it would.

"They're going to probably take your trach out tomorrow seeing you have left your valve on for the night. Sleep with it again tonight, and we will take it out, okay."

I nod excitedly. With the trach out, I will finally be my own person again. Independent of anything. Plus, I will be given more food choices.

The next morning, I tell the nurse that the doctors are going to hide under my bed and rip my trach out when I least expected it. They are probably ninjas hiding behind a corner waiting for me.

She laughs as she readies me for the gym. To begin we take the long loop around to get extra walking practice. As we near the gym one of the physical therapist's is hanging by the door smiling so that all of her teeth show.

"I can't trust anyone that is that perky in the morning." I growl at her.

"Jesus, KaDawna can't you be nice." Mom snaps. "Sorry about that."

The physical therapist laughs it off. I think Mom would like to pinch my oxygen cord.

I sit on an exercise bike. I push my heavy legs to go in a slow rhythmic pace. I feel dizzy as my lungs work to keep up. The physical therapist pushes me to go a little faster.

To my surprise the doctors come in. The physical therapist, who I told that I am expecting the doctors to jump out, and get me at any moment, laughs at the sight. They just need me to sign a paper.

When we arrive back to the room it isn't long before my respiratory nurse comes in. I like his visits. He always makes me laugh until I cough something up. It is much better than being deep suctioned.

He explains to me he is the one going to pull out my trach. It's that simple. He unsnaps my trach collar. He tells me I have two stiches in my neck. I must have fallen asleep when my trach was downsized, because I have no recollection whatsoever of getting my neck stitched. He does simply pull it out. Then he places a big bandage over the hole.

He sets up an oxygen hose that loops around my ears and goes up my nose slightly. Now I'm an old lady. It tickles as I'm not used to it. At least the horrible loud gurgling that the trach oxygen hose made is no more. It's so quiet now.

Mom sits on the couch, and we chat for a while to pass the last bit of the day. Now that I have the bandage every time, I talk it blows up like a bull frog. Mom laughs. I decide to sing the beginning lines of a bullfrog song leaving her ribs aching with laughter.

Valentine's day is not to be passed over as I thought. There are hearts on my white board. Drawn by a sweet nurse, with great handwriting. I think that will be the extent of it. If the bed alarm wasn't on, I might have wiped them off. I even considered pelting them with spitballs.

Mom comes in smiling ear to ear followed closely by a big red heart balloon. I tie it on the bed next to me. We make bets of when it will lose its air and attack me. It never does. It hangs lower and lower, but it never falls. It never tries to suffocate me.

She also gives me a plastic red bag containing: a coloring book, crayons, bubbles, and a card. My favorite gift is a little stuffty goat. I can't believe she did so much. She's my mother, of course, she would. Also, candy! I could eat it. No trach to get in my way. My life is so much better.

I ever so slowly unwrapped my chocolate from its pink and red foil. The first time I'm going to eat chocolate since I don't know when. I place it in my mouth whole, and just let it melt. I don't care if I look like a drooling rabid chipmunk. This is mine. My moment. With a love card and a balloon, and a mouth full of chocolate. I am doing this. This life thing. My bed alarm is on, but I gaze past the bed out the window.

This is just the way life is supposed to be. An exposed nerve, a show of the strength under my shaking white knuckles. I dry heave into a bucket after working as hard as I can. I still have the nurses and their compassion. She is looking at me with those milky golden eyes as she places a cold cloth on the back of my neck. I try to smile, as I convulse slightly. My body revolts against my constant abuse.

I finally catch my breath. I stop. I ask for paper and exit the bedside commode. I crawl into bed. I ask for oxy. I sip water and sleep. I wake at two. I move slowly. My stirring wakes Mom. She smiles at me as we weakly gather ourselves. There is the little. The sweet smelling little just four floors down.

They offer the wheelchair. It would be so easy. I decline and go for my walker. The belt around me. My mom is pushing my oxygen, and quietly watching my every movement as we creep down the hall. The lurch of the elevator is excuse enough not to talk right now. I smile at her though I am biting my tongue to stay focused. She reaches out for me. I want to collapse into her. My heart aches at all I have put her through.

I roll out of the elevator down the mess of halls. I reunite with my heart. I snuggle and clumsily try to feed. I am here right now. I want to be in bed. I want to drink grape juice and eat more oxy. I want to ignore my rough re-introduction to motherhood.

I smell her hair. I touch her feet. I run a finger around her chin. She opens her sleepy eyes for a moment. My stomach lurches with joy, and pain as those eyes meet mine. She is still supposed to be rocked in the warmth of my womb.

My eyes begin to burn as I choke back tears. A heavy dose of hot liquid pain escapes down my cheek, and splashes on her forehead. I wipe it away. I chance a glance at Mom. If she has seen she knows the right thing to do is pretend the phone is way more important.

The morning is no longer gym. Instead it is physical therapy with Meadow. I just had a blood thinner shot in my stomach, but I bite my lip as the nursing pillow presses on my bruising. The baby is handed to me. I am told to pull off her clothes. I follow slowly unwrapping her. I had hardly touched her. I still have not even changed a diaper. I startle at the thought. I haven't changed one diaper.

"Put her on her belly for me." Meadows physical therapist startles me back to focus.

"Huh?" I say coming back to earth.

Then my body responds slowly turning her onto her belly. I am taught how to rub her back top to bottom. Then I turn her on her back. I massage her head. Then I bring her hands to her midline. Next, I massage the belly, and finish with some gentle bicycle movements. She is too tired for feeding. So, I hand her back.

I can now see her twice a day at 9am, and 3pm. The next morning, I don't go to the chair. I stand at her tiny little crib (a tiny plastic container on a dresser). My physical therapist stands behind me. I am glad. I look to Mom.

Even as an experienced mother I understand I need to follow their way. Mom gathers all the stuff slowly so that I am aware of where things are. She walks me through this new routine. New diaper under her. Open old diaper. Spray and wipe with dry wipe. Use a strange thick substance called ilex. Lift up and remove old diaper. Gently down on new diaper and fasten.

I am wiping at spot on her thigh. It won't go away. Mom leans in and smiles.

"It's a freckle." She says causally, avoiding my eye contact.

I feel more tears coming to me, but the focus I need to complete this task pulls them back. I stand legs screaming as I take her temperature.

"Celsius!" I bark. "Who the hell does Celsius?"

I pull her outfit off and have to pull it down her oxygen cord. Then I have to feed a new onesie back through the oxygen cord, and over her head. I am biting my tongue now to keep focus as I fight with the cords and snaps. Mom snakes a finger around them to give me a tiny amount of help.

I pause. There are three people around me. I scoop up my baby. I press her against my chest. The three sets of arms are close with hands open and ready. Tears fall as I use the strength of my upper legs, and slowly wind the cords to my chair.

My baby. My baby. My baby. I clutch her to me. I smell that baby smell. I feel the nursing pillow come to rest on my lap. I don't ever want to let her go. I lay her down. We begin the clumsy and uncoordinated dance of feeding. We still go nowhere.

I hand her to Mom. She reads her favorite story. I get lost in the words, and the most comforting voice on the planet. I wake to a gentle nudge. Time has slid by me. Meadow is in her crib. Mom and my nurse help me up, and they both give me a bit more support to make it over to my walker.

We eat lunch. I can finally have salads now that I have no more trach. I can understand why. I had a bit of choking moment with cheese that stuck to my trach. I could see lettuce being a problem too. I also got a full fruit tray. It is ridiculously big. I try to get Mom to eat some of the fruit with me. By the end of the day I have only managed one fourth of it. The nurse won't let me keep it any longer. I smuggle some melon and grapes away for later in the night wrapped in a paper towel and hidden in a side compartment of my table.

I watch what I can of the TV. Everything is new to me, so I can always find something that isn't a rerun. I get hooked on a show of surviving in the wilderness. It makes me ache to be back in nature. I enjoy watching how he can forage, and bravely drinks water from almost anywhere. There is also a show on tree houses that I love for the same reason, the same ache.

I pick up the phone, and I give Jewell a call.

"Going to be released soon, huh?" Jewell answers happily. I hear a baby goat in her lap.

"Yep!"

"Meadow is still off a ways?"

"Yes indeed. She cannot eat yet. How is everyone?"

"We're surviving. Do ya wanna talk to the girls?"

"Yes." I say.

I wait for the little voice that signifies Lotus. I give her my reassurance it won't be long now. Rayne sounds exhausted and depressed, but she's masking it like I am. Like mother like daughter. There is a slight lol in the conversation.

What do I say to her? I have nothing in the way of timelines. I can't fake anymore promises. I just want this right now. To hear her breathing. If only I could take away her pain. I ask to be handed back, but I am rather wordless everything is still so up in the air right now. I say I love you to everyone personally. That's all I could offer right now. I hang up.

I twirl the cord around in my fingers nervous and alone. I want to sneak to see Meadow. The time is 6pm. No nurse now would want to help me. Plus, I am too tired to move more than pulling off my clothes and putting on my tried and true hospital gown for pajamas.

I have to go. I really have to go. The bed alarm is on, so I groggily poke the nurse button. In few moments in bounds the small round male CNA that was in the ICU with me. I immediately go on edge.

He hugs me and while I am still in his arms, he drags me to the end of the bed. He tells me how excited he is to see me here. He puts my slippers on before pulling me to a complete stand. He walks me to the bathroom and balances me on the bar. He turns and stands outside the door.

I still eye him. Maybe I was crazy. I know I was fully present. I also know I can forgive. I click when I am ready for the help back. He tucks me in tightly. I understand how babies love to be swaddled. I quickly fall asleep.

The next day Meadows main nurse, Marry Anne, is busying around. When I roll in, she smiles at me so brightly it lights up the whole room. I wonder how she came to meet, and love Meadow so dearly. Was she their when she was born? She has seen me on ECMO as she was the first one to place Meadow in my arms. She knows the story. Maybe she knows more than even I do. She always gets first dibs to take care of her.

We are going to give her a bath today. I have stripped her down and rewrapped her back in her swaddling blanket.

"Let me show you how to set up the bath." She says redirecting my attention from Meadows open and bright eyes.

She pulls down the bright pink bath that has been carefully inscribed with Meadows name in sharpie on the side. Someone takes lots of time to create these beautiful masterpieces. A nurse has decorated her room with her name and feet prints laminated and taped up. It really helps me feel like this is my personal space.

Anyway, she shows me the perfect temperature, and how I'm supposed to check it with my elbow. The real shocker is the fact that she takes the baby in her swaddled blanket, and gently lowers her into the water, on the mesh hammock. We soak her down. Then we slowly open the blanket to expose only one body part at a time for washing.

She tells me she is going to give me the bottle of shampoo/body wash, and the sponge brush thing. I am so grateful for everything.

Then the baby is hosted up by her, as I don't trust myself and a wet baby. She lays her in her little bed. She talks of how she wants to take her home and keep her, but that would cause a divorce. She tells Meadow how cute, and how hard it is not to want to keep her for her very own.

I stare at Meadow. I don't want to speak. I want to memorize this moment. Here is my child naked. This is what she looks like. For the first time I gaze at her without a feeding tube, and oxygen cannula. No stickers on her face. She does have my nose. Her hair might be Jewells. There are lots of fat rolls, and an outie belly button. I poke at it because it's distended.

Mary Anne watching me explains that it's herniated. They are supposedly common, and there is nothing to worry about. She is so perfect. I am so thankful she has survived. I shudder to think if she didn't.

I hold her head still for the feeding tube. My stomach lurches, and I look away with clinched teeth. The nurse does a fast-efficient job. By the time, my eyes are back on her it is taped down. I help with the oxygen sticky patches on her face. Wires on her left right and belly. Pulse oximeter wrapped around her foot. I pull a cute onesie through the oxygen cord, and over her head. I wrap her tightly up. I touch her soft round face. No feeding tonight. She is exhausted. Me too.

I sit now alone as the dark presses on the window. The clock now ticking down the hours, before my release date that is scribbled across my white board. I am coloring pictures in the book, Mom got me, for Lotus and Rayne.

My mind flicks to the last time I touched their soft hair. Their small shoulders, and tiny hands. The last moments before they left the hospital in Alamosa. The broken promises that I was okay, and I would be home soon.

It was two months ago, and still a third must pass before they release Meadow. I wish I wasn't so far away. So, trapped by time, and distance. I feel as though somehow, I had let everyone down. I had failed. Meadow wasn't even to be born yet. What could I have done different? Was I just a victim of a freak circumstance?

I carefully pack my crayons and look around the room I am to leave tomorrow. I have clumped what I can together. I know how slow things work here, so I'm not expecting to be out before the afternoon.

February 18th, Mom comes in with Kyron. She takes pictures of my graduation flyer taped to my door. The doctor comes in to talk to me. He says they want to keep me another month but being as close to the hospital as I'm going to be, and having Mom trained to watch me, I'm bound to get even more exercise and practice at being normal.

Occupational Therapy makes me take a shower as a test. No chair or bar. Just her hawk eying me to make sure I can bathe myself. She continues to watch me as I dress slowly, brush my teeth, my hair, and put on my slippers. One of my strangest tests by far.

The Physical Therapist begins by having an oxygen specialist give me a walk. Sitting I ranged at 93% oxygen. Sadly, five steps out of my room without it, and I am down in the lower 80's. I didn't want to be on oxygen, out of the hospital.

"Let me catch my breath." I say to her pleadingly.

"Look!" she says waving her hand.

I turn to follow her hand as it waves toward my room. Its only feet away from me.

"There are your reserves. I'm sorry but you need to continue to be on oxygen." She is firm in her voice.

I place my nasal cannula back on. We continue our walk trying to causally chat, mixed with Mom interjecting that I'm going the wrong way. It seems that 2 liters of oxygen will be okay, or 3 liters if I get tired and disorientated.

I'm also going to be released with a bright red walker. I came up short on my goals of getting out of here fully independent. Healing is slower than I thought.

The Physical Therapist for the day is the women that had caught me when I first got up off the ICU bed. She is so happy to see me. She gives me one hell of a hard test of walking me all over the hospital, and without my walker. I lean against walls. I sit halfway through trying to breathe and push on.

I want to be done, but then she leads me to the gym. The nurse explains to me that one of my most important tasks using a walker is getting up. I may fall alone, and I need to work through the first couple of times with a watchful eye.

I don't think I can handle anymore. I watch as she lays a big mat down. She tells me to sit down.

I sit and instantly regret it. Everything goes out of whack, and I want to vomit. I have to lay down now. Oh, how I want to be sick. Now I am instructed to get up without holding onto anything. I try in earnest remembering the days when this task would have been laughable.

I slip and fall; more than once. I can't coordinate my body. I'm still not as strong as my body weight. I am confused. I fight and flounder trying to figure out how to get off the floor. I struggle to keep from puking as everything swims in front of me. I fight to keep tears from my eyes.

Mom wants to help as I struggle and fight my body. We meet eye to eye. She sees the determined angry fire in me. She retreats to biting her tongue and crossing her arms.

I lay exhausted. I remember how toddlers get up. I copy them slowly. I manage up finally. It has taken me 40 struggling minutes to do it once. Then I do it again with muscles that are burning, and a brain that is screaming at me that I can't do it. This time it takes only 20 minutes to get to standing.

I stagger back to my room. I flop on my bed, and thankfully turn my oxygen up to 3 in a feeble attempt to get some strength and focus back. I am fighting the urge to puke. I am terrified of the world that awaits me. I am still so helpless in a system that demands so much. How am I ever to pull anyone else to standing if I cannot even hold my own.

Kyron has filled all my prescriptions. I am embarrassed to see the big brown bag resting on my walker seat. Next, to it is two oxygen tanks. A third one is in a cute little dolly. This is what I still need. I guess there is no shame. The healing process is slow. At least I'm alive, right?

"Thanks!" I smile, but my face crinkles like something smelly is waiting in that bag.

"That's a lot of medication, but the pharmacy tech said it's one of the smallest bags of meds she's seen for someone who spent time in the ICU."

I finally have earned my discharge paperwork. I place it carefully in my bright red binder. I gather everything I want to take. I am ready to go. New normal meets the world.

The nurse cuts my band off of me. I am free to go. I don't want anyone to see how scared I am. I raise my head up high, and I push out of the room. I stop at the nurses' desk. I thank the doctors and the nurses over and over.

I step into the elevator. Without hesitation it jolts and descends to the bottom floor. I march straight to the door, and happily wheel out.

$\mathcal{I}$ am Strong

I am strong because I wasn't expecting another pregnancy, but I loved her anyway.

I am strong because at ten weeks pregnant I said goodbye to my dad who died of cancer.

I am strong because I had to find the ambulance that cold December morning.

I am strong because I didn't lose hope of having Christmas with my girls.

I am strong because I didn't lose hope even as they life flighted me at six months pregnant to Denver.

I am strong because I woke up three weeks later without a voice and without my baby.

I am strong because I have family that didn't lose hope, even on Christmas morning when I died, and they took the baby in 97 seconds at just 29 weeks gestation.

I am strong because Mom was there every day, I was on life support holding my hand and then going to care for my baby.

I am strong because Jewell fiercely loved and cared for the girls.

I am strong because I fought every day to heal my body.

I am strong because I started breathing again, I learned to walk and eventually talk again.

I am strong because they had to dry up me up, and I could not breastfeed for the first time.

I am strong because I missed most of the firsts with my baby.

I am strong because it took three weeks before I could even hold her.

I am strong because as soon as I could I was in the NICU with her.

I am strong because after a week of having her and I both home and reuniting the family she had to go back in the NICU for RSV.

I am strong because being strong is my only hope.

New Ropes

Mom and Kyron think nothing of the shuttle as it slows to a stop and hisses to announce its parked. My heart races, as I stand outside. I'm leaving a safety and sanctuary I have grown used to. I smile over at Mom softening my face to mimic happiness. I feel terrified that I am now fully in control of myself again. Especially being so clumsy, slow, easily lost, and confused. She gives me one of those squeezes on my shoulder, that centers me. I think she seen through the fake smile.

We have lots of my hospital stuff to deal with. Along with three oxygen tanks, my walker, and my mess of a self. I came here naked. A baby nestled inside a body that was dying. A life for a life, and yet here I stand.

I have clothes, and toiletries. I have my tablet, and my bear. I have snacks, and a bean bag goat. There is a coloring book with crayons. A red balloon, a bag of medication, a plant, and my coat. I have a $100 to my name (A gift from girls on a social media group).

They haul it all up inside with a swift hello to the driver for the day. Mom comes back for me. She waits behind me. There are three stairs I have to get up. I panic for a second. I grab one leg and place it on the first stair. I feel when my ankle is ready to cooperate, and then I pull myself up white knuckling the bar. I lift the other leg. It is embarrassing and tedious.

I finally make it shakily to the top and hold on to the first chair I can grab for balance and breath. I ignore the eyes on me. I find a seat a few rows back next to the window, so the oxygen bearer can sit.

This is Mom's world now. She has dropped everything to stay by my side. She lives here. She knows the driver, and she chats with him. She knows the scenery. The stoplights. The old pine fence that winds forever. Apartments hidden in the twists of the road. I have never been in this part of Denver.

We are delivered only blocks away from the hospital to a brown building. It stands three stories tall. The shuttle driver pulls up to the sidewalk. It is not as big as a motel, but not as small as a house. It seems cozy.

I manage down the stairs. I am met with the creepy clown that sits on the bench I had seen in the picture with Mom. He is frozen there. From what I can see of the outside yard protected by a black iron gate is lots of little playhouses, and a nice walkway.

Inside is a large living room with a couple of tiny playhouses, a large stuffed giraffe, a large funny looking stuffed zebra, and a kangaroo momma with no baby in its pouch. There are lots of couches of different sizes. Chairs some big and soft (perfect for reading and cuddling), some hard (like you would find in a doctor's office), and a couple soft benches. Two pianos, decorations, paintings, a train in a glass box, lots of wooden red wagons, and a couple child sized wheelchairs are scattered throughout creating a maze of comfort and chaos.

Mom announces with pride how I had survived to the lady at the main desk. She has short blonde hair and small glasses.

I smile faintly as I push my walker past the brown wooden desk she is sitting at. I don't want to talk about it.

Mom shows me their library with free toys, hats, and packs of crayons with coloring books, and blankets. There are movies, books, and games to check out.

From there I wheel my walker back through the living room past a large replica of Alvin and the Chipmunks. I reach out to touch their hard-plastic noses and look eye to eye with them.

Next, it is the playroom. Being a kid at heart I am excited at the sight of all the toys and play stuff they have. I wish I was stronger. I wish my kids were here.

We go through the playroom, and into the kitchen. Mom points to her designated shelf. I can tell immediately that it is hers. It is stacked with heath food galore, and my brother's favorite junk foods. There is a large fridge and freezer that everyone on the bottom floor shares by marking their names, on masking tape with a sharpie.

Through another door on the other side of the kitchen is a hall. Down it is our laundry mat. It is tiny with one washer and dryer. Our room is not too far off. 2B, my new home, with no need for question.

Mom holds the heavy wooden door open for me; I roll into my new world. I am still miles away from home, and a good month before home can be reached. I imagine bringing my sweet baby home, and dream of snuggling her. For now, I'm glad she is in the NICU, because I'm still easily confused, and badly need my walker to do the simplest things.

In the room there are two beds divided by a small nightstand. On the nightstand is one large fancy lamp fighting over space with a large black office phone with lots of buttons. I can tell just by the setup whose is whose. It is easy to tell where my niche will be. Mom shows me the dresser drawer that is empty for me. I put my clothes in kind of scrambled. I don't have much, but Mom of course offers her shirts and socks.

I sit on the bed in semi shock not knowing what to do. No obnoxious noises from the ICU. No hustle and bustle of nurses. No warning alarm on my bed to keep me from randomly getting up. It's just me. The rub of my C-section scar. The hiss of my oxygen. My choices. I feel scared and unprepared.

There are no bars in the bathroom. The toilet is surprisingly lower than expected. I need all the deliberate motion, strength, and balance of my walker to reach it. I have to keep the door ajar in case I need help.

What do I do now? I lay on the bed with my tablet, and doodle around ignoring the vast ocean that I am now swimming in; with nothing but a walker, and my new nurse maid Mom. They trained her well in watching me if I turned blue or have a fall. She would know. Mom reassures me that the hospital, being so close, would have someone out in moment's notice if something went wrong.

A ring of the phone scares me. I look at Mom who motions me to answer it. It's the oxygen guy. He wants in the door. Mom explains to the lady at the main desk that it was us who sent for him. Moments later he is barging in with a lot of new things, and some not so new things.

The oxygen machine I knew from dad being on it. That familiar hum and pop is now mine. He shows me two tanks. He walks me through charging them, connecting them, and even troubleshooting problems. He gives me a 50ft cord that seems crazy in such a tiny room. He also gives me two bags to carry the tanks in, and a smaller oxygen cord for travel. Then he hands me his card, and leaves.

I am in charge of myself now. As much as possible. It is daunting, yet laughable of what I am scared of now. This feels like a final exam that had no margin for failure. It's overwhelming. I am in need of sleep, and food. I am starting to become snappy.

With patience Mom sets up the oxygen tank. She helps me onto my walker. It's time for dinner. I don't want to move out of my new sanctuary. Mom holds the door for me. I don't argue.

I follow them as they walk back through the living room with the large TV, through the main living room, and into an elevator. Out we go and twist this way and turn that. I get lost, and it takes some coaching, but I finally enter the busy dining area.

There are lots of people. I feel the wind suck out of me. It's too much. It's too overwhelming for me. I know that one day everyone in this room will die. I know that everyone in here is here, because their kid is sick, premature, in need of surgeries, or dying.

I back up wanting to run. Tears are streaming down my face. Mom reaches out and comforts me. She keeps me from running away.

She ushers me to a table. She turns up my oxygen, so I don't hyperventilate. I am shaking. I try to focus on the smells of the food.

People cast glances at me. I feel like I'm the new kid in high school. Not in the new meat sort of way, but in an intrigued way. I can't make eye contact. I don't want to be touched or bothered. I stare at the table and make myself small.

I have food and something to drink brought to me. Kyron and Mom sit down next to me. They talk and laugh. This is their new normal. I look out the window. I can see the hospital lights looming out there. I see the blinking that is the lights for the helicopter pad. It makes me a little nauseous and scared. I can't wait to see it in the daytime up here, and yet it feels like I'm peering over the deepest of cliffs.

I want to be included in the conversation, so I try to smile and laugh. It is still too much for me to handle. I'm starving. I eat as much as my stomach can handle. Mom hides some dessert for us to share later in my walker pouch.

We head back to the room. Everyone is happy and giggly. I am so tired my legs want to give out. I pinch the back side of my tongue between my molars to remain focused. I mimic Kyron and Mom, so I don't seem out of character.

They want me to watch a new movie that came out while I was in a coma. It is so enjoyable. I feel apart for once.

Finally, its dark. Mom rolls over to the other side of the bed. I snuggle against her back. Warm and free. I'm so happy that I can turn almost anyway I want except for the oxygen cord that will wrap around me.

I am right by the air. I love the flow of air around me. Stale non-moving air for some reason scares me. I need to know it is there for me, and I'm not drowning.

I wake up faintly as Mom shoves my oxygen cannula back up my nose. It is time to get up. A late wake up for me its 8:30am. Mom is already drinking coffee and eating something yummy she found in the kitchen.

I rise and I take all of my medication. I get out of bed like a robot might. My calves will not relax easy, so I stiff legged limp to my walker. I ready as fast as possible. Mom calls the shuttle, as she continues to move me along.

I unhitch my oxygen tank. I set it all up in its bag. I place the bag on my walker, and we leave. Mom has the walker finally figured out. It folds up in the middle making it easy to load and unload.

Here we are again. The hospital. I high tailed it out of here yesterday and didn't look back. Now here I am facing the other way rolling back in. I get to see the hospital for the way it really is. The ICU where I spent most of my time, can be spotted. The second floor. There is the hospitals motto written across the bridge. It was such a strong Deja-vu.

I veer left into the cafeteria. I sit in tears as a major panic attack waves over me. I am hyperventilating. Mom is almost ready to get me a paper sack to breathe into. She doesn't want to leave me to go in search of one. She turns up my oxygen. She squeezes me hard. I look into her eyes. I begin to ground. My breathing finally steadies. I am still shaking.

The last thing in the world I want is to walk back in this hospital. I will walk through the gates of hell to get to my babies, and this is exactly what I'm doing. I shakily grab hold of my walker. My small strides lead a screaming mind to the elevator.

I roll in steady myself and hit number four. Off we go with hardly any lurch. The door pings open. There are the cardboard people smiling at us as they give maternity advise. I want to hit them.

Instead, we take a sharp turn right. The lady recognizes us right away. She unlocks the door. We scamper through quickly hardly looking at the waiting room on the right of us. Someone is always in there. More often than not, someone is trying to sleep. There is a nice bathroom, and vending machines there. Lots of uncomfortable benches with a T.V. going all the time. There are racks of magazines, and some are free to take.

Past the door that threatens to close on us in a heartbeat, is another door down a hall not too far out of reach. Beside it is one of those big cardboard signs saying watch for flu symptoms, do not enter if you have any one of these symptoms. The list is amazingly long.

Through this sweeping door is another very small hall. This one is where the lactation consultants lurk behind the doors of a small room on the left. Once past there is another nurse's desk straight ahead. They will watch you like a hawk as you stop to visit the sink recessed into the wall. Usually, they welcome us happily as we wash in hot water and put a paper mask on.

At 9am we are ready to change Meadow, check her temperature, attempt to feed, and love her. I want to jail break her so badly. She is still on oxygen and just starting to learn how to eat. Not very well. We are waiting patiently for her due date, and a visit from the nipple fairy. I can now pick her up knowing how to watch the cords. I have memorized the feeding tube, the three wires telling what all her stats are, and her oxygen cord stickered to her face by two large brown bandage looking things made especially for babies. Under it all is my sweet little fighter.

I snuggle her and hold her as best as I can. Everything still seems to hurt. I'm always tired. It's a fight, but one I'm waging with all I have to offer.

I pull her close and squeeze her. I run my fingers along her tiny hands, arms, and face. I listen to coo, and breath. I put our hearts together kangarooing her. Finally, I hand her back to Mom. She holds her for a while talking and cooing. I smile watching her so bright, so at peace. I push myself to fight off a dizzying grog. I try to smile as bright and alert as I can. I turn up my air.

Mom lays her back down to sleep. I prep myself for leaving. For the first time I feel myself leave her. I am leaving my baby alone. It felt okay when I was also in the hospital. It's a whole new sensation to turn my back on her and wheel out.

I lift my head higher for what it's worth. I smile at the nurses who still gawk at me. Mom guides me out. I am numb as she pushes me along chatting.

We are home. She holds the large door open for me. I wheel in wash for the third time, and then collapse on the bed. I dump pill bottles on the bed and begin the mid-day routine. Gabapentin, and Oxycodone are my most important meds. The pain I am still in with my feet, and body is almost unbearable.

"That reminds me." Mom says shattering my concentration. "Do you want to come to the store with me to get Kyron's medications?"

"Okay." I say cautiously.

"Well hurry up we don't want to miss our three o'clock meeting with Meadow."

I trade out oxygen tanks. I push along with my walker back out into the bright sun. Mom tries to put the walker in. It won't fit no matter what we try. She gets the little step ladder and helps me in. Then she goes and drops my walker back off in the room.

It's great to see other parts of Aurora. The traffic is nerve wracking. I feel semi sick, and overstimulated. Thankfully, it's not that far away.

I turn up my oxygen, as I wait patiently for my new nurse to help me out of the Jeep. Her strength is always amazing and comforting. I feel her support my wonky body as I heavily lift my legs down. I lean against her, and she steadies me for a moment against the Jeep. She throws the step ladder on the seat and slams the door.

Then she grabs my arm with her less dominate arm and steadies me with her other one as we walk through the parking lot. She guides my hands on a cart. I want to retract from touching it, but I know I will fall if I do. I push the cart around like a bulky hard to move walker. I sit and rest staring at all the people. No doubt they are staring at me in my slippers, oxygen cord, and dazed look.

Mom finds me 10 min later in the baby section. I am holding a pretty pink band with a ribbon for her little head. I found a shelf to sit on, and I am sorting through outfits and other knick-knacks I found to stare at.

She pulls me up and steadies me. Back through the same routine to get me in and out of the Jeep. I want to sleep but I feel dirty. I ask Mom for help showering.

She places a rubber mat and readies everything for me. I had a horrible nightmare about this. The door is open, but I am scared. I dreamed I had suffocated in here. I don't like the curtain closed. The water gets in my cannula.

I turn off the water. Mom asks if I want help out. I reassured her that the walker is there. I can hear her by the door, but quiet as a mouse.

I move slowly, consciously, and ever careful of my balance. I lift one leg out and onto the mat. I spread out my toes, and carefully shift weight before bringing out my last leg. It may be painfully slow, but I at least manage okay.

After heavily medicating we head back to the hospital. I am growing extremely weak and clumsy. I don't know if my body will keep moving. I am so tired. I bite my tongue. I lean over to Mom for comfort. I just keep pushing through the rest of the day. I eat all I can for dinner in a quiet stupor before we head back down to our room. I wash again and crawl into bed.

I stare at the celling quietly. I know its roughly 3am. I have been out of the hospital now for a week. Overall, I am feeling more comfortable in my new situation. I uncurl my hands on my chest and roll to my side, giving my oxygen cord a yank, and snuggle into Mom's back. I hear her soft breath as I try to sleep.

I close my eyes and let time slip by me waiting for sleep to come. My thoughts are flooding in too intensely. I feel as if I can't breathe. I begin to twitch, so I decide to roll back to keep from waking her up. I reach for my tablet.

I sit up. For the first time I dare to go to the pictures she has put on there that are me in a coma, and Meadow at her most vulnerable and small. I thump through them. This is the first time I have been able to look at them. I struggle to put pieces together. Finally, I exhaust myself enough to sleep. The air has kicked on, and it feels so good to feel the air on my face.

I see on Meadows white board that she has gained a pound putting her at 6. Today they are going to give her her first set of shots. Meadows nurse tells us not to worry about our three o'clock feeding, because she will need to rest.

That leaves us with the afternoon. She takes me to a store where I can by a diaper bag. I think that will help me realize I have a baby. I bought one for each baby I had. Each of them I thought was my last baby, and I gave it away when I was done. I look and sort through the selection. Mom offers to take me other places. I shake my head. I'm too tired to go anywhere else.

I settle with a gray canvas one that is lime green inside. There is a big plastic pouch for stuff and lots of space to organize. I clutch it as we drive home. I zip and unzip it. I smile. The first thing I have bought for this baby. Maybe more for me then her.

It isn't the only thing I have. The NICU is giving me outfits. They are also giving me the pink tub they bathe her in, and the sponge and soap. Mom and grandma had squirreled away enough free diapers, and wipes for months. Meadows main nurse had bought her first set of bottles; a special kind for babies like her. Mom had bought blankets. She also gathered a bunch of free stuffties, for her, and the other two girls as well.

I also have two boxes of baby clothes from friends mailed to me. It is truly an amazing surprise.

Stuff is coming together slowly. I still have two maybe three weeks before she will come home. I know I have more to do. I can't afford formula, and a car seat. That weighs in my stomach like a lead ball.

I lift the phone and called WIC. They say they can help me buy formula, and if I get a note from the NICU they will even order special formula for me. I breathe a sigh of relief as I set up an appointment with them.

I go in the next day to see how Meadow is doing after her first set of shots. I have a strange nurse who seems to immediately set me off. She wants us to room in with her tonight saying she is ready for the feeds test. It really throws me off, but I cannot say no to taking my baby home.

I have to bottle feed her and room in with her in an attempt to have her to eat most of her formula. Its more watching. To see how I handle my baby. How do I take care of her? Am I a good mother?

Right now, I'm still in need of all the help I can get. So, Mom rooms in with me taking over a side of the bed. I am sure it is an odd sight as most pairs are wife and husband.

We listen to music and play scrabble together to pass the time. Anything to ignore the fact that I'm in the hospital. I sigh as I began to twitch again. Mom sits up and rubs my back.

I look over at the breast pump I had dragged into the room. Every chance I got I was pushing one of them around with me. I know I am probably never going to breastfeed. Breastfeeding was such an important part of my mothering experience. With milky baby breath, the nightly cuddles, and watching them grow with what I had to offer. I couldn't yet let go of the tiny spec of hope. It was such a huge part of me.

All hope of getting Meadow out did fade quickly. I know it was a rough attempt. We did try. We took turns waking up, and mixing formula. We tried over and over again to feed her. There was no way of her taking all her feeds. By the morning we are utterly exhausted and frustrated. We ask the main nurse to not let that nurse take care of Meadow again.

At the end of the week we struggle through town trying to find the tiny building where WIC hid. People are out front smoking. Mom yells at all of them that I am on oxygen. They scatter giving me more space. I sign in and wait. Babies of all kinds and sizes are all around me. Fat healthy babies all around me. I look enviously at each sleeping, and fussing baby as I wait my turn. Finally, I'm called in. I sit in the cramped room, and we go through the paperwork . I will have formula delivered here one week before she comes home.

The hoops I have to jump through are hard and tedious. I know it's for her safety. So, I slowly cross off everything and pray some where I can magically get a car seat. Mom has no financing and is surviving barley with help from others. Jewell cannot work and is taking care of a farm and two kids. There is no one to help. No one to help relieve this pressure. We are all caught in a tight bind. This large looming Gregorian knot that I have yet to untangle.

Part of this hoops and ladders game is a child safety class. I cram in a room with two other mothers who gawk at me. I leave my walker at the front as the room lacks the space I need. Mom helps as I struggle to the back where they can't stare at me. I can tell they are normal baby mothers.

I chew on a new pen that was handed to me along with a small binder filled with paperwork. I thump through it as the nurse situates herself for the class.

"This is dumb." I whisper under my breath at Mom.

The nurse then begins. Seeing the eagerness from the woman on the right of me I can tell she's a first time Mom. Her introduction proves me right. The women on her left is slightly annoyed because she already has a two-year-old at home.

As the nurse goes over things like temperature checking, feeding, burping we all try to ask questions. I am getting nothing from the lady teaching the class. She only tells me to check with my nurse at everything I ask. So, I fall silent and try not to doze off.

I write down what I remember my nurse has taught me scratching out, and altering the information given to me in the binder. I am a seasoned mother so most of this is old news anyway.

I'm chewing my pen to shreds trying to stay alert. She begins to talk about RSV. I perk up, as I have never heard it before.

RSV is a really bad cold in kids. I write down notes on the information because Meadows immune system is going to be compromised coming home. It sounds like it could get super scary. When I finally get out of there my head is spinning. I shove the stupid binder in the walker. Mom helps guide me to Meadow. I want to be with her.

As I come into the small room Mary Ann looks up at me and smiles. I park my walker and snap both breaks down. I turn off my oxygen, yank the cord out of my tank. Then I slowly manage across the room with my oxygen cord in hand. I hook it up to my spot on the wall and turn it up to two liters.

I turn to my little baby now in a swaddler strangle blanket with Velcro straps to hold it in place. She looks like a burrito in a

Rubbermaid tub, placed on a fancy dresser with wheels. It's funny to look at.

After all the nurse work is done, I take my baby to the chair and lay her on my chest. I smell and rub her head. I run my fingers over her tiny body, as she snuggles into my warm breasts. I know she is sleeping to the sound of my heart thudding in my chest. I feel the bond slowly coming around. Not intense, like the last two. I am ashamed to say this feels more like I'm adopting her. Something is lacking, something is missing. I know time will heal.

I feel anger at times. I sometimes hold her so overwhelmed, and so grateful that there is always someone watching me. I am suffering from my normal PPD (Postpartum Depression). Now it is compounded like a vice on my heart and stomach.

Holding her is hard. I hurt. I know it is not her fault, but I have no one else to place blame on. I know it was the virus that went AWOL. I truly believe, in my heart of hearts, that is was her that saved me. The main reason they life flighted me to where they would save me. But it is also me that that sometimes blames her. Her who saved me.

No good deed goes unpunished. I run my fingers over her tiny back. I wonder what her hair will look like. What will her eye color be? I hold her close to me and fall off to sleep. Mom will not be able to trust me. I feel her gently nudging the chair with her foot. This will keep me in a light doze, or worse it will keep me ping-ponging between sleep and consciousness. I want to hurt her.

I have anger issues. I suffered Post-Partum Depression in the past. I hid in my house when Lotus was little. I was alone to deal with it. I got medication, and simply hid out until the storm passed. I would just post some mushy baby pictures on social media. No one was the wiser. Except Jewell. She understood.

Being here has left me exposed down to every nerve. Everyone is watching. Always watching. So closely. They monitor everything. Not a moment alone, and not a tear unnoticed.

Deep inside I'm glad she is ever watched. Even more than her is me. I'm glad I'm watched. The thoughts that race through my mind makes me want to hurt myself. Obviously, I know that numerus hours, money, hope, and faith that had been spent to keep me alive. I'm not dumb enough to throw that away. At times it's almost too tempting though. Moms ever watchful eye watches me. I'm grateful, and I hate it.

The social workers will come around. They ask about our plans. She has a clipboard and an air of importance. I want to tell them I'm going to punch them in the face if they come around again. I usually can say most of what I want to with just a glance. I don't want to get marked as unstable and possibly violent, so I will give in. I will spin tales of how we are planning everything to the detail. Arizona is our goal.

I'm too weak to go back home. I'm scared of the high altitude. I'm scared of the left-over germs. I want that book to be closed and stay closed for good. What will that leave me to do weak as I am? I don't want to tell these people that. They might take all my babies away.

It's all still too much, and too overwhelming. So, I count my mid-day pills, and I curl up on my bed. After an hour of sleep, I groggily come around to the sound of the phone. I sound like a perky happy momma to the two girls giving them updates on their new sister. I ask how each one is doing. Then I give my round of 'I love you's before being handed to Jewell.

"How are you sweetie?" She begins.

"I don't know? Can I come home? I'm so weak. I can't climb those stairs. I built those stairs, and now I can't climb them. Yet, we have no money. I can't work. You can't work, because I need help, with everything! What are we going to do?" I finish on a panicked exasperated tone.

"Try to fill out the Social Security paperwork for Meadow, and you." She begins in a soothing tone. "It's going to be fine. I will help with all the kids. You know that. Rayne and Lotus are doing okay. I'm cooking better now."

I smile, and she begins to speak again.

"Don't worry about what you can do. I will carry you up and down the stairs. Not a problem. We can figure out where your walker fits in when you get here. You just need to relax. You will be fine here. This is your home. We built it together. I will start doing research on the best oxygen equipment to get, okay? This is the safest place for you and Meadow."

I hang up feeling some sense of peace again. I feel it in my heart that I want to be on my farm. I see no other possible way with financing, and the fact that Mom didn't have a chance to get a home herself before being thrown into this mess.

March is here. I want her out by her due date. I've filed paperwork for Social Security. I sit on the internet in vain trying to look over some of my application. The internet keeps flickering out. Mom finally gets mad enough to slam her computer shut, startling me.

"Let's see if the computer room is working." I say wanting to break the monotony.

"Fine, they have a good one upstairs." She smiles at me.

I decide to go without my walker. My home appointments with physical therapy are advancing me in literal leaps and bounds.

The young guy, my age, was rather shocked that I'm so young. He worked with me two times in an attempt to get my "swagger back". I had advanced from tiny steps, and heavy reliance on my walker, to longer strides and my body finding more balance than ever before.

Mom still decides to hold my oxygen. I lean against everything but manage into the elevator and finally to the computer room with minimal help.

As I sit there, I read over something funny. Instead of just the tickly happy feeling something rumbles from my chest. Its horse and strange as it comes out.

"Holy Cow!" I yell in reaction.

"Shhhh, this is the computer room. What's so funny?"

"No, it's not the funny. Did you hear what I did. I just realized it's the first time since I got sick that I did it."

"What?"

"I laughed. I have found things funny since the accident, but I haven't laughed out loud. You heard it right. When was the last time you heard me laugh? Do you think it's because of my lung healing?"

Mom looks at me startled. She stares at me lost for a second then just turns back to her computer. When we finish what was needed with a solid connection, I hobble back down to the main room to do laundry and wait for dinner. Life is almost normal.

Getting up and going to the hospital is now routine. Its predictable: coming home, eating dinner, watching movies, and taking my meds. It is all too comfortable. I know I will have to come face to face with the outside world, and I am still nowhere near ready for that.

I am finally ready to come face to face with the chapel. It is on the main floor before the elevator. For some reason it elected the same emotions as the helicopter pad. I am scared to even look inside.

The door is open. I push inside. I get to about where the alter is. There is no one, but Mom who has found a seat. I let the walker go out from under me. I fall hard on my knees. I silently give thanks. For as long as I can bear to be on my knees I pray. I reach out toward Mom to thank her as well.

I scoot back toward my walker, and I claw my way back up to standing. Why had I even been given a second chance? Me, this broken mess. I feel like for everything I have been given I haven't felt worth it.

I will take this second chance and give all my energy to my babies.

Meadow's nurse has given me another long oxygen cord. I now have enough length connected that I'm able to walk wobbly legged out to the group of doctors as they do their rounds. I am ready to banter with them. I have been in the NICU long enough. I have somewhat figured out what could be holding Meadow off from her feeding.

It is time I start advocating for her. Mom has been amazing to this point, but I need to do this. To do what I think is right. I'm demanding a new formula. One with less lactose.

I stand strong, and I make eye contact with every doctor. They agree that a change might make a difference. They look at me with what seemed like admiration or shock, as I slowly shuffle back to Meadows side.

The shift in formula seems to help as soon as its switched. There is less spit up and less bloat. Now we have more interest in eating. Has the nipple fairy finally arrived? Could we finally be coming out of stagnant waters?

The nurse for the day introduces herself to us so full of life. She leans in and tells Meadow that she is her waitress for the night. We laugh. She sits with us and talks because she only has one other baby for the day.

I noticed that there is a baby next to us that got a huge crib. I haven't seen the mom here but one time. The nurse can't say anything to me, and I understand. I ask if I can at least cuddle with him. She looks at me saddened and tells me it's against policy. That crib is a sign that he is going to be here for a very long time.

She shows me how to mix the new formula, and warm it. We are all finally getting this down to a science. Next, the tight bundle, and the special preemie baby hold. Suck, suck breathe. It's going so smoothly.

Meadow chokes in my arms. I don't know how to react. I am scared. Should I turn her sideways to let her throw up as I was instructed, or is this new protocol? I froze.

Meadow lay blue in my arms. The nurse takes her from me. She quickly sits her up, and whacks at her back. She breaths. I almost don't want to hold her anymore. That ends our feeding session for the morning.

Later in the day we need to go to WIC. This time to pick up my box of formula for the baby's coming home. I sign in and ask the desk lady if she knows where I can get a car seat. She shakes her head at me.

I take a seat in an almost empty office. I pick up a magazine and pretend to thump through it. A man stands up when he sees his wife and baby appear at the door. He talks to her in a foreign language that I can't understand. I know what Spanish sounds like, and French. This I have no clue. They banter back and forth in the foreign tongue. They stop. I realize they are staring at me.

I shift in my chair. The receptionist calls me up. I put down the magazine and break eye contact with them. She hands me the box of formula. Mom takes it for me. I glance at the strange man now coming over to me. It startles me, and I want to get away.

Calmly he tries to piece English words together.

"Car seat. Car seat." He says to me syllable by syllable. "I have one. No need. You need?"

I nod. "Yes."

"Come. Follow in car. Home we have one. Too small, too small. Come? Follow?"

Mom and I exchange glances. I nod yes again. We all walk out together struggling to communicate. We pick up that they are from Iran. They climb in their tiny car, and we climb in the Jeep.

They begin by taking us on main easy roads. We keep turning and winding going deeper and deeper into the heart of the city. Mom and I exchange uneasy glances. They keep driving it seems forever; until we are sure there is no way out. I dig around for her GPS unit, and I can't get it to work. We tail them for 25 min. I'm about ready to call it due to my oxygen demands.

We are about to give up when they finally pull into a small cramped apartment complex. Nervously we pull in, and park next to them. The young women, beautifully dressed, bounces out of the passenger side and quickly disappears into the maze of stairs and doors. He gets out of the car and pulls out his car seat with a big baby boy inside. He looks huge to me. I try to tell him he is beautiful. He smiles at me. I think he understands.

Now she is coming back. In her hands is another car seat. Much smaller. I almost want to laugh at the size difference. No way this big baby could fit in there.

"We used for first week. Then no fit. New." She says.

Then she hands it to me. Coffee brown with black designs. Simple, and cheaply made. My eyes well up with tears at my gratitude. It is perfect. There is a small head rest. She will fit in here so nicely and have plenty of room to grow. There is a base to it, so that I can snap it in, and out of the car. It also has the new buckling system that has become popular just in the last year. I don't know if hugging is okay with her. I do my best to convey my thanks over and over again.

I bring in my car seat to the NICU. I am ever so proud and happy. To my shock they had moved the baby. This time I'm room sharing with a beautiful black woman who as well doesn't speak English. We smile at each other and understand each other's struggles here. I ogle over her baby and she does the same.

No more nurse Mary Ann. She is focusing on helping a 1lb baby survive. Meadow is finally ready for her feeding test. Now Mom is going to leave me alone with the baby. I'm terrified, but this will be a good bonding experience. Why should I be scared to be alone with my baby?

I want to lay in bed with her. The nurse won't have it. I think about the room layout, and how I might pull the queen size bed toward her. It looks as if they have covered every which way, I could sneak her into bed with me. I wish I could sit on the bed with her, and just stare at her. I want to strip her down and look at her. My baby. I want to give her a bath. It's all still too overwhelming. I just sit on the bed, and stare at her from afar weeping quietly.

I know it isn't going to be easy. I dry my eyes. I get up go over to where she is hooked to her leads. I stand as long as my legs allow simply to watch her sleep. I run my fingers through her tiny fine hair. She shifts and opens her eyes. I feel myself falling deeply in love with her. I take the tiny hand that has escaped the tight burrito.

Finally, a moment alone. All alone with her. This was my baby. My beautiful little baby. I pick her up and sit in the chair. I rock her. There is a rush of emotions. For once an ecstatic joy, blends with excitement and rushes over me. I squeeze her. She coos at me mouthing her hand. I place her back down in her crib. I drag my oxygen cord around to where the tiny sink and fridge are. I prep her a bottle.

As it heats in the bottle warmer, I put my attention back on Meadow. I slowly unbutton her cute little outfit. I take her temperature. Then I change her diaper. I check the leads, fix the pulse oximeter and redress her. The bottle warmer dings.

I take the warm bottle, and quickly set up a space for feeding. I pull her back out. We lock eyes. I smile. I sing my favorite lullaby. It catches in my throat as my mind wonders to other littles sleeping in their beds without me.

I hold her tightly in my arms. Long after she dozes off. I don't want to fall asleep in the chair without help. So, as tiredness finally takes me over, I gently get up with her in my arms. Rocking and humming I lay her down. Then I snug up her little swaddler. It is simple, but I'm doing it, and alone. I didn't even bring my walker.

I don't take any meds that might make me drowsy or disoriented. I lay in bed all night watching her sleep. I am watching the monitor. I can't stop staring at the numbers and the lines. It's hypnotic. I set my alarm and rise up to feed her. In the middle of the night the main nurse comes in and checks her out. I proudly point out how much she has eaten.

In the morning with the help of the day nurse I change her diaper and outfit. Mom comes in. As if in celebration Meadow pulls out her feeding tube. The nurse wants to put it back in. I refuse to let them this time. We have done it. We made the quota with feeds. Mary Anne stops by to see how we are all doing. Mom and her have a nice chat while I mainly focus my little Meadow.

Brown Matted Dragon

Brown Matted dragon with the shiny red wings.
I have watched you every day.
I hoped you would get a home.
I imagined a little boy falling in love with you and
carrying you away.
He would hold you in his heart for years,
maybe you would see grandkids.
I came in every couple of days
to rummage through puzzles, DVD's and coloring books.
I would stop for a moment to run my hand over your
green felted spiky back.
Toys were there for kids to take
to ease pains and heart ache.
Lots of bears, dolls, and a few exotic animals like ostriches.
All of them coming and going.
You sat there hardly moving at all.
Did nobody want the matted brown dragon with the red
shinny wings?
As time fades on
you never slumped.
You always waited
with one beaded eye on the door.
At last I granted you the gift you wanted.
I took you in my hands.
I had already taken you in my heart.
I stuffed you in my bag and away you went,
with me to the NICU.
I gave you the job of protecting my most valuable treasure.
Brown matted dragon.
You never let me down.
You never slumped or looked away.
For that I give you a special spot on my shelf, and in my heart.
My kids will love and play with you.
I will see to it that you are well taken care of.
Maybe even grandchildren will hold you.

Catch and Release

March 11th, 2014 her due date. The waiting game again. I fidget with her coming home outfit. A mishmash of colors. She is wearing rainbow socks that go up to her thighs. A cute dark blue onesie, a pink coat, and the cutest little white knit hat with two bear ears.

The nurse is back with my paperwork finally. I have to make a pediatric visit next. I don't have a cell phone, so she lets me use the nurse's phone. It feels like forever to get through and set the appointment. I get it done, and the nurse is finally happy.

Meadow is eating. She passed her car seat test, with a small nudge from me. I have jumped through all of my hoops. The discharge paperwork is massive. We don't have a lot of stuff to take home as we have been doing that slowly over the last couple of days. The nurse follows us to the main door. She gives Meadow an RSV vaccination. She gives us all hugs and wishes us well.

Fitting her in her car seat on the bus was as interesting as the first time we brought my walker on the bus. As soon as we are home I charge through the main door, and into our room. This is my little. My precious gift.

"Kyron, watch her for me." I say as I finish hooking up her oxygen tank. Two cords will be winding around the room. I know that this is going to get crazy really quick.

I shower to get all the hospital off. When I come out of the bathroom Kyron is still in the same spot on the edge of the bed in the same position as when I left. He is literally watching her. Meadow is asleep in her car seat. I laugh.

I make the perfect bath for Meadow. I get her a new outfit all set up, and towels. I pull off all of her clothes, and then gently place her in the bathtub.

I count and wash ten cute little toes. Her chubby body. She looks up at me with her dark blue eyes. Ten cute little fingers. Two tiny chins. She still only weighs in at 7 pounds. I play with her hair and rub her little head. It still looks as though she is going to be a blonde.

I call Mom in to get her for me. It will take me a moment to get off the floor by myself. Doing that with a slick wet baby is a laughing matter. Mom smiles as she picks up Meadow and wraps her in a warm towel. She places her on the bed for me. I dry her off and dress her. Two new sticky patches to hold her oxygen safely in place.

She wakes to eat. We are all slowly sinking into a new rhythm. We take turns feeding her at night. We go out for walks in the fresh air. It's heaven. I put her in the wrap that Mom bought me to take her up to dinner. I still need to rest here, and there but at least I'm walker free. After a week and two pediatric visits Jewell and I think it's safe for a visit.

The familiar lights of the Jeep come into focus. They turn into the cramped parking lot. I run out. The stars are singing. Alive is the air as it ruffles my hair. I hear the doors creak, and out they come. With no regard for anything they bolt toward me. In the dark without shoes. They run for me.

Lotus collides with me first. She jumps right into my arms. She has grown, and the new weight almost catches me off balance. Her arms around my neck clutching. She buries her face deep into my neck and begins to cry. Rayne is around my middle squeezing and crying. I wrapped an arm around her. I'm weeping and shaking. My nose finds their hair earthy, and soft.

We exchange wet kisses. Louts finally let's go. Jewell who has held back embraces me so hard I feel all my pieces come back together. She kisses me. I bury my head in her shoulder and breathe deeply. I snuggle into the scratchy crux of jawbone and neck.

Mom has come out. She grabs my hand. I must be turning blue again. I am escorted back to my room. I sit and breathe while the kids eagerly say hi to their new sister. Mom runs them a bath. Jewell gathers some clothes for the night. They all have to fully scrub and change, before I will allow her to be held.

The room is cramped to the max. Four adults, and three kids all lay together talking and laughing. I snuggle next to Jewell on the floor with Rayne on the other side of me. Lotus, Meadow, and Mom sleep on the bed. Kyron has his own bed.

The next morning the Ronald McDonald House is having some

kind of party. It's almost seems perfectly timed just for us. Marty and Cindy have come to join us and share in the festivities.

They offer free family photos. I feel so proud to have all my children here. A family photo with the newest member of our family. Even still on oxygen she is the cutest thing ever.

We don't take her out of the room for more than the pictures. Mom stays with her, so I can get some one on one time with the two other girls. The front room is crammed with people. There are fake tattoos, which I get one for Lotus and Rayne. Then we stand in the line for face painting. The girls play in the playroom and run around outside. Keeping up is impossible. I don't care. I'm so happy I can finally be with them.

We eat corned beef and hash for the fourth time that week. It's hard but manageable, and they did a good job on it this time. There are green cupcakes. Finally, Cindy and Marty say goodbye. It feels like longer goodbye. I may not see them for a while.

Lotus and Rayne dog pile on top of me while we watch a movie. They will not let me out of there sight for one moment. They enjoy Meadow. Rayne and Lotus both carefully take turns holding her and snuggling up to her.

The next morning Jewell wants to take me alone around Aurora. I take my extra tank just in case. It is comforting being in my old car again. Old habits lead us to a nice thrift store. We always enjoyed clothes shopping there. I am slightly more independent now. At least she doesn't have to half drag me to a cart. My walking is still very slow, wobbly, and lefty still lacks control.

We thump through the dresses and skirts. I pick some new things out for myself. I get a new purse as mine had disappeared somewhere in the crazy accident. Mom is carrying the only two items I have right now. My driver's license that Jewell gave her while I was in a coma, and my used gift card.

We talk about ideas of what we should do. It seems that they want the baby to stay here in Denver for a while longer for pediatric appointments. I know that if we did go back to my home there won't be the kind of care we can get here. I want to make sure she is completely stable and growing normally before coming back to the farm.

The thought of being here until April grates on me. Mom agrees. We still don't know where Kyron is going to land. He was in a group home when Mom took him out. Mom will not be able take him, because she is going to live with her mom once I can prove independent. That is Mom's plans until she can finally get a place of her own. Kyron refuses to live my rugged farm life. I guess being an hour away from a normal city is too frightening. Everything is still a tangled mess with delicate immune systems in the balance.

Lotus has gained a cough. It comes on quickly with a runny nose. Here in this small cramped room. She is sick, and Rayne is following right behind her. What am I supposed to do? I bark at her to get away from the baby. The ice in my voice is sharp against my own skin.

I had them. I had them all in my arms. Now Jewell is packing. She has brought me some clothes. She left me with the suitcase. She left me with my favorite comforter. She left me. She left me in haste, so as not to get Meadow sick. She left me. I knew it was coming, but it is too much like the last time I saw her in the hospital. She left me. She left me.

My arms are empty as I watch the red of the taillights fade into the dark again. Five hours away from me. I won't see them again for another 2-3 weeks. My babies, and my family severed again. God, I didn't think it would hurt this much.

Now I'm alone. I sit in the living room tucked away from everyone crying. I know it is for the best, but time had gone to fast. The ache is almost unbearable. The unknowing future. This painful tangle that never seems to end.

I wake up coughing. I have a runny nose. My lungs hurt. It almost drops me too my knees to sneeze. Hugging myself hard seems to lessen the pain. Mom is slower in catching this bug, but I can see it in her eyes; it's catching up to her.

We have to handle the baby. Her nose is dripping too. I hear Meadow cough in the middle of the night. Her feeding is slowly dropping. I sit her up, and I try and try until we are both exhausted. She isn't eating. The sucky bulb, vitamins, nothing is working. I can't stimulate her to latch. She is too lethargic.

I have Mom watch Meadow breathe with me. Her ribs are pulling in hard. Her nostrils are flaring. The coughing is horrible. I reach into my green diaper bag and pull out my nurse number.

The lady on the other end answers. I am in a daze as I explain my situation. She gives me some things to look for: flaring nostrils, and the pulling in of ribs. Indeed, Meadow isn't breathing right.

I buckle her into her car seat. I tuck lots of blankets around her. It's a bitter night. The Jeep Mom has is barely legal for the car seat. We drive past the University Colorado Hospital. I am half tempted to take her there. I know that it's just a fantasy that I could put her back in Mary Anne's arms. We are told to go the Children's Hospital of

Colorado. The E.R. is warm and inviting. The germs, and the thought of her getting sicker and sicker makes my skin crawl.

We are herded into a small room. The floor is sticky. Everything feels so dirty. The nurse is kind and looks her over quickly. It involves stripping her down. We get admitted to the hospital. We wait in one of their tiny rooms while for a doctor to make the final call.

The nurses wear awesome cartoon shirts and are full of bright happiness. I wish my hospital was cool like this. I tell them I am on oxygen, and I can't just sit here. The nurse hooks me up to the wall.

I call Jewell crying. Its March 23rd, her birthday. I want her to feel my pain. I am hurting beyond words. More than the hard and tiny chair I am stuck sitting on. More than the resurfacing of my trauma. I want her to be with me.

Still we wait. The clock ticks on for an eternity. Finally, the doctor comes in. She tells us to strip her down again. With her cold stethoscope she listens for a while. With a pained look she tells us it's RSV. She needs to be hospitalized. My heart sinks. I hold back the urge to puke.

She tells me that she is going to get a NICU room set up for us, and we have to wait it out a little longer. I dress her slowly as she leaves the room. I hug and hold Meadow. As time ticks by I try in vain to feed her again.

We arrived at the children's hospital around 8pm. It's now going on 2am, by the time they are ready for us. I'm expecting a crib to come rolling in, but it's a bed. It looks like an adult bed, or at least one that could fit me easily enough.

They instruct me to sit on there and hold her. I clutch her to me as we begin a new labyrinth. Into an elevator up and up we go. This way. That way. Finally, we stop. This hospital is different. The NICU here is just like my ICU unit. Separate rooms for all the babies. All behind sliding glass doors.

Ours is very small. There is a fancy crib with a heat lamp for her. They strip off all of her clothes, measure, weigh, and listen to her heart and lungs as usual. They give her and surprisingly me a hospital band. Then the nurse wraps her up in a tight blanket. She is sleeping. Gurgling as she does. The nurse offers me the couch. I can't stay. I am worried I will get her sicker. Plus, I'm on an oxygen tank that is running very low.

They explain how to get out of here. It doesn't help at all. We are so disoriented, and tired we wander around for a while before finding a way out. I mark the way with things that stick in my mind. For instance, a large aquarium is in the new waiting room. I step out and get dizzy. The barrier between us and the stories below us are a glass half wall. To make matters worse there is an all glass elevator. I step on and close my eyes as tight as I can. This is torture on top of torture.

On the ground floor, I still try to piece together a route to her. I am still collecting little things in my mind to trigger my memory later. We still don't have any idea how to even get back to the Jeep. We creep along the white walls silent, until we find signs that lead us back to the E.R. Finally, we step out into the blasting cold air. Mom helps load the empty car seat, the diaper bag, and me into the Jeep.

My baby is gone again. The fight begins again. I feel like I am being thrown backward. Red rover, red rover, has just fenced lined me. We are silent as the Jeep pulls out of the hospital, and winds back to the place we now call home.

Its dead silent. We quietly stumble to our room and close the heavy door slowly, so it won't slam. I stand in the room empty and lost. I put the car seat in the closet slowly like I am letting her go again. I lean into the cold wall. I cannot even cry right now. I feel Mom hooking me up to my main oxygen condenser.

There are unclean bottles on the counter, and old milk I have to now throw out. I wind up her oxygen cord untangling it from mine. Then I turn it off. I turn off my feeding alarms.

We curl up in bed. I fall asleep. My nose runs. I have a fever raging my body. Our eyes are puffy. I'm catching the cold. Sneezing hurts like hell. After what I had just went through this simple cold is utter terror to me. I awake coughing. I hug myself as I sneeze or cough to ease the pain. I try to keep positive.

This is hell. I lay in bed gathering all my strength. I need to see her. I need her to know that I have not abandoned her.

I stumble out of bed. Mom is moving as deliriously slow as I am. Hardly any words are passed between us as we ready to go see her again. I brush my hair and feel the new band slid down my wrist. Its glossy and orange with strong black letters. I was told not to cut it off for any reason. A new handcuff.

I know fair well what could be worse than this. It's another maze. Another fight. It unfurls like a nightmare. One with nicer private rooms, and nurses demanding much more from us. I am holding her now with a mask a trying to keep her away from my clothing as much as possible. Now, I am also fighting against the restraints of my oxygen tank because they won't let me hook up to oxygen here. I need proof from the doctor. I will fix it on my next doctors visit.

We have full blown come down with this monster. I'm restless, but I know I shouldn't be around her right now. We watch movies and try to sleep. The nurse calls us wondering where we are. I tell her I cannot come in right now because I'm sick. She seems impatient with me. I half hang up on her. I lay back down and let the world spin.

After a couple of days, we go in to find her gone. I panic. The nurse simply tells me she has been moved. They didn't tell me, and I feel an angry rage welling up inside me as I stomp off in my fuzzy blue house slippers dragging my oxygen tank alongside.

"Wrong way." Mom says. "Wrong way again."

I mumble every swear word my foggy brain can think of. I continue on following Mom this time. Finally, we make it to her new room. She has graduated to a crib.

A real crib. Its metal and white. The long side facing me drops. The tiny mattress crinkles. I use the hand sanitizer and mask up for her safety. Every nurse that comes in here has to come in with a yellow scrub cover, and a mask. I vaguely remember them in my ICU unit. I also see to my horror its back: her feeding tube.

The nurse says they are giving her a break from eating. I drag her over to a very comfy chair. Mom has taken over the couch for now. There is also a TV. It feels very personable. I cuddle up on the chair with her. It lifts up so that I can fully stretch out. Like old habit I fall asleep with her. My baby. My little miracle. An hour or so later I wake. Mom can't kick me over here.

I am not allowed on the couch to sleep with her which seems odd, but I guess understandable. She smiles in her sleep, and I melt. I see pink gums flash up at me as her little rib cage rises and falls. This is her normal. She is comfy here. It is okay. We are going to be okay.

I glance at Mom. She is fiddling on her phone. She looks tired. So, tired. She has also gained many gray hairs.

I wonder if we are going to get out of here by the middle of April at least. The thought of three weeks of this. I look at her. I wish I could take this pain away.

"Are you okay?" She looks up from her phone having noticed me staring.

"Just tired."

"I know. You have cussed out everything that has so much as looked at you today."

"I'm sorry. I don't mean to be such a jerk."

"We'll get through it. We have made it this far, right?"

I smile and nod. I tuck the blanket back around Meadow. She

would be a newborn right now, had everything been normal. I wouldn't know that the black lead is on the right the white on the left and the green on her belly. I wouldn't know how to change her pulse oximeter. My worst concerns were never about teaching a baby to eat or watching her turn blue in my arms.

She is gone again. What is with them moving her around so much. Another week has passed. This room is kind of cramped. The hospitals new rhythm is becoming natural to us. The rules are quick to learn. For example, when you see a group of life flighters flying down the halls you duck, run, and get out of the way as fast as humanly possible.

There is a room for families to decompress. I have bumped into a lot of the mothers at Ronald McDonald here. It has an awesome machine that has a large selection of yummy drinks. You just pop in a small bag. In a moment you have hot coco, or coffee. In my case hot coco with lots of sugar. They also keep a fridge full of snacks.

After our two-week mark here, Meadow is cleared of RSV. They bring in a sweet treat for her. A super comfortable baby swing. She loves to spend lots of enjoyable time in there. It helps pass the time as we get through their hurdles to bring her home. They include the car seat test, that I can mix and warm formula, and the biggest one of all teaching her how to eat again. She again has to eat so much in a 24-hour period.

She has turned blue in my arms. I again freeze in terror. I hear the scream of bells the squeak of many nurses' shoes. Her main nurse has whisked her away and is bagging her. The other nurses are waiting pressed against the wall waiting.

The bells stop. The bells stop. The other nurses leave. My nurse still bags her. I get up and go over to her. The nurse smiles at me. She tells me that it happens with preemies, and we will have to resume trying to feed her tomorrow. She tucks the blanket around her, touches my shoulder for comfort, and fades into the hall.

Where is Mom in all this chaos? She had retreated to the couch. She looks as spooked as I do. I continue to watch her sleep. After a long painful moment of watching her breathe I motion to Mom that we should probably go for now.

We pack up our things, and I disconnect my oxygen from the wall. She picks up my tank for me. I take her other hand and give her a grounding squeeze. I feel her wristband. They gifted her one after she barked about it. I don't blame her one bit. She deserved that wrist band. The right to go see Meadow anytime was a right she had to fight for.

In the beginning days when I was in the coma, she had to sneak in.

Sometimes she would get kicked out. No matter what nothing kept her away. She fought like hell for this. I heard it was a rough couple of days until Jewell sent a copy of his license and released the right to let Mom see her.

Back on the bus. Back to the Ronald McDonald. Its lunchtime. We go up to the second floor to find some leftovers. We respect anyone's stuff that is marked. Anything not marked is free game. We don't have time to grocery shop, let alone the money for food. They offer one good meal here. Mostly dinners. At least we can get one hot meal. The rest we make up with leftovers and donations. We don't eat much as it is.

I have found a box of mac and cheese. As we are leaving, we meet two beautiful Vietnamese women. A mother and daughter team no doubt. We chat with them as they make their lunch. I lose concentration and wander over to the soda machine. I fish out a quarter and get my favorite soda to fall with a satisfying cluck.

When I come back the food smell is amazing. We smile and say goodbye. They want to share what they made with us. We feel flattered, but don't want to impose. They insist, and before we know what to do they hand us each a bowl of amazing noodles and veggies.

Sadly, they can't sit with us as they have a baby in the NICU as well. We sit eating in silence. I stare at the Helicopter pad. If I had any idea of what was going to happen. That I would still be here in April staring the very spot I landed in December. It still causes terror in me to even look at it. My stomach clenches at this simple landing strip. If it wasn't for them, I would be dead.

It was such a delicate dance. Beautifully orchestrated and carried out. I can't imagine how that many people managed to work together to keep me alive. Now the dance is hopefully in its last scene, and Meadow will catch on to eating quicker.

She is in my arms sleeping and smiling her newborn gummy smiles. There are so many differences between her and my full-term babies. Her body is not all scrunched up like she had long outgrown her surroundings. She doesn't suck her tongue in her sleep. She doesn't root for milk from me.

Her eyes brighten up when she sees me. She loves our snuggly times. I am strong enough now that dressing her is getting more enjoyable. I got her some cute rainbow leg warmers and purple dinosaur socks from the gift shop.

Once we get past the RSV, they manage to wean her off oxygen at last. That really makes dressing her a lot more fun. I also know how to attach leads. The nurses now trust me enough to unplug her at the main computer, so I can sit with her on the couch.

It is wonderful to see my little baby now only with that feeding tube. It feels good to hold her, and not think of all the stupid wires, and beeping noises. We are so close to getting out for good.

The main focus is eating. Meadow is on Zofran, because her eating is met with a lot of gas and constipation, and it also comes up as reflux. They switched formulas back to the one that was too much lactose. She needs the one that had less lactose, because I'm also lactose intolerant. Many doctors don't believe in lactose intolerance. So, I have to fight with them on changing the formula.

I wait for them. They are making their rounds at the room next door. When they creep up to my room, I pull off my oxygen cannula, to meet them face to face.

I tell them that I want her switched to my preferred formula. They agree if we get her a swallow study done. I agree. Between the both of us, doctor and mother; we slowly start to get somewhere.

Swallow study shows at least that she does not have stridor. We have to just keep at it. The change in formula does greatly reduce gas and spit up. Out of the blue she finally starts catching on.

She starts responding to the bottle quicker this time. More and more every day. It's exciting to us. Then she pulls her feeding tube. They want it to put in immediately. I demand a little bit of tough love. I want her to get hungry. I feel she had no real reason for eating because at the end of it all she still gets a full belly.

I stay the night with her to make sure nobody tries to put it back in. I stay awake until 2am when my body finally gives out. I hear the swishing of starchy fabrics. I open my eyes to slits. Out of them I see the nurse rocking and feeding the baby. No tube. Meadow eats hungrily for her. I doze back off. I rise at 6am or earlier for another feeding. This is what we need.

She is taking her feeds. We are making progress in leaps and bounds. They don't have to put it back in as long as she keeps on this road. We on the other hand have to pass all our tests again. The I can mix formula test is easy. Meadow's car seat test. She does better this time. I don't have to nudge her.

We are slowly getting ready to spring out of the Ronald McDonald as soon as she is released. Everyone decides that going back to the farm is best. There is no way I can make a new start of any kind in this condition. Meadow and I's immune system are still too weak.

Most importantly it is home. It is where I had Lotus and raised my babies for five solid years. It will feel so good to be back on the farm with the family together again. To get my life back again.

Kyron doesn't want to come to the farm with us. There is no way he wants anything to do with the rural life. Thankfully for him he has family support in Arizona. I hug him and thank him for his support. Mom takes him to a bus station. They are going to help him find a place and get him situated in his new chapter of life.

The room is quiet. It is finally pitch black at night. I need this right now. This quiet healing time. The outside world awaits me. I am scared, but I most of all don't want to stay here.

I think it's time I weaned down on some of the meds. I am alone. I am hiding in the laundry mat. I don't remember what I did, except that I yelled at Mom. I don't know why. I just got frustrated. I think one medication is making me more aggressive than I should be. I know she is crying in the room. I didn't mean it. I still feel like a monster.

I gather my clothes and face the music. I apologize. Her face is puffy, but she smiles and reminds me of dinner. She needs a break too. She needs to put this behind her as well. We are all tired. One thing I got to give her credit for is the fact that she is going to come to the land with me, to help me for as long as she can. After all I put her through, she never gives up on me.

After we eat, we decide to take a night run in the Jeep to see our baby. The air and the stars are so refreshing. Nighttime in the hospital is quiet and peaceful. The lights are dimmer. There are a lot less people.

Meadows evening nurse is a sweet guy who looks more like someone's very fit grandpa. I scoot some of the little toys the nurses are letting her explore and play with, so I can change her diaper. I stare into her eyes. I play with her hair.

In the morning, the cute red dragon I left with her has its own pillow and is tucked in beside Meadow. The nurse confirmed for me last night that he was indeed a busy grandpa with lots of little grandkids to keep him on his feet. He was sweet, and I might not see him again.

Easter is around the bend. April 20th, to be exact. I want her out by then. She is eating like a baby should, and we have passed all our tests. The doctors agree. We finally begin the finishing touches on leaving.

April 19th, 2014. They let us leave. The day before Easter. We pack everything and load it in one of their cute little red wagons. This time we put her car seat in there. Along with my diaper bag, and all her cute stufties. We are ready. We are done with this. No matter how scary reentry is going to be I am completely done with hospitals, and not being in my own house.

The waiting game again. Me sitting there fidgeting with her cute little leave the hospital outfit. The nurse comes in. She gives me instructions, and lots more paperwork. I tuck it in the diaper bag. The nurse puts Meadow in her car seat checking the straps again for me. Then she hugs us. Mom picks up the handle to the wagon, and we trace our way out. Out of the labyrinth. The sun is much warmer. I feel like I am coming out of the nightmare finally.

We pack as much as we can for the rest of the day. Thanks to the nurses I have: a nursing pillow, bottles, diapers, and outfits. I have everything I need to give her a bath. A couple of friends mailed me small boxes of clothes, and gift cards. I bought a little bouncy chair, some clothes, her night baby wraps, and a diaper bag. Mom bought me a Moby wrap to carry Meadow in, blankets, and portable bed for her. We have the free car seat. I have a couple months' worth of formula.

Jewell and the other two kids are here by late night. We don't say much. We are all just focused on one goal, and one goal alone: leave. Jewell holds Meadow and feeds her. It's as if they have never been apart.

In the morning, the girls open Easter baskets. There is toys and chocolate for them to enjoy. There is no time for egg hunts or even Easter diner. Everything is thrown into Mom's Jeep or mine. This day is a rebirth in its own right.

Me being on oxygen isn't so easy. I have managed to graduate to one litter which helps. About three days ago I had an oxygen person come over and set me up for the trip. There are lots of tanks. Some went into Mom's vehicle. Some went into mine. It is going to be a five-hour trip. I want extra in case we get hung up in traffic or lose a tire.

Jewell had researched on her end of the trip. I will be set up on condensed liquid oxygen because we are on solar power. Someone will have to come to refill my tank twice a month. I will have a smaller condenser that I will just carry around with me. This is my last fight with the big bulky tanks.

Everything is set. Meadow is fed once more, burped and changed. I lay her gently in her car seat. Jewell balks about how tight the straps are. I reassure her its where it needs to be. Rayne hugs me, and gets in. Lotus is so excited she can hardly hold still long enough for Jewell to buckle her in.

I am in now. I can smell hay, and dust. I buckle. Jewell climbs in the car. We drive out of the parking lot, and onto a main road. Mom's yellow Wrangler is always behind us as we wind our way out of the city. We have found the highway, and we are now moving even faster away from Denver. I reach behind me and hold hands with Rayne.

Meadow is asleep. I watch for a few moments making sure her breathing is normal. Then I extend a hand to Lotus. It won't be long, and the car will rock her to sleep as well. Jewell reaches over and rubs my head. Finally, together. Finally, free. Blessed and ever so grateful, but I need to get back home. To be with my babies.

After a couple of hours, we decide to stop, and get something to snack on. We go into a tiny little general store. I get some weird looks with my blue fuzzy slippers, and oxygen tank in a cute dolly trailing behind me. Jewell has Meadow. Lotus is all over the place, while Rayne eyeballs anyone that gets in my space. Just like old times old habits die hard. Same old choices of snacks. We get energy drinks, for us, soda for the kids, and chips.

I hand sanitize and make the girls do the same. I switch tanks. We care for Meadow making sure she is doing fine. Which she is. I'm just in hyper protective mode. I snap her back in, while Jewell wrangles Lotus. Rayne is going to ride the rest of the way with Mom.

The scenery is now familiar territory. I do what I can to pass the time. I look over long and hard at Jewell. She takes my hand in hers and squeezes it.

I ask her where she went for that phantom hour in the hospital. She ignores me. There is more to it than food. I can see it in her eyes. I change the subject to the new baby goats. She opens back up and begins to talk again.

The last hour finally ticks by. I see our town come into view. Two new stores, but not much seems to have changed. It's warm and there is no snow. Onto the old highway. Its bumpy and rough as usual. At last we hit the old familiar dirt road.

Dirt

I clicked my nails.
Slick black and long they clicked to the rhythm
of a song. The bridge
tying it all together for me to witness
the visions of things I can never be tears
me down. I turn it off and fade to sleep.

I know they can't sleep.
They saw the dirt under my nails.
Why I tear
everything down to the rhythm
of intoxication's call. They all witness
the crumbling bridges.

I will suffer the burn as I waltz on the bridge
of intoxication. I am a zombie in a sleep
in a tangle of witness's
watching me drive the nails
in my coffin; to the rhythm
of my tears.

I let the tears
fall as I dance on the bridge,
to the rhythm
of the call of sleep
the desire to drive the nails
deeper in with me as my witness.

My bony fingers draw out confessions. I witness
alone the bruises and tears.
I drag my nails
slowly down another as I sit on the bridge
of intoxication, trying not to fall asleep.
I dance to the rhythm.

What is real and what is the difference of rhythm,
between the beat of healing, be my witness.
I fought against the urge to sleep.
All the boundaries have blurred. There are tears
that run in little black rivers like the ashes of the bridges.
I halted the hammering of nails.

As the world sleeps, I sway to the rhythm.
My nails keeping time as I witness
The tearing down of my bridge.

Moon, Stars, and Oxygen Cords

Ashes to ashes. Dust to dust. Life is the question. Death is the must. It is four months since I sat pregnant, cold, and out of breath. It was the dead of winter. My breath small as it was left frozen crystals against the window.

Now, I am soaking in the dry snow free land coming alive with spring. The earthy smell as the sun slowly shakes everything awake. The puppies that Coon had while I was in Bullhead have grown to full size. Spot himself never got to greet me. I feel a deep sadness to hear that he got hit by a car. Goats have three-month old babies.

As soon as my door opens to this once familiar landscape, the herd queen, a four-year old black Lamancha goat named Coal, immediately comes to me. She inhales me deeply, and looks into my eyes as if saying, where were you? I reach out to comfort her. I run a hand over her soft muzzle, as she eyeballs me.

I open the front door. The Christmas tree is long gone. It is a little messy, and unorganized. Jewell had quickly done everything she could to make the house perfect for my new needs, and the preemie baby in my arms. It's cozy. I am home.

My kitchen is the same. Just the way I would have kept it. Greased cast iron pans on the stove. Dishes left in the dishpan to dry. Bread, cans, cereal are stocked in the pantry. The fridge has plenty to offer. There is plenty of food to last us long enough to adjust without having to go out too soon.

A flower bursting with orange has grown from its tiny green pot on the counter. It has reached up tangled and weaved its way around a wire shelf. It has a tough thick stalk. Some of its leaves are browned in places. I reach out and touch this stranger. I run my finger over its woody stalk, and graze over a leaf.

"You grew it last summer. I kept it alive as a token of you. It's a fighter and survived the winter just like you did." Jewell says.

Everything is almost like it was when I left. It is so comforting, and so disorienting.

Even though I don't need to be carried I do need support up and down the stairs for the first month. After that I learn to lean, and let the wall be my support. If need be, I will sit on my butt and reorient myself. Carrying the baby is still a task left to Mom, Rayne, or Jewell.

I make it upstairs with help from Jewell. I just need someone to balance heavily on while I slowly step my way up there. Our hands intertwine. I look at her worried she won't be patient. She just smiles at me, and her fingers squeeze mine encouragingly. Those same dark blue eyes that I fell in love with eleven years ago. I never thought for one second this is how the pieces would fall.

We did talk about what would happen when she would die. She is almost thirty years older than me. The thought of me going first never entered our minds. If so, it was so fleeting that we never really took it seriously.

Jewell makes sure I am good and steady at the top step before we unlock hands, elbows, shoulders. She goes for the baby. I shuffle winding my cord to the old spot on the couch I call mine.

Rayne is coloring and pretending that she isn't watching me out of the corner of her eye. Lotus is using my walker as a fun scooter buzzing back and forth across the room.

It is as though I had been gone half a day, and Jewell moved all my stuff up in the attic as a joke. No laughing, no just kidding is waiting for me. I'm 4 months later, and in a different galaxy from who I was when I shut that door in December.

I have brought home a preemie baby and two boxes of formula. I at least have the minimal of what I need to care for her. I have lots of support in her care which I am grateful for.

I'm scared the germs are still here. I sit in my living room conflicted. I cry. It's so awkward. I can't be still. Yet, I don't know what to do. I'm tired. I feel as though I have stolen the identity of a little arrogant mother who never thought the proverbial shoe would drop.

Jewell sits next to me. I snuggle into to her as she tries to be a comfort. She can see how restless I am right now.

"Um, I will let you use one of my pillows." Jewell breaks my silence, "And we need to get you a new toothbrush too. I took your pillows, and your toothbrush, and I burned them. I also got rid of the old mattress. The flu had me so freaked out."

I laugh it off. I smile though the tears as I curl up in the same spot I had for years. Jewell hugs, and snuggles the tiny new little. She gladly changes her diaper and feeds her. She stares at Meadow soaking in every little detail.

Mom finds herself a nice little sanctuary. It isn't long before she has marked her spot. She hugs me and snuggles Meadow. I feel she is in as much a shock as I am.

I venture into the attic. Slowly, I crawl up these stairs one at a time. I grab stuff that is mine. I don't have to wonder what she would have done with it had I not survived. We are so intertwined. I doubt she would have done anything more than I am looking at right now. I find a small tattered cardboard box. It's still strong enough for at least one rough ride. I gather what I call mine. I fold up the top and push it down the stairs. Then I follow on my butt.

I make a space I call my own, and quickly cover it in papers, and pencils, and books, and the tangled mess of my headphones. Just the way you know that space is mine. Organized chaos.

Up in the attic I also find games that are hidden away. They are wrapped but untagged. I kind of know who they belong to thanks to the different wrapping paper for each child. I push them down the stairs too.

We have a mini-Christmas right then in April. We dye eggs and hide them around the house as a late Easter. I want to reclaim some of the fun we had missed.

I smile and laugh with everyone. I don't think anyone can see it. The disconnection that still feels like I am in a different dimension yet sitting right next to everyone I love. I can touch, but I want to hold back fearing connection. A part of me still holds raw anger and fear. I want to smash all the windows and break all the dishes. Sometimes I just need to breathe and cry through it. The girls are also dealing with topics that even as adults we struggle through.

I am glad they never got to see me that weak. As I fumbled through the early days with my walker. As I soaked every inch of my feeling in medications, and oxygen. The trauma and grief are still too real. Maybe they did need it. They felt it. The true nature of our impermanence. They dealt with it every single cold and bitter day in January.

The reason why I will never promise to them again that I will be here tomorrow. Lotus has tried to get me to pinky promise I won't leave her. She has seen a glimpse of how false their mother goddess really is. That in reality I never had control. We only think we do, and we parade around with our false powers.

No one except angles have immortality. I was told once that it is through mortality, we can feel love. With immortality we can take each other for granted. Days can flutter by. Hatred can fly freely.

Maybe we are all fallen angels who have freely traded our immortality for the elixir of love. Sometimes sweet and drunken. Sometimes bitter, and painful. Through the experience of love, we gain are immortality back. Through my kids eyes I live on.

Sometimes I stop just to run my fingers through their hair or run my thumb over their cheeks. I hug as much as I can. My communication skills still are weak. I can speak of course, but nonverbal is my strongest points. I have a mash of purrs, coos, and a strange loud trill that I alter for different moods/meanings.

We are all crashing back together in a dance that blends all personalities and perspectives. Our energy's melding and churning in excitement, fear, and unconditional love. I feel we all twirl in and out of this dance as we heal. To pull in and embrace with love and gratitude. Also needing to push out with confusion and grief as it hits. They feel it now with me. Everyone who experienced this, is dancing with me, to the drumbeat of the impermanence of our existence.

I am falling back into my favorite habit of going outside at night after the babies are in bed. The first night I see the moon for what it truly is vast and looming. I missed seeing her every night. Luna is growing brighter and larger. The stars are all dancing prominently in the sky. There is no pollution to block your view. Every night you can see the milky way. I shiver as the air bites at me. I feel that connection, that prickles my skin, and makes me connected to every little thing. God is me. I am not God. I am a temporary fragment flickering away madly like one of those stars.

Here it is. I look around at the pieces of my life that had been thrown in boxes and tucked away. Ta-Da here I am. I move carefully so the anger can't be seen, the fear isn't detected. I slowly put one foot in front of the other.

It looks like another scraggy mountain to climb. This time with three kids in tow that won't let me out of their sight even to pee and shower. I move slowly completely surrendered to time. I put on my best face.

I spit on my hands. I reach up to the sky. I begin the journey. I may have been completely shattered, and glued back together, but the kids still held onto me with the same faith, and same trust as the first day they lay in my arms. I'm always the spearhead pushing the family forward. I set the pace. They don't seem to mind the slow crawl we are going at. At least movement has begun again.

I first concur back my kitchen reorganizing everything. I take note of things that are in there. I make a list of what I need. I season my cast iron skillets. Jewell bought me a new bigger cast-iron Dutch oven with a lid. It is heavier than I can lift. I can now feed more. She bought me jars of different sizes to complete my organizational needs. She also bought me new dishes to brighten up the place.

Mom does the cooking in the beginning, and I slowly fade it into my day. I begin to do what I did before. Sweep the floors daily. Wash the dishes. Read books, and color with the kids.

I organize the kid's clothes. Everyone has grown, and I need to resort their mess. I take away sizes 6-9 of Rayne, and 2-3 of Lotus. I put them in bags for hand me downs. Some of Rayne's shirts, dresses, and pants are now Lotus'. Lotus' baby clothes are washed for Meadow. I brought more clothes from Denver that have their new sizes. I took advantage of the amazing thrift stores while I was up there.

Next, I begin to concur the house. I start to get them into a loose schedule. I slowly reign everyone into a predicable rhythm. I have times for when meals will be done, school will start, and when we will wind down for bed.

In the morning I'm never very good. Even before the accident mornings and I were never a match. It's Jewells time to bond with the baby of the house. I remember back when she would take Rayne, and Lotus out of my arms when they were tiny. Now, it's Meadows special time. Jewell feeds the kids and brings me coffee.

I drink slowly savoring the quiet and working through what needs to be done today. When I am finally ready for the day, I first have to stretch out my stiff legs. After my crazy wobbly dance, I thread my oxygen cord back through the house up the stairs, and to my spot.

The kids will all pile around me with books. I insist they sit with me in the morning and read. They love it as always. I am slower and stumble for once on words. For me personally, it is healing my cognitive and speaking glitches.

I find my binder with all schoolwork for them. Eventually I throw in some math work for review. Slowly we will have all subjects rolling, and we don't need a summer vacation now. The calendar I did in November with new ink and hopes is now useless. I rip it out. I crinkle it up and toss it away. Me in November would have had a kitten to see me do this now.

Lotus needs to wait to start school. Rayne is the one I need to focus on. The trauma she had to endure caused her reading to fall to a Kindergarten level. Her dyslexia has grown into a large looming monster mocking her movements. She has let it grow, until I'm left not knowing if I can unwrap her from its coils.

Rayne is tall and lanky. Finally, growing out of her baby fat. She sits at the very tail end of childhood. When I tucked her into bed the night before I got hospitalized, she was wearing the dog collar she wore every day since she was five. She got it from her first and favorite little goat she raised named Rosy Flower. Now after almost five years I find it under the couch completely forgotten. She gave me the five teeth she had lost since I had been hospitalized. She lost two right before she came to see me, one on Christmas, and the last two as she waited to see if I would make it.

She acts tough like nothing fazes her. She is just like me. Expect with a feminine finesse and poise that I could only dream of. She masks her insecurities with a go getter attitude, and a determination that can block out emotions for a while.

I can see it through her blue and green eyes. You can see it in her body. Her shoulders close in, and her hands start to fidget. I can't sort out what is the normal baby steps into puberty from the sharp pangs of separation anxiety.

She is there close by at all times. Sometimes it causes me awkward dances in an attempt to avoid stepping on toes. The occasionally elbow in the ribs, and misstep on a toe become second nature to me. She watches me. Even when I think I have skillfully adverted her and crept away.

I am heading up the stairs in one of those rare moments alone. I have found new books for another homeschool lesson. I miss a step. Things fall like raindrops raining loudly all around me. I look up for a second on hands and knees, face burning. Just my breath. I think that no one has heard. I reach down to gather all the things that went thump and bump, when above me appears my watcher. With such class she comes over like she was heading this way and just happened to pick up a couple of books as she went. She flashes a smile at me.

I never have to ask. She just knows. I will never have it all together. Maybe I never did. There she is waiting now at the top of the stairs for me to rise back up. Nostrils flare as I fill my lungs. I grab my books, and I stand. Fire and determination pass between us like synapse and nerves. Even though I try to keep the child as a child, and me as the mother, she will not back down. She has earned her place. Therefore, stubborn as two well rooted trees; elbow to elbow we inadvertently intertwine.

She rose as the mother of the house when I was gone. She took a leap of faith, a leap of growth. Her childhood came flooding out squeezed and twisted like a sponge wrung dry. She made hot coco every night just like I showed her: warm the milk, add coco, sugar, and cinnamon. She took care of the wild creature Lotus. She got her dressed and brushed her hair. She helped with dinners. She made sure to turn the lights out at night. She even became a ruthless spider killer. It encumbered her taking care of herself while continuing to grow into a woman.

She thankfully had Jewell. Together they learned to cook. Between the two they tightened the loose threads of the family. There would always be a void if I never came back, but they did a good job of keeping it together.

I decide to clean Rayne's room. She has become a packrat. After just moments I find my old purse. I find pockets of my clothes. Some are hidden under her pillow some are stashed under the bed. I find my makeup, and my jewelry. The last book that we were reading before I fell from grace is right next to her bed.

I can't go any further once I find the book. I break down crying. I leave her room to go outside. Leaning against the fence sobbing uncontrollably I hear the front door close. I try to wipe it away and stand up straighter thinking its Rayne.

Its Jewell. She squeezes me tightly. As she rubs my back, I can hear Lotus playing in her in little world. She is outside playing some wild game with the dogs. Giggles erupt on occasion from the other side of the house. It has finally warmed up.

The May breeze feels nice but still a little cool. The sun is climbing slowly down the mountain out of sight. I feel arms around my waist. Lotus has come to comfort me. I pick her up and hold her tight. She snuggles into my neck, but only for a moment before she wants to play again.

My beautiful Lotus has also grown taller. Her baby fat was gone by three years old. All muscle, and ears. Her face is splashed with freckles and dirt. Brown straight hair that has grown long thanks to Rayne working on it every day. She is all elbows and crusty noses. Lotus now teeters between loving and kindness that encompasses innocence. She has an artistic left hand that creates curves and bumps that I cannot recreate. She mixes colors from a cheap watercolor set onto paper that curls up in response. Her hands also now destroy. They break and shatter to signal frustration.

It's rough sometimes at night. I try to play or read, and yet she flows through my fingers, and into her destructive angry side. She slams her head into the wall. The anxiety burns inside her. Her lip bleeds. I use a tissue to stop the bleeding. I am angry and confused too. We all are.

I pick up the mix of freckles and elbows. I hold her to my heart. She snuggles into my breasts and listens to my heart. Her breathing slows, the tears dry. She places her hand on mine. I smile and tell her she's growing every day. Her fingers stop at my last knuckle. We both have the same tiny hands and long fingers.

I keep calm and flow with them as much as I can. They are my main focus. They still need room to grieve, to be angry, to cry, and hopefully dance with happiness. For the first two months they sat with me while I went to the bathroom and even showered. I could not close the door. They literally would never let me out of their sight.

I have gotten used to Lotus getting up and finding me at night. I try to be tough, but not make too much a deal out of it. She eventually wound it down to twice a week. I would let her sit with me for about thirty minutes, before shooing her off.

My 29th birthday left me feeling really torn. Everybody happily celebrates. It is a major milestone. I feel like I have made a big hurdle. I am also still too raw and aware of what will eventually happen to me.

I was never raised on big birthdays with gifts and parties. I am happy eating carrot cake with cream cheese frosting standing in the kitchen. It seems to be my new favorite spot leaning against the sink. The counter is one piece making an L shape. I like to hang in crux. I think it is comfort of habit and extra support. My favorite gifts are simply everyone taking time to hug me and saying how thankful they are that I am alive. Simple and easy just the way I like it.

The inside is coming together. The house is now running at some sort of a rhythm. Things are organized. The children are all settling the best they can. Jewell and I are reconnecting. Mom has found her niche.

The outside world on the other hand is still a big frightening mess. The first couple of times going into town is too much for me to handle. I take heavy meds and doze as I sit for the 45min ride.

Then we have to unload three kids. Rayne often helps carry my purse, and my tiny oxygen device. Jewell will hold Meadow, until I can put her in my wrap. Lotus can have my free hands.

I must look strange with oxygen, a baby tucked into me, and blue fuzzy slippers. I will brush my hair, but that is always the extent of my grooming routine.

In the store Lotus will flex between touching everything and griping onto me. Rayne holds steady like a bodyguard watching everyone that would come around me. She is always a hare's breath away from me at all times. She is also a master of my body language. She will slowly take over more and more, as I wear out. She helps to direct me in indirect ways.

I want to chase her off and tell her to go play. Go be a kid. I can't hurt her like that. She is too invested in me. I will just have to eventually find things to distract her to gently give her those last years as a child.

Jewell realizes rather quickly that I can't remember most of my neighbors or friends. I have been here for years, so people will come around and say hi. They will state how well I look, and how scared they were for me. Jewell learns to say hi, and their name for me. With luck it will click. My memories will start to come back.

If I am caught alone when someone approaches me, I will just have to apologize, and ask for information until I can get it to click. I had some surprised and hurt people, but I can't control it.

It's a small town. The information about my accident leaked directly from the hospital. As Jewell hid out on our mountain alone a few people called him to ask how I was doing.

It was a rather rude shock as no one, but immediate family was supposed to know. It didn't work that way the whole town knew rather quick of the pregnant woman who was life flighted out. Against our wishes we were the talk of the town. Being a small town, we followed the thread directly to a nurse in the hospital. I thought about suing.

Gary would still have the family come over when I was sick. He would make dinner and get updates on me. He understood that we didn't want our information out there, so he kept it to himself. He would help brush the girl's hair and try to support Jewell any way he could. That is all I know.

He won't have anything do with me. I think he feels guilt some way or another. He doesn't know how to deal with me anymore.

It really hurt to have him pass me up in the grocery store. The loud sigh and shaking of his head. I want to talk to him or hit him with my oxygen tank. I want to have closer if that is what we need.

We do need to go to Gary's for the trailer. Jewell needs hay. I pop out just to give him the opportunity to say something. He sees for the first time up close my trachea scar. It freaks him out. He can't make eye contact. I get back in the Jeep and do my best to just let it go.

I lose friends. They don't understand me anymore. I can't hold long conversations. I can't remember past conversations. When I speak to someone my back is better facing them, until I am ready to turn around. I space out back and forth. I forget what people say, and it is still hard for me to grasp a lot of things. I am not good at reading body language.

Communication back is slow. I need time to process. I need time to find words. If I can find the words I am looking for. I often repeat things that I don't remember I have just said. I say things that are scattered and disjointed.

I have one friend who has stuck through it. She even talked to me once or twice when I was in the hospital. Barb is one of the most patient people I have ever met. She has a little boy who is the perfect age to play with both Rayne and Lotus.

As we are sitting around talking, I realize I'm facing away from her. I realize at that moment that I face away from everyone I talk to (excluding the immediate family).

I really don't want to do it. It takes me a moment to find the strength I need. I slowly swivel in my chair. I turn toward her. I take a deep breath, and for a moment meet her eye to eye. I squirm in my chair. She smiles brightly pausing to silently celebrate. I space out on the designs in the wood on the table. When I come back, I notice she is watching me every so calmly. She is smiling and simply waiting for my attention.

The brain fog that I'm still in is still rather stifling. I need to be reminded to do things. I sometimes lose concentration and wander around lost. I'm nowhere near able to drive. I drop dishes and cups full of coffee. By now everyone just accepts it, and me just as I am.

Its June my look back date. This is the time I was looking forward to in ICU. For once I can touch back on where I was when I set this time frame. This is what I was looking forward to in the hospital.

I have a watermelon I am trying to hack at. I still love watermelon. Lotus reaches for a piece with muddy fingers. I shoo her away and point to the sink.

I cut a piece that is safe and seed free for Meadow. She is swinging in the swing we picked up at the thrift store. She loves life. She smiles her toothless smile at me as I place the cold watermelon piece in her mouth holding on to the rest so she can check it out without choking.

Rayne as usual is here helping with something. She hands a piece to Lotus before taking a couple for herself. Jewell comes inside. I make her wash her hands first. She happily grabs a few pieces. When she is done, she puts on a baby backpack and places Meadow in it.

Jewell helps me take walks. With oxygen in hand, and her carrying the baby she gets me outside. We walk our foot paths around the property. It is challenging, but no one minds the pace. My lungs are hard to build up. I sometimes wonder if I will ever get to where I want to be. I push on, and I push harder. I am determined to get off oxygen soon. I also know that I will not be able to do much in the heat of summer.

I'm weaning down on oxygen, but I am still watched to make sure I don't get too tired or spacey. I still drag my cord around with me everywhere. I am leaving it off more and more for light tasks and as I sit on the couch. That seems to be what I do the most is sit on the couch. I snuggle with Meadow. I find little things to keep myself occupied. I'm doing better with reading comprehension as things are coming back.

I decide to try to cook more. It is a propane stove. It sometimes doesn't light without a little bit of help. I have incense sticks that I use. I don't want to use a lighter directly. I use a lighter to light the incense, and while that's lit, I light the stove. It seems safe enough to do while wearing oxygen. No major spark is involved.

I light the incense stick. I realize a terrible mistake is made. Instead of getting the predictable small flame, it explodes into sparks and hisses. I tear off my oxygen, and I dance around the kitchen to the sink to put it out.

I had bought sparklers to celebrate July. Somehow, I had mixed the two together. I jerk my drawer open to look at what I might have done. Mom is still doubled over laughing at my amazing dance skills.

Even after my light show in the kitchen, we still go to see the fireworks. The kids really enjoy the small show they put on in my town. We are finally enjoying warmer weather. It is still not warm enough for Mom.

I know that is what she says, but I know she is done. She needs to go to try to get herself back in order. She helped Dad in his last months. Then she gave me eight months with no questions asked, and no strings attached.

We have delved into the darkest depths together, as she has watched me die. She has helped me grow again from a helpless newborn. She has encouraged me to learn to walk, talk, and breathe again. She has watched as I try to clumsily step back into my role as a mother. She took Meadow on without hesitation. She is just as open and loving for Lotus and Rayne. She has dealt with my rants and anger.

She has wiped tears off me. I squeeze her, but there is nothing I can really say that can explain how I feel.

I miss the yellow Jeep. I know she has her own hurtles. She in her own way will have to re-enter back into her own world. I know this has changed her to her core. We did not even have time to unpack Dads death.

Time slows for no one. The sun arcs even higher in the sky. My right lung fights against the heat. I have a much harder time breathing. I still try to get outside.

I try my best to garden and be with the earth. Jewell buys a nice big pool for Rayne and Lotus to pass the summer in. We take out Meadow's bouncy chair, so she can also enjoy the sun.

It feels so good to feel the dirt in my hands. I can still grow just about anything. I have started too many tomato plants. I try to patch up some of my relationships with friends by offering strong hardy starts. Everyone is very thankful.

Summer is just the way I want it. Everybody growing together. Everybody enjoying the simple things life has to offer. Tomatoes, squash, and lettuce are growing in my garden. Rayne and Lotus work on creating a tree house. Angry chickens dodge baby goats, doggies, and kids as they run and play together kicking up dirt.

I'm Okay

I forgot the sugar in the banana nut bread.
I dropped and broke two new dishes.
I am okay.
I spilled my coffee, shattered the cup.
I forgot where I was driving to.
I am okay.
I lost my balance.
I shut down from you.
I am okay.
I am out of the hospital.
I am all better.
I am okay.
I am scared to close the curtain in the shower.
I am afraid to sleep without my oxygen.
I am okay.
I am overweight and out of shape.
I am okay.
I may wake up screaming.
I may claw at my scars.
I am okay.
I medicate.
I understate.
I am okay.

Dead Sunflowers and Birthday Cake

I fought the war and I won. For now, anyway. The losing card I will someday lay. It haunts me every day. It picks at me. It pins my feet.

I can feel fall in the air. In the morning, the air is sharp. Another cycle of seasons. The impending cold. Another winter creeping closer has me freaked out. I don't know if I can do it. I can't imagine the cold getting worse. Sometimes in the morning it is sharp on my right lung. I have weaned myself off oxygen except at night.

This time it's Jewell who unloops it from around my neck as I sit up. I snuggle into her chest. She rubs my shoulders, and arms. I stare at the wall we put up and painted in another lifetime. She begins to finally tell the tale from her perspective.

The phantom hour where she had disappeared is finally laid bare. As I had originally thought that food would be the last thing on her mind. She had spent that time with God in the chapel praying for me. That was her true nature, and also very understandable that she wouldn't want to share such a private moment.

"Christmas morning, I don't know what happened, but my phone had gone dead overnight. When I got it going again there were a ton of messages on it. I called the Doctor who said that you had died, but they brought you back. They told me that you would probably not survive the night."

"We had a baby girl who was now fighting for her life. She would probably survive. Three girls. Three motherless girls."

"I was so crushed. I pulled my favorite chair over to my window, and I just sat there for hours. Rayne had overheard and she laid in bed. Lotus knew something was up, and she just wandered aimlessly from me to Rayne."

"I opened up a can of soup, but the dogs were the only ones hungry that night. Everyone just cuddled up to me. We slept for over 12 hours."

"I kept the faith that you were going to survive. After a couple of days, I tried to have a Christmas. Rayne got the lion share of the toys though."

"January was a rough month. I honestly believed you were going to make it. You just kept fighting for every moment. I could feel your spirit. I could see it in the kids."

"When you started communicating with us again it was remarkable and relieving. The kids loved every rare second they could get from you."

"I wanted to come up. I honestly tried but the car situation is always so shaky. Also, it was too hard to figure out what to do with the kids. After Louts was so sick, I was leery doing anything with them. I didn't want anyone else getting hospitalized. I also didn't want to traumatize them any further."

"Us getting to meet Meadow was amazing. The kids were so heartbroken that we all couldn't go home together. They just didn't understand."

"I guess everyone made it through ok. I did the best I could to keep everything running smoothly. It's not easy keeping everyone fed, and warm in the winter. The kids were so distraught and freaked. That was the hardest thing to keep reigned in. Their minds, and spirits." She lets out a sigh, and nothing more.

I can tell she is still dealing with what happened. I can also see that her heart is full of guilt and pain. She blames herself. Her pregnant wife got sick, and both child and mother almost died. It eats at her making it tough to processes through what happened.

The past is the past. We could have both done better. We could have both been better. Would it have changed anything? Would that change have been positive?

Maybe I should have got my flu shot. Maybe we should have insulated the house better. Maybe I should have spoken up when I was too cold or too hungry. Maybe nothing would have changed what happened.

Nothing could honestly now change what happened. It's all in the past. The only thing we can do is shape our future by dealing with the present. The me right now is never going to be the me I was last year, and there is no "maybe" that is going to change that.

I don't know if it was on purpose or not, but around September I found the small book that covers all the rules and laws of the road. I read it until I felt that I had relearned most of what I had forgotten.

As soon as I had landed here Jewell had renewed my driver's license for me. With my oxygen restraints, heavy medication, and horrible memory I didn't dare drive. Now with the success of weaning down on all my medications and oxygen I am becoming more grounded. I think my brain has also healed quite a bit. I feel like I can begin the process of starting to drive again. It starts simply, by scooting around the property.

Jewell warns me about a problem spot, and how I need to veer to the right to avoid it. Well, I'm so focused on driving I forget her warning completely. I run right into where the road has washed away. Both front tires hang in midair while the front bumper rests on the other side of the road. Beautifully stuck. Jewell pops me out with her van no problem.

I began to drive around the country roads. Once that feels comfortable, I start to drive into my tiny town. Mainly just the mailbox, and the general store. I can now drive to my therapist, and doctor. Simple and easy.

After a month I finally feel I'm ready to drive myself into the larger town. Jewell will only say yes if I drive with her a couple of times for a safety check. Then I have to let Rayne come with to watch me and navigate when I get lost.

I realize why I still need Rayne at least to help me get around. I still get fatigued easily. I lean against the seat belt and breathe. It took a minute to locate the car. Or, should I say Rayne located it. This is pushing me to the max.

All I have to do today is go to two stores. I am so overwhelmed and tired. I try to caffeinate. I know a quick sugary drink will give me enough energy to get back home. I have to drive the highway safe, because I have Rayne. Another reason she made me take her. So, that I have to be careful.

Rayne knows I'm stressing out. She comforts me with some stupid joke then laughs. I turn to meet her beautiful eyes. I can do this. I have to do this.

"You want to pick up a pizza for home." I say smiling.

I don't even need the happy response. I can see it in her eyes. Fast food is still something we don't do much of, but who can say no to pizza.

She carries the hot boxes to the car, and I follow her. I don't even try to fake that I am not lost. She will know anyway. I just keep the conversation going as she walks us to the car.

We talk about Halloween costumes. It keeps my concentration focused as I drive. I don't have a lot of money, to spend on them. I can tell though that she is okay wearing last year's costume. Lotus still fits hers okay, but Rayne is very much on the border of not being able to fit comfortably. For this year I think it will work just fine.

The only difference is I have another child. Last year Meadow and I fit into a costume together. I was big. It was a stretch, but I made it work. I thought about the quick snapped picture that was taken last year as the sun set. It would have been one of my last two pictures ever taken.

Fear is finally giving way to pride about what I have survived. I start to talk more about it. Late at night when all are sleeping, I can venture to the pictures, and videos that were taken.

I look over at my beautiful new baby bouncing in her favorite pink rocking chair. She is on the cusp of being mobile. She has no teeth yet, so she is allowed to gum my oxygen cord. She drools as she chomps away. I know it's not long before her first teeth come in.

On the couch I sit oxygen hissing. I have music playing to cover the quiet. I talk to Meadow while I crochet. I make hats. Lots of warm winter hats to pass the time, and hopefully rebuild some of my memory. In the mix I have created Meadows simple cute little costume. It is also a beanie, but it looks like a cute caterpillar from a popular kids book.

Rayne who still is always there has also taken up the craft. She has gotten so good that she crochets little animals and toys for herself. I didn't know for almost a month that she is using the stuffing from the couch cushion.

Lotus has immersed herself in music and coloring. It seems to heal her hurt, and it slows down the destruction she can cause. I know it hit her hard, and she has less internalization processes. I wish at times Rayne hadn't internalized so much.

"Come see Momma." Lotus looks at me excited.

Black washable marker in hand she motions me to her. I put my crochet hook and yarn down. I get up, and I stretch my stiff legs. In her room she points to the wall.

"Shadow Man!" She says.

I sigh and decide to tell her it looks great. I will paint the walls again, so it's no big deal. Shadow Man was someone who started coming to her while I was in the hospital. I think it was Dad, as his presence has always been intimidating, and I can see it as scary for her.

Later that night she gets up to pee. I curl up in her bed to wait for her. I lay on her pillow just like she sleeps. I glance at "Shadow Man", and quickly realize she has drawn it perfectly to look like it is coming up from behind her bed from this perspective. Despite the fact that she had drawn it standing next to the wall.

I tuck her in knowing she could have nightmares like me. That she might fall out of bed with a horrible thump. I scoot a couple of large and soft stuffed animals by the side where she sleeps to cushion the thump if it's one of those nights.

I feel Rayne is up again, and I am right. She is lurking in the living room fidgeting with her hands. I make her go back to bed as well. I have a surprise for them and would like them to have a decent night sleep.

In the morning I have them put on their costumes. It's a week before Halloween, but they have the pumpkin patch train. The girls are excited to ride the train again. We haven't had the luxury of a pumpkin patch train in two years.

Beside juggling 3 pumpkins and a baby, with Jewells help, normalcy has pretty much returned. I still don't have energy to do everything. The most important traditions for the holidays I will try for. I'm going to keep it easy and simple.

Trick or Treating is only a couple of blocks. The good thing is with three kids the candy is enough. I still make everyone dump their buckets in a big garbage bag, and we all share the loot. On the occasion that someone gets something they really want in their buckets they can hide it away.

What only Jewell and I know about October is that I have thought long and hard, and I realize that I can't do it again. Three is my number. I know deep down that getting pregnant again would be horrible for my already weakened body. I always wanted my tubes done by thirty. Just the trauma of another pregnancy is not bearable. I have signed the paper and waited the required thirty days. I have been to the consultation.

November 5th, 2014. Somewhere I never want to be I am going again. Into the hospital. They know that I have a real fear, and they treat me with respect. I sit quiet in the small surgery waiting area comfy yet nervous.

The anesthesiologist likes to sing. He sings "Knocking on Heaven's Door" for me to announce he knows my story. I warn him not to panic, because I like to wake up in surgery. When the time comes to wheel me to the operating room, they give me a fast working dose of meds that keep me calm, or I might have jumped right out of that bed. Into the cold surgery room, I go. I can do this. They waste no time in putting the mask over my face and I am out.

When I wake again, I have a nurse sitting beside me. She is laughing at something I realize I had said unconsciously. She is feeding me ice chips as the blurs become shapes, and everything makes sense again. I look at her. She is still giggling. I don't know what I have said, but she feeds me a few more ice chips. Then she asks if I think I can do it myself now.

I nod. Things are still coming into focus. I reach a heavy hand up and grab the cup. I spoon a few more chips into my mouth. This is what I thought coming out of the coma would be like.

After almost an hour has passed, I feel weak but in control. I slowly climb out of bed. I pull on my clothes, as I see Jewell coming with the girls weaving around her.

The nurse wheels me out. Jewell helps me in the Jeep. As soon as she gets in, she rewards me with the best chocolate ice cream I think I've ever eaten. The kids are already worn out. Lotus is dozing off already.

The surgery has me down and weakened for a good two weeks. The worst thing I got out of it was a split lip because the anesthesiologist slipped. Probably because I woke up and he panicked. I am more at peace that this part of my life has come to a close. It is a little bittersweet.

The sunflowers on the side of the road have all lost their petals. They are dead. Dried twisted and frozen, with their heads up toward the sky, begging for one last day.

It is getting colder and colder. The impending winter is daunting. I am lathering my hands in hand sanitizer and showering in hot water when I get home. I am scared. I think I will always be scared.

The air is colder. Sharper than ever on my lungs. As we creep closer to winter, I try not to let my mind wander to deep. Jewell gathers wood, and hay. I try to be apart as much as I can. It feels almost normal. I know I'm no better than one of the kids right now. I am so far away from throwing 80lb bales of hay and splitting wood,

I shiver feeling this coming on. It feels like a giant panic attack. Would I survive this winter? Would I survive a winter five years from now? I get gloves from the dollar store that way I can cover my hands. I also load up on hand sanitizer.

I wipe down a grocery cart thoroughly before even touching. I notice a lady watching me. She sighs semi disgusted.

"Young people don't die of the flu." She states matter-of-factly.

I am enraged, disgusted, and shocked. I let her continue a moment of eyeing me snobbishly. I begin to glare at her, but my mouth is dry. She pushes her cart on her way. I restrain the urge to whack her with mine. It would make no difference anyway.

She is in her tight little safe American bubble. Full of expensive coffee cups, and the illusion that what she has gained in life is hers tell she dies. No one seems to understand that we are all one car crash, one diagnoses, one layoff, one death of a family member or spouse from losing it all. That what we have today we may not have tomorrow. I wish I didn't know this sometimes.

One thing that very little people understand is my body feels more like a cage. The mirror lies in so many ways. I'm honestly my worst enemy. I keep my mind medicated. Less now then the hospital days. I still need it. I hurt. I honestly feel still trapped in a body that still isn't healed enough for me. I understand that the old me isn't coming back, but that doesn't stop the frustration I feel.

I rage more out in the open now. I shatter dishes on purpose. I throw books. I push Jewell away. I have break downs. I also fight to push thoughts of suicide out of my mind on more occasions than I want to admit.

Jewell has to now deal with someone who can fly off the handle at a moment's notice, or someone who would often disassociate. She has to deal with night twitches. She can no longer touch my feet, as we had as a connector all though our years together. She has to deal with me waking up wailing or screaming. I can go back to the ICU any night and be back on ECMO. I can forget I am breathing. A main fear I have is waking up afraid I'm not breathing.

No one can understand me. I fly off the handle so much that I hardly know how to get back there. Back to the calm. I can be nice to you. I can also turn on you in a second. I don't even understand it.

I want to be more in control. So, I go to a therapist for help. I need to learn to control the fears, the nightmares, the spooking, the depression, and the disassociation. I want someone to silence the constant ticking of my mortal clock that I now hear in the dead of night.

She tells me I'm playing into the short-term memory. I am milking my hospital experience. So, I believe her. I really want to. It would make my life easier. Just admit I'm faking it. I'm milking it. All I have to do is let go of the tit.

I make Thanksgiving dinner with this premises. I'm doing just fine. Then, I drop the green bean casserole. After I had made my own mushroom soup. We are an hour away from town. I cannot rectify the mess all over my floor. I can only be happy I didn't burn or cut myself which I do regularly in the kitchen.

Then I piss of Jewell so bad she won't even eat with me. I want her to be with me in the kitchen. I want to talk, and not be alone. Alone is where I land. The kids even turn their noses up at the mess before me.

I undercook the turkey, and I have to put it back in. I burn it. I border line ruin the mash potatoes. They are lumpy and glue like. I burn the stuffing. I forget to make rolls. The gravy completely becomes inedible. This isn't me.

I was a great cook and usually impressed everyone I could get to come over. Everything always came out so good, and right on time with one another. All I did right this time is a sweet potato pie.

I lean against the kitchen sink, and eat a little bit, while crying. Alone is where I landed. This is milking it?

I cut ties with her. She is not the only one, on my list. I cut ties with my doctor who thought I was just riding a good drug. With a three-question survey she deemed me an addict. I was furious. I had proudly weaned myself off so many medications, and down on my opiates. I was doing 6 oxy pills a day out of the hospital. Now that I take one a day, not even every day, she is calling me an addict.

I even wean myself down all the way to nighttime only on my oxygen. I did it without help. From the large brown paper bag to a few bottles a day. They don't know. They never deal with people like me. I am in a small town without even a pediatrician to help me with Meadows development.

Little Miss Meadow has Christmas birthday I need to prepare for. I have snuck into town by myself. At the grocery story I stop to look at the cakes. The lady working at the bakery sees me staring. All the cakes in plastic domes, so cold and pretty. I can smell the sugar. She comes over and asks if I am looking for a birthday cake. I tell her I have a little girl born this month. She noses around as to when. I tell her on Christmas.

"Oh!" she says excited. "A Jesus baby."

Lady, I think behind my smile you have no idea. I fight back tears. I'm falling apart. I try to breathe through it. I don't make any eye contact with her. She pauses watching me. Finally, she decides to leave me be, with a simple I'm here if you need anything.

I sigh and move on. Most of my Christmas shopping is done. I just need some sweets, and knick-knacks as stocking fillers. Maybe a turkey for this Christmas instead of a Ham. If I don't fuck it up again. I want something different. I don't want to have a redo of last year.

I want more meaning and less fluff. Everything I wished for is at home tearing up the place, waiting for pizza. This is my first trip all alone. Jewell finally decided I am safe enough, and understood I wanted some Christmas knick-knacks.

I went online to avoid most crowds. Black Friday. Not a chance. People are still nails on the chalk board to me most of the time. Their eyes. The germs. They push forward so blindly. They want plastic. What they watched on TV. The newest this and that. To be the best gift giver.

I know that I am not the best. I do not desire to be better. When I am dying again no one will be lamenting on the new monitor I couldn't get for Christmas. The kids never cried over not having enough stuff from me. They cried because they did not get enough time with me.

Time that is granted will be savored. I am doing more to revamp the school to be more hands on and fun. With lots of stuff that they want to do. Books to enjoy as they cuddle up with me. Projects that would put us shoulder to shoulder learning and creating.

A geology unit with pretty geodes to break open. Paper airplanes to fold. Fluffy pompom animals to create. All real goods. All more than plastic that will be broken within a few days. It will be small as Jewell hasn't been able to work much with me, and the baby to tend too. Everything is streamlined down. What is important to me is taken in small increments.

Up in the attic just like last year. I am wrapping our small bounty. This time Jewell has insulated and made sure I have enough heat up here. She comes up a few times to make sure I am warm enough.

I have even more fun with my memory issues. I yawn and decide for now that I am done. My concentration is slipping to much right now. I'm just frustrating myself. I still scoot down on my butt. Rayne is not happy I have separated from her for a whole hour. I think she will live.

"What are you doing up there?" She says glaring at me.

"Feeding the snakes. I have dangerous snakes up there right now."

I flop down on the couch and put my oxygen on. I am tired as fuck right now, but I will never give up. I love every moment with my babies. I begin to doze off. I feel Rayne sitting down beside me. I can tell she is crocheting her little thing. I hear Lotus in her room. Jewell has Meadow.

This is new me. Strong as I am pain still overwhelms me. I am slower, and I need this small nap. Nights are hard. Dozing off scares me. I am still afraid I will stop breathing. I am scared to have the dreams swell up and devour me. I am scared to let go. Rayne is here with me now. My strong anchor. I shift slightly so I can touch her. I doze off.

I am never ending surprised how many people prayed for me. So many people would have been impacted by my death. They use me as an example of why pregnant women should get their flu shot at the hospital and clinic. There were numerous people watching me and getting updates on my progress.

The first time I grabbed a hold of my walker and pulled myself up I was doing it only for my family. I was doing it because there was a little girl in the NICU, and two girls who needed a mother who could be strong enough.

I didn't know that anyone cared about this simple homesteading 28-year-old with wood smoked, messy coffee hair, and hazel eyes with little suns around the pupils. As I laid in bed fighting with all I had I couldn't imagine how many people waited with bated breath. I did not think the nurses would internalize my pain as deeply as they did, even as they passed me from hand to hand.

I push on because I have love. The strong love from my mother that pulled me forward. Without her there the shock may have been too much. It also gave me someone to look forward to seeing. I had someone I trusted taking care Meadow. My mother's gentle touch to help in my care. If she had not been there Jewell would have taken over, but that would have completely uprooted the other two children.

My wife still looks at me and shakes her head.

"I cannot believe you made it." She says.

"You died." My family doctor says to me once as she runs a finger over my trach scar. Over a road map most never travel, and even fewer come back from.

I want to tell her yes, and it was lovely.

"You cannot get over that that easy." She continues. "Do you want something to reduce your scaring?"

I shake my head No.

I will carry these badges with pride. They are my proof I have survived. My neck will never be pretty. Right down the center is a puffy pink disorganized scar. There is my beautiful x mark scar at my collar bone where my ECMO was, and three puffy scars up the right side like a ladder rung where they stitched it to my neck. People will stare. I don't give a shit. I am beautiful. A spirit walker. I have felt a fragment of God. A fleeting moment of how small I am.

I know the peace that awaits me. The understanding that I will one day shake off this body, and yet still be so alive. I have learned that I am more than my body. Odd as it feels I understand that this is a temporary vessel for me.

It can be hard not to pull the trigger and push the car just a little too far. I know I will be There again. It was like tasting the best honey ever. I sometimes want to stick my hand back in that jar.

For now, I will enjoy every granted moment with my girls. I pray my thanks every day. I also beg that I die before my children do. I still cannot carry the weight my mother carried around every day in the hospital as her child and grandchild teetered one hairs breath away from a eulogy.

We silently celebrate and mourn my hospitalization date. The morning exactly a year ago that they woke up and found me gone, they came crashing in on me. They must have felt something for I made no mention of it. Rayne against me so tight I can hardly breathe. Lotus on top of me keeping me anchored here. Poor Meadow fighting for her space here too. I pull them all so close. I want to feel all of our heartbeats together.

I have to keep reminding myself of the way it used to be. Full of joy and happiness that the big day is approaching. That is how we are expected to feel this time of year. I need to be careful. I need to use the happy excitement to mask over the building rage, and irritability as December wears on.

This holiday season is a mix of emotions. If I am not wanting to break something; I want to cry. If not that then I am excited to be alive. I am trying not to go into full panic mode, or full rage mode. I want to open my arms, and let the storm take me. I tuck into my coat and learn to weather my storms in more silence. I know I have overdone it taking it out on everyone. This is what it is. Gratefulness has dried up and crusted over.

I look into Jewells eyes; so tired, and still trying so hard. It broke my heart. What she had been though, and I continue to put her through. I place my hand in hers trying to touch at her soul to heal something. Had I broken it all?

"It's like old times, huh?" She says feeling my hand squeezing her.

"I love you." I whisper.

"Love you too." She makes genuine eye contact with me and smiles.

We have a rare day of just the three of us. Meadow sitting in the seat of the grocery cart. The other two children are playing at Barb's house. Jewell and I holding hands gazing at a sale on ice-cream.

The tiny little strawberries on the front beg me to grab it. I look over at Jewell. I can tell she feels the same way. I reach out and grab one. As I place it in my cart, I sense eyes on me.

I look up to see three girls with backpacks, and bibles staring at us. My face goes from instant freeze to curiosity. They take this as an invite and come over to introduce themselves. Their bibles are heavily worn, marked and tagged. They on the other hand all look young and vibrant. Full of life and promise.

They begin chatting about the bible, and how they are concerned with the world. We banter back and forth. They follow us as we shop. They want to baptize us. Crazier than that, we agree, and follow them to a tiny motel.

Meadow goes first. She is my lamb, my sacrifice, and my miracle. Next is Jewell. Finally, it is my turn. Wearing nothing but a white robe I kneel in their bathtub while they pour water on me and recite the bible. It feels so enlivening I have given my heart truly to God. I am truly thankful every day.

Slow and tired as I may be stockings are hung. We screw the Christmas tree into the floor. Not only did we have a baby that was crawling all over, but we have four new kittens. The kids all help hang bulbs and string lights.

It looks as good as its going to. I am truly happy. I wrangle the kids into pretty dresses and brush out their hair. I want to capture this.

I have Jewell take some pictures of me and the girls. I take one of all three girls together. Then I take a picture of each child separately. Lotus and her strong freckly face. She wants remote control car so she can hit her sisters. Meadow is just enamored with the tree itself. Its Rayne's turn. I hold my camera up.

"What do you want for Christmas?" I ask ready to click.

"I have my mom. I am happy." Rayne smiles. Her whole body comes alive.

Choose

I can choose to carry this trauma around.
Wild and unhindered, tight leashed,
ready and rearing to rise and spring.
It will snap and growl at everyone.
I can keep it like a pet to parade around.
I can keep this pain close at hand.
To use when things get rough.
To excuse me from tough situations.
To keep me from being accountable.

I can choose to bury it.
Somewhere deep and wooded.
I know deep inside it will not stay down.
For trauma never dies.
It will claw its way back to the surface
dirty twisted and decaying.
It will come for me,
and never stop its ruthless hunt.

I can place it on a shelf.
After I have molded and shaped it.
A trophy of what I've survived.
Something when gazed upon
that will always fountain up emotions,
and stop my heart for a second.
I can sit with it.
Touch it.
Share it.
Live with it.

The Other Side of the Curtain

Part 1. A Mothers Grief, written by Nancy Blevins.

A mother's grief is silent, alone and very misunderstood. For it is through her own heart she perceives a painful experience that only she knows and only she understands. It is closing in on nearly four years now. Still the holidays arrive and so does the flood of memories. Memories of a time when I became numb. That numbness changed all that I was and used to be. All my perception on life. All that was living that surrounded me. I no longer could perceive me.

I am taken back to the memories of talking to my child. My only daughter on the phone from her hospital bed. She was telling me that they were going to send her out to a larger more advanced hospital, Colorado Springs, Colorado. I told her that I would be on my way. I would be leaving Arizona and heading to Colorado in the coldest month of the year, December.

I did not think there was any real urgency. Speaking with her it just seemed like she had a bad case of bronchitis or pneumonia. It was later confirmed they were flying her out of the Alamosa hospital to Colorado Springs. I only knew that they had more advanced care for a pregnant woman, as sick as she was. I was yet to be told the whole story or even know what was truly going on.

So, I hopped in my old Jeep and left for Colorado Springs, Colorado. I was coming from Prescott, Arizona. I drove all night finally surrendering to the freezing cold and getting a room at 2:30am. I was only able to sleep an hour or so.

I was awake by 4:30am. I sat straight up out of bed in a sheer panic, as if my daughter was calling for me. I gathered everything up and headed back on the highway. I got a call somewhere on the road that they had life flighted her to Denver. That's when I knew things were more serious.

By the time I reached Pueblo I talked to her husband (I, KaDawna, use female pronouns, and her female name Jewell in the book. Nancy has chosen male pronouns and her male name Jimmy.) who said the hospital in Denver was trying to reach him and he could not get through or was able to call. I called and spoke to the head nurse who told me my daughter was in ICU, on life support, and was not expected to live. She requested the family to come. I had her repeat and verify she was indeed on life support and ventilator. I choked back my tears as I called her husband. I told him he had to come and struggled to convince him of the severity. I called my mom who was in Prescott, Arizona and told her. She was on her way immediately.

I drove the next couple of hours into Denver and managed to get to the hospital where my sister was waiting for me. She took me in to see her. There was my beautiful daughter lying in a medically induced coma, paralyzed with tubes, wires, and machines everywhere. I thought to myself, how can this be? I was having a real hard time accepting that she was not expected to live; but they would try to save the baby.

A life for a life so to speak. I felt as if my heart was ripped out of my chest and torn into a million pieces. I could not imagine my life without my daughter. I was afraid of who I would become if I lost her.

I stared down at her lifeless body, numb from how this could be happening. My mind whispering into her sleeping spirit as I am not allowed to touch her.

Sad Faces

Sad faces.
Droop with loss.
Pain in places.
Strangle
Pause....

Mind drifts distance.
Heart pounds to mend.
Within all resistance.
Hand reaching in.
Hand reaching out.
Pause...

Healing my sad face.
In order to,
heal sad faces.
Mending the pain.
Pain in places.
Frozen in smiles,
so, no one knows.
Pause....

Hand reaching in.
Hand reaching out.
Pause...

Will you take it?
    My hand.

I went out and sat in the waiting room in shock and frozen. I glanced around at other families gathering to battle for their loved ones, their child's lives. Pain, dripping into the silence and words are unspoken. For their faith, their hope, is all they have left to cling to.

I sat there as the infectious disease team was running all kinds of tests (38 plus). The Doctors were puzzled how to treat her, because she was pregnant, and they were uncertain of what was now attacking her body. An OB/GYN team kept tabs on the baby's health and prepared to take the baby at a moment's notice. They had the ICU room next to my daughter set up with incubator and emergency baby stuff.

Late in the evening of the 23rd of December Jimmy her husband arrived along with her two girls, Lotus 4 years of age, and Rayne age 9. They clung to me as if they could feel my broken heart. If I could absorb their fear, their pain and confusion I would. Jimmy took the youngest one in to see Mom; Rayne did not want to go.

Afterward Lotus the youngest crawled up on my lap and repeatedly asked "Mommy's dead? Mommy's dead? Mommy's dead?"

I thought I would completely fall apart, but I quickly stuffed the swelling sorrow deep inside, deep in the numbness of the overwhelming pain. I knew I had to take the girls in to see their mom. I could explain. I could give them hope. With love maybe I could erase their fears. I lead them both into mommy's room where she laid hooked up to machines and noises.

I told the girls, "Mommy's sleeping so she can heal and get better. She is just sleeping."

Lotus repeated several times "Mommy's sleeping."

Back in the waiting room my sister was still with me. Jimmy says he is going to see if he can rent a room for the night and leaves. My sister stayed with me, and we slept in the waiting room of the ICU.

By December 24th, Mom had arrived. The family was all there. Before everyone left by the end of the evening there had been no change in her condition. Jimmy was leaving and heading back home with the girls. My mom made him sign a medical release, giving me some medical rights to my daughter.

I was there alone with her, and it was Christmas Eve. The nurses had made up a bed next to my daughter before going to sleep. I sat beside her and read her Christmas stories. Stories of joy so she would not miss Christmas even if she slept through it. Somehow or another every Christmas story I would begin to read aloud and in between all the noises, seemed to go gangster on me. I would stop and try and find another. I wished her a Merry Christmas and let her know I would be by her side. I finally managed to slide into sleep on the makeshift bed beside her.

Christmas morning December 25th, 2013 I am awoken to chaos. There were a team of doctors trying to save my daughter's life. She had flat lined. She was dead. Another team was rushing into the room to take the baby. In shock I grabbed my shoes and phone. I struggled to find my way out of the room telling whoever could hear me: "I am going to the waiting room."

I found my way to the waiting room, which was empty and silent. Everywhere all over the world families gathered with each other. I sat alone opening my phone to call my mom, and my sister to let them know that I believed that my daughter had died.

I know nothing of the baby. They said they were all on their way. My sister was coming from Fort Collins. My mom from Parker. I tried like crazy to reach her husband which proved hopeless.

I went to the bathroom, and when I came out the whole Neonatal crew was pushing a baby quickly down the hall. I ran after them hollering "That's my baby."

One of the head nurses stopped me. I do not really remember what she told me other than it's a girl. She took off running after them.

I sat in the waiting room. They told me they were going to do a heart and lung bypass to see if they could save my daughter. I was devastated, I had no idea the condition of either mother or child other than both were now fighting for their lives. I was fighting to hold it all together.

As I passed by the hospital chapel, my hand clutched the outside of the doorway. My body froze. Frozen not to feel and anger rose then fell into emptiness. I refused to enter. I refused to pray. Struggling to come to terms with a higher power, a God/Goddess. For all the hope that flowed into my veins ceased and faith was no more.

Diminished was my faith, numb and hollow was my soul. I couldn't even think. Time, days, and hours all blurred into one. Now in this hour I waited to know if my daughter was even alive or my new granddaughter. My sister finally arrived, and we searched for someone who could help us find where my daughter was taken. Her ICU room was now empty. No bed, no machines nothing but a lady mopping the floor.

Finally, a male nurse, would take us to see the baby in the NICU, and then take us to a different ICU department where my daughter was taken. Where over the next few months I would battle for two lives. One little girl born at 28.5 weeks and another reborn at 28 years.

My Journey to Prayer

A battle between God and my heart.
Take my child if that is your will.
Bleed out faith, drain thy love.
So, it's I no longer feel.
Empty, cold and harden blood,
leave thus body soulless, numb and still.
Crawl as I might,
under thy rain of prayer's,
for you child, still I fight.
I take a stand if I dare.
Not to drown in thy mighty shower.
Bathing in thy love's glory.
Rejoicing in the healing power.
A miracle, a story.
Written into life by God.

January 18th, 2014

The journey has been long filled with emotions and heartache. Like the scale of Libra, the weight of life and death is held firmly with one hand. In the other hand is held universal doorways scattered like stars waiting for entry. One is to be chosen for the pathway to be set. A timeline recorded. As Libra stands in the shallow waters of the female energies three girls cling to her side waiting for her to choose a doorway.

Once the door is chosen it will create paths and doors for each one of the three girls. Some may be prewritten. Maybe a prerecorded twist set in stone before their entry into the third dimensional world. Along with the mother as their vessel, and the spirits to embrace while on their earthly journey.

Leaves that fall gently into winter's cold air. They dry into dust and are carried away into winds grace. They spread the seedlings of renewal that beckons Springs calling for rebirth. A birth that holds the three girls in the clutches of the Libra clinging to a new life and new beginnings.

For it is the rains that fill the shallow waters in which they all stand looking up at the scattered stars. In the doorway they wait for Libra's chosen door to open and lead them into their future.

August 12, 2019.

Six years have passed, as I stand here in the present moment of my thoughts. There's no miracle cures or magic dust for grief, to expel its hauntings. I have just completed a grief course. I'm much better than I was. I still feel as I am one of those mothers that dangle in the emptiness of a hollowed-out world, filled with words and emotions. Yet, left to a silenced voice and no expressions to make others understand what I have gone through. Just triggers.

At times I see the pain and the struggle my daughter goes through. It leaves me swinging from the end of my rope that I dangle from in thoughts. What quality of life was she left with? I see the unrealistic-ness of a world filled with youth and vitality, that she will never again fit into.

A world with so many that do not understand nor could grasp what it is that this young woman, young mother, has gone through. Merely to look at her in judgment and as well as myself. I can hear the whispering of thoughts dancing in the quiet winds of their own mind.

"Geeze, you need to get over it, she lived."

Yes, she and her daughter Meadow lived. I also survived broken and mended, as never to be the same. I don't have any answers, just triggers. Dangling in a world that beckons me to let go and move on. I have in many ways. Yet, I still feel so alone. I am somewhere caught and dangling in the void of the between.

Part 2. Torn Family Ties, written by Jewell Lotus.

How often has the near-death experience been described where the subject of the story leaves their body and travels to an indescribable, splendid "heaven" like dimension, or on the other hand, a hellish place. The lesson for them in the latter case may be reasoned that God gave me a second chance in life, and if I don't do better that is what will await me at my final hour. In the heaven like experience KaDawna has indicated she felt the lightness of being and freedom from pain, but ultimately felt the pull back to this earth plane.

To know if there's something on the other side of the "veil", so to speak, seems one of the utmost importance for many of the souls that are traveling along the cycles of birth, life, and death. Most religions are based on such inquiry.

To be swept involuntarily into a dimension beyond the veil, and yet still be partially aware of your surroundings as well as partially in the physical body is quite a radical feat.

I remember the urgent feeling surrounding the events that night the girls and I arrived at the intensive care unit in the UC-Health University of Colorado in Aurora.

The fear she was quickly on the way out. The girls were thinking maybe she was already "dead". That "machine" she was on had taken her over; they thought.

I tried to make talk and contact with her. Even touched heads to communicate. Was she still there? I felt she could communicate somehow.

The life threating events that unfolded over the next 24 hours would be an experience of the other side of that veil, not just for KaDawna but for me as well. Going into the chapel to pray as well as communion with family members was ever so needed. Her condition seemed to be stabilizing. As we left the hospital late the next day (Christmas eve) several doctors tried to sooth my worry with the hope that her critical condition was stabilizing. As I left the hospital a very strong surreal energy waved over me. Like a Deja Vu.

Should I go? Should I stay? Would we ever be together as a family again? Have faith an inner voice tried to say. She will pull through. The 200-mile round trip to the hospital and back that Christmas Eve was difficult. Rayne, my nine-year-old, seemed to be very brave through it all. Lotus (age four) was very traumatized.

We arrived around midnight. The house lay cold and empty where just a week ago there was a family of four, with a pregnant mom expecting the fifth member. Exhausted sleep came quickly for us all home again and safe. Was Mom feeling this way too?

Dreams of KaDawna reaching to me out striving to communicate, filled the night. Was she saying she was alright, or was she saying goodbye? In some ways the other side of the veil seemed to be bending into this one allowing some communication of the most intuitive nature between us.

By the time we awoke in the morning. News came crashing in that KaDawna's condition had worsened to such an extent the baby had to be taken very prematurely. She was put on life support in an effort to save her life.

Was she ever to return from that "other side"? This became for all of us a daily meditation and prayer. The fight had begun for everyone to truly realize in utmost sense that our physical existence in this world can be shattered in a quick moment in time.

For the next week or so I would receive daily status reports from doctors and nurses. There was always an element of hope along with the warning that there is a rough 50-50 chance she will not make it. Halfway in this world and halfway into the afterlife? Not only for KaDawna but for the kids and I as well.

January came in all its cold splendor. For at least a week time passed in a very strange way. Basking in the southern exposure of our large picture window, the sunshine becomes therapeutic, a meditative endeavor to stave off the emotional and mental energies of the medical trauma. Soon we would be almost assured that she was going to make it. Even more hopeful was the news that they felt like they could finally remove the ECMO machine. She was coming out on the winning end of the 50-50 chance.

There still left unanswered were the lingering doubts even from the medical community whether she would be whole again. Only time would answer how damaged she would remain.

It didn't matter. Even if she couldn't walk again at least we would have her by our side. We made through this; I felt we could make it through anything God would give us.

It seemed like a good month before KaDawna's mother was able to put us on a phone call with her and the kids here. It was very emotional for everyone. We realized soon that we may get the opportunity to go see her in the physical.

So, we made our first trip to the Ronald McDonald House. It was a joyous moment for everyone. It felt like a reunion that may never have happened but did. The girls knew it. That this moment could have easily never come to pass. That they might not have ever felt her embrace again.

When I first laid my eyes on Meadow, I could immediately feel the trauma and the confusion that she had been through. Little did I know that Meadow would be returning to the hospital in a few days. Her newborn struggles were not quite over yet.

I held her tiny body and watched her breathe. I longed for the time to be able to see her play with the goats and be with the land like the other kids. I felt this would be a definite possibility.

As I held her, I imagine her finally being out of stuffy rooms. Cast free to grow on the farm. The bright sun, and breeze on her face. What a blessing we have been given to watch take her first steps in our living room. Arm in arm with the other two children, she will slowly get stronger and grow wild as the cactus flowers.

I can't wait to have to flush her out of the barn so she can eat dinner. I can't wait to have her come running in muddy to just to cuddle. I can't wait until all three kids are snuggled up to momma as she reads to them as the night winds down.

I knew it was going to be hard. I knew these dreams were going to be work. I could see how weak and confused KaDawna was. She was on oxygen with a huge possibility that it may be for a lifetime. Only time would tell how much healing could do for her.

I knew she was going to be dependent on her mother and I for a while. She was nowhere near being able to drive, and she didn't trust herself to walk with the baby in her arms. She couldn't walk up very many stairs, and she required help to balance herself. How permanent was this? We as a family didn't really care, so long as she was with us. Her even coming home was a God given gift. We would work through the rest moment to moment.

Lotus was young enough to not think of the possibility of long-term health consequences. She thought Mom was just fine maybe just like before. She was just happy to be in her arms. Mom was coming home soon.

Rayne on the other hand could sense the change. She knew that KaDawna's personality had shifted. Rayne was insecure and wanted to protect her mom at all cost. She sensed how delicate the situation was.

The first six months were difficult to say the least. KaDawna needed lots of help and fought for most of it. The damage was intense.

She would never be the same. She wasn't a vegetable, or completely crippled. Everyone was blessed about that. All the blessing and gratefulness didn't stop the war that was now hers.

This was her battle. Neuropathy, cognitive impairment, and chronic pain were her new normal. She had to relearn some of the simplest things. Growing up she was always taught you don't get sick; you don't slow down. There was shame. She pushed herself to hard. She broke things, mostly on accident, but sometimes the emotional energies would overwhelm her.

She would try to hide it from the kids. I could see it plain and clear. Rayne could see it. She was only fooling herself. She would medicate to try to bring her energy up and pain down. That way she could grasp tiny bits of what her youth used to be. I thought about this as she would buzz around the farm. This used to be a normal occurrence. Sun-up to sun-down. Busy happy little bee.

Now this came with a cost. She would eventually spiral down and get very tired. At night, the pain would be revealed. Could she sleep? Would she just thrash around, and give up as was becoming normal?

She forced herself to wean off oxygen, and most of the medications she was on. It may have been too early. She would push herself to exhaustion. In a blink of an eye everything she had worked toward had collapsed.

We were struggling now that our farm business had collapsed. With the help of adult temporary assistance and food stamps we were barely making ends meet. I couldn't work the typical job. Instead I picked up odd jobs doing solar, construction, and oddball farm jobs. I had to take care of our farm, kids, and her. It was overwhelming especially now that I was nearing 60 years old.

Her life which was full of dreams and goals had all shifted. She was starting all over again. It can be a blessing. The ability to start again is a gift.

KaDawna tried to start again here on the land. She honestly did what she could to pick up the pieces. Lack of support from the community and doctors made it more difficult. The cold winters, and the high altitude. Everything was pushing against her.

I also know that there was still too much residual trauma in the house. Like a ghost it haunted her. It mocked her. She tried to lock it down. She tried to ignore it.

She left us in 2016. She needed a new start. I gave her my blessing to leave. She was still horrible weakened. Everything seemed stacked against her, but she didn't give up.

I never blamed her. I understood that she needed to work through some of the trauma alone. I knew she needed to piece herself back together. She needed to reset her foundation. To create new dreams, and goals.

She started a life from scratch. She began to learn how to communicate again. Her job understood her blocks and pushed her to grow. She shared rooms with people she knew and even spent time in a homeless shelter. She managed to gain a trade. She is now building on that trade to make a comfortable life for her children.

She left the kids. The kids were angry and confused. I understood that what she had to do could not incorporate them. She wanted them to remain free in their fleeting childhood. I know she will circle back around when the time is right.

PTSD and KaDawna's psychological ability to deal with her past and present must be very challenging as to what the future holds as well as why she was "given" a second chance. A new dragon stands before her as a new virus spreads. I think she is doing well with her second chance despite the hard roadblocks that are constantly placed in front of her.

www.ingramcontent.com/pod-product-compliance
Lightning Source LLC
Chambersburg PA
CBHW020926090426
42736CB00010B/1056